# JESUS

# JESUS

## A. N. WILSON

**W. W. NORTON & COMPANY**
*New York    London*

W. W. Norton & Company, Inc.
500 Fifth Avenue, New York, N. Y. 10110
W. W. Norton & Company Ltd.
10 Coptic Street, London WC1A 1PU

# CONTENTS

# PREFACE

THE JESUS OF History and the Christ of Faith are two separate beings, with very different stories. It is difficult enough to reconstruct the first, and in the attempt we are likely to do irreparable harm to the second.

Jesus, or Joshua, which is the same name, means 'saviour'. It is the Christian belief that one of the many men in history who bore this name was literally the Saviour of the World. And it is for this reason that the Western World divides history itself into the time before and after the birth of Jesus. Millions of people throughout the world still subscribe to the belief that Jesus was the Saviour. For them, he was the incarnation of God, coming down into a Virgin womb, and being born in a stable in Bethlehem to save the world from its sins. Revealing his identity only to a small band of followers, the Saviour taught the human race how to live. But this teaching alone could not save men and women from the consequences of their sin. They could not be saved unless the price of sin was paid; and this price was the supreme sacrifice which Jesus made when he died, a painful and humiliating death on the Cross of Calvary. Three days after that, to reveal his triumph over sin and death, Jesus rose again from the dead, revealing himself to his friends, before ascending through the clouds back to heaven again where he sits on the right hand of God. At the end of the world, Jesus will come again to decide which members of the human race deserve to enjoy perpetual happiness with God, and which deserve to be sent for everlasting punishment in hell.

This is the Christian faith. For those who are not Christians, it must seem very puzzling that such beliefs could be entertained about an historical personage. Even for those who are Christians, the figure of the historical Jesus poses problems which are not easy to solve. What are the sources for our beliefs about Jesus? How do we know whether or not they are accurate? Is it possible for a twentieth-century reader of those sources to get close to this man, or to envisage with anything approaching accuracy, what he might have been like? How far does the Christian faith depend upon history? Would Christian faith collapse if it could be proved, for example, that Jesus did not exist, or that he did not rise from the dead; or is the Christian faith an essentially imaginative exercise, focussed largely upon myths which have been fashioned out of historical material, but remain only myths, which are not susceptible to historical analysis?

These are all questions which it is worth asking; and the Christian Church has certainly been asking them during the last two centuries. With varying degrees of sophistication, I have been asking them of myself since I first heard the Christian story in childhood. Like all Christians, I was aware that my religion claimed to be rooted in history. There were certain stories, with verifiable dates attached to them, on which my faith was founded. But I did not become a Christian because I believed those stories. I became a Christian as an infant when I was baptized. Year by year, at the great festivals of the Christian Church, I heard these historical claims rehearsed. But even then, I absorbed the stories because they were so powerful in themselves, and not because I had tested them by means of historical analysis. So, at Christmas, I heard that the Angel Gabriel went to a town called Nazareth and told Mary that she was going to give birth to a baby, and she was to call him Jesus, the Saviour. Without having had sexual intercourse with a man, Mary gave birth to the boy, not in Nazareth, but in the town of Bethlehem. Mary gave birth to Jesus in a stable, because there was no room for her and her fiancé, Joseph, in the inn. The birth was heralded by angels; and when Mary had laid the little child in a manger, the Holy Family was visited by shepherds and by wise men from the east, who had been led there by a star.

This story had taken hold of my imagination long before I ever studied history at school. So powerful was it that I would not readily subject it to the ordinary processes of historical analysis, in the way, for example, that I might ask how we know that Napoleon was defeated at Waterloo in 1815. I continued, however, to suppose that it was a story with a real historical setting. The Gospel according to Luke dates it most specifically to a time when Caesar Augustus required that everyone in the Roman Empire should take part in a census. It happened at the time when Quirinius was governor of

Syria.[1] Herod was King of Judaea at the time.[2] This would seem
to place the birth of Jesus very accurately, until you discover that
Herod died four years before the Common Era began, and that
Quirinius was not the Governor of Syria during the reign of Herod.
No historian of the Roman Empire makes any mention of a universal
census during the reign of the Emperor Augustus, although Flavius
Josephus tells us in his *Antiquities* that there was a census in Judaea
in the year 6 of the Common Era.

The story of the baby being born in a stable at Bethlehem because
there was no room for him at the inn is one of the most powerful
myths ever given to the human race. A myth, however, is what it
is. Even if we insist on taking every word of the Bible as literally
true, we shall still not be able to find there the myth of Jesus being
born in a stable. None of the Gospels state that he was born in a
stable, and nearly all the details of the nativity scenes which have
inspired great artists, and delighted generations of churchgoers on
Christmas Eve, stem neither from history nor from Scripture, but
from folk-lore. Once we go into the matter, we discover that the
real Jesus, the Jesus of History, is extremely unlikely to have been
born in Bethlehem. It is much more probable that he was born in
Galilee, where he grew up. Yet, which is the more powerful figure
of our imaginations – the 'real', historical Jesus of Nazareth, or the
divine being, who in his great humility came down to be born as a
poverty-stricken outcast?

Most of the stories which are associated with Christ-mass derive
from the deep world of folklore. They have infinitely more power
over the imagination than facts could ever have. If this is true of
Christ-mass, what of the Mass, or the Lord's Supper, or the service
of Holy Communion, the central rite of Christian worship in which
the priest or minister takes bread and wine, and blesses them? The
faithful worshippers who partake of this sacred meal believe that
Jesus is indeed present in their midst as they do so. The sacrament-
alism of Christianity is the supreme expression of its belief in incarnation – God became flesh, God penetrated the material universe,
and the material universe, in its turn, can be redeemed and sanctified.
The symbolism of the Christian Eucharist has nourished and stimu-
lated millions of human lives. But, here again, there is a paradox.

[1] Luke 2:2.
[2] Matthew 2:1.

Christmas is not just a piece of folklore; it claims, in Christian story-books, to be part of history. Likewise, from early times, Christians have claimed that Jesus invented the Eucharist. It is an important claim, because by so doing, it could be said that he also invented Christianity, founded the Catholic Church, or however you choose to express it. Here, once again, we stray over from the area of religious observance into that of verifiable historical claims. And we come to a difficulty. Paul the Apostle, whose Letters are the earliest Christian documents, had a very distinctive set of beliefs about Jesus. He was writing for Gentile, or semi-Gentile, audiences in such places as Corinth, Thessalonika, and even Rome. One of his beliefs was that Jesus, in dying on the Cross, became a new Passover Lamb. Just as the Jews, in commemorating their deliverance from Egypt, killed and ate lambs, so Christians, commemorating their deliverance from sin, ate the body and blood of Jesus, symbolically represented by bread and wine. This tradition of offering bread and wine as the Christian Passover, this eating of Jesus's body and drinking of his blood, goes back, says Paul, to the night when Jesus was betrayed. This seems like an historical statement, and since Paul was making it perhaps only twenty years or so after Jesus died, believers have tended to assume that he was telling the truth. The Four Gospels attest that Jesus died at the Feast of the Passover. They all say that on the night of his arrest, he gathered some friends together for a Last Supper. But here our difficulties begin, if we wish to believe in Jesus as the inventor of the Eucharist, or as the founder of Christianity. If you take the first three Gospels, they claim that the Eucharist was instituted during or after the traditional Jewish Passover meal. If this is the case, then every single event which follows – the arrest of Jesus, his trial, his execution, must be a work of fiction, since it is unthinkable that the Jews would have broken their most sacred religious observances in order to put a man on trial. The Fourth Gospel tells us that the meal took place well before the Passover. It was not a Passover meal, and in this account there is very conspicuously no institution of the Eucharist. This is perhaps the most glaring inconsistency in the Christian claim to be an historically based religion. The truth is that even if we were to believe the fantastic claim that Jesus wished to found a new religion, with a sacramental order of bishops and deacons, we could not believe that he had instituted the Eucharist at Passover time as Paul and the Gospels aver.

If the birth in the stable at Bethlehem makes an appeal to the deepest religious emotions, how much more can this be said of the Last Supper! The Christian Eucharist is the mystery of mysteries, feeding the hearts and imaginations of men and women for two thousand years. The great cathedrals of Europe and of the Americas were built to house it. Wars have been fought over its significance. It is no small thing to recognise that it has no historical connection with Jesus of Nazareth.

And this is partly because of the extraordinary power of the Gospel narratives concerning the arrest, and suffering and death by crucifixion of Jesus. No one could read that story without their emotions being powerfully engaged. Such torture and suffering were not, of course, unique, and that is surely one of the reasons why Jesus in his suffering makes such a universal appeal. Historians can read the stories and sift through which parts could conceivably be true, and which must, without any question, be inventions. It is true, and indeed very likely, that Jesus caused some kind of disturbance in the Temple, overthrowing the money–changers' tables, though Christian interpreters of this event are likely to have mistaken its meaning. This event happened in a crowded city, in which the Roman authorities perpetually feared an uprising of the people. The Jewish religious authorities, the High Priest and the Sanhedrin, feared such uprisings, too, since when they happened, it was they who were made to suffer by the Romans. There is nothing more probable than that they sought out the arrest of Jesus, though exactly how and why this took place, we shall never know.

The Gospels are intent on blaming the death of Jesus on the Jews. This is because Christianity started life as a Jewish heresy, and there had no doubt been quarrels between the early Christian missionaries and the synagogues of the Diaspora. It is a curious fact that, although there were severe penalties for blasphemy, religious persecution of dissident groups within Jewry is unknown in Jewish history. Christians invented the idea of the embryonic church being persecuted by the Jews. Out of this invention grew their stories, related in the Gospels, of Jesus being condemned by the High Priest, or the Sanhedrin, for his religious ideas. But by their own accounts, all Jesus's friends ran away at the moment of his arrest, and could not possibly have witnessed his so–called 'trial' at the hands of the Jewish authorities. We return to the realm of probable history when we see

Jesus on trial for his life before Pilate, since it is only too likely that this incomprehensible trouble-maker from Galilee would have made the Roman governor afraid. Who were his friends? Was it true that he had among his followers members of the Zealot group, who were committed to armed resistance against Rome? In such circumstances, Pilate would not have been interested in discussing Jesus's ideas of the kingdom of Heaven. The very word 'kingdom', or 'empire' (the same word in New Testament Greek), would have set up in Pilate's mind uncomplicated political fears.

We can envisage the kind of thing which happened to Jesus in his last hours when we read Josephus. In the year 62 of the Common Era, some thirty years after Jesus died, and four years before the first major Jewish uprising against the Romans, which led to the destruction of Jerusalem itself, there arose a prophet in the city. By coincidence, he was also called Jesus – Jesus the son of Ananias. During the Feast of Tabernacles, the Jewish authorities had this Jesus arrested for causing a public disturbance by uttering prophecies of doom over the city. They had him flogged. With great sanctity, Jesus the Son of Ananias did not cry out or protest, but nor would he refrain from prophesying. Still fearing that this Jesus would inflame the mob (and it was a mob uprising which was eventually to lead to the wholesale starvation, burning and slaughter of the population of Jerusalem by the Romans) the religious authorities handed this man over to the Roman governor. The Procurator Albinus had this Jesus flayed to the bone. Still he prophesied doom and woe to the city; at which point Albinus released him, having decided that he was mad.[1]

Jesus son of Joseph was in a very similar position thirty years before, but he suffered death. The horrible scarecrow sight of a man being crucified would have been a familiar one all over the Roman Empire. It was the usual Roman method of disposing of criminals. No one who witnessed the death of Jesus of Nazareth could have guessed that this image, of a man on the cross, could have become the emblem of a world religion. Today, wherever you travel in the world, you are likely to find this image. For the believer, it is the emblem where all mysteries meet: the clash between absolute evil and absolute goodness; between the love of God and his omnipotence. For all of us, believers or non-believers, it is also the point

[1] See Geza Vermes: *Jesus and the World of Judaism* (1983), viii–ix.

where we feel the strongest clash between the mythological Christ of religion and the historical figure of Jesus of Nazareth.

The mythological Christ, who was pre-existent as the Second Person of the Holy Trinity, was born in a stable, instituted the Christian Eucharist, and founded the Catholic Church, is not the subject of this book. He does not need books written about him. He is there, to comfort and to save those who turn to him in faith, and to baffle those who do not. This book is written with the hope that it might be possible to say something about that other Jesus, the Jesus of History.

Before we start this investigation, it is necessary to have two things very clear. The first is that the task can not be done without reference to the New Testament. This may seem a very obvious thing to say, but scholars of that strange collection of books will, I am afraid, find my approach, my actual methodology, sadly illogical. I start by admitting the premise that the task is strictly speaking impossible. Anything we say about the historical Jesus must be prefaced by the word 'perhaps', and as this narrative progresses, you will find that in order to avoid wearying the reader with repetitious 'perhapses' I take the New Testament more and more on its own terms. In my account of Jesus's last days, I do tell a narrative, based on the New Testament, which would not be satisfying to the most rigorous historian. For the sake of trying to convey what I think Jesus stood for, and what sort of a man he was, I adopt the New Testament order of events. I hope that I have not written fiction, but I am aware that strictly speaking we cannot say as much about Jesus as I have said in the final chapters of this book without an infinity of perhaps, perhaps, perhaps.

The second proviso is in some ways more important, and I would urge anyone who has not entered, however tentatively, the territory of New Testament Scholarship to take note of it.

You cannot simply pick up a copy of the Gospels and read them as if they were history. Nor is it possible to read them as if they were imperfect history – as if, let us say, we chose to believe that Jesus really did teach his disciples the Lord's Prayer, but did not really perform miracles. As I have stated in my first proviso, I do in fact commit this 'error' myself at various important junctures of my book. I do it deliberately for the sake of providing the book with a narrative frame in its second half. From this illusion, I believe that it is just possible to reconstruct, I hope plausibly, some picture of the historical Jesus. But I have never lost sight of the fact that it is an illusion. The Gospels are not history-books. They are narratives framed by communities of believers who entertained certain beliefs about Jesus which they took for granted – such as that he founded a 'Church' for Gentiles, that he rose from the dead, and will come again to judge the earth; even, in the case of the Fourth Gospel, though not in the case of the first three, that he was divine. The smallest details which might look to a modern reader like believable historical facts or incidentals turn out to have been fashioned by the evangelists because of their presuppositions about who Jesus was. For example, Matthew believed that the Messiah would be born in Bethlehem; he believed that this fact was predicted in the book of the Old Testament prophet Micah. So, he tells us that Jesus was born in Bethlehem. As we have already seen, this is less than historically probable. It is difficult to draw up any criterion by which to read the Gospels which would enable us to sift the material, and see behind the Gospel narratives to their possible sources. Sometimes we might think that we can do so. Mark, who believed that Jesus came to admit the Gentiles to the kingdom of God, gives us the surprising information that Jesus dismissed the Gentiles as 'dogs' to whom he had nothing to say. Here we might plausibly suppose that a fragment of oral tradition survives of the real Jesus which has been clumsily preserved for us by the evangelist even though it flatly contradicts his purposes.

But getting into the right frame of mind in which to understand the New Testament is not easy. I have therefore taken the risk, for the sake of those who are not New Testament scholars, of spelling out the difficulties in the opening chapters of this book before we get down to a narrative examination of the life of the historical Jesus. Some readers will find this wearisome and will wonder why they have been asked to read a chapter on Paul and a chapter on 'How to read a Gospel' before reading the story of Jesus's childhood. To such readers, I would say, 'Skip to chapter four. Then, maybe, come back and read chapters one, two and three if you find yourself in difficulties.' Certain textual and methodological complexities need to be understood before you plunge in and decide the nature of the material we are considering.

To many New Testament scholars, the nature of my task will seem pointless. There is the Christ of Faith, and we find him evolving and emerging in the pages of the New Testament which were written for his disciples in the Mediterranean between, say, 50 and 100 CE.

(Incidentally, in this book, I use the abbreviation CE, the Common Era, and BCE, Before the Common Era, rather than the religiously biassed Before Christ and Anno Domini.) Why, the scholars will ask me, attempt the impossible, and write a book about the historical Jesus?

It was not in fact until they came to doubt the divinity of Jesus that historians thought of writing his life at all. It was the unbelievers, Strauss[1] in Germany, Renan[2] in France, who set off on that quest for the historical Jesus which was to prove so illusory. They were hampered, as all their Christian predecessors had been, by prejudice. Unbelievers, no less than believers, create a Jesus in their own image. Even Albert Schweitzer himself, who tried to dispel the myths of the demythologisers,[3] created a story of his own, about an apocalyptic prophet who died tragically disillusioned. Schweitzer's story strays far beyond the narrow confines of what can be proved. In subsequent decades of the twentieth century, the preponderance of Biblical scholars have steered clear of any attempt to reconstruct what the historical Jesus might have been like. For such a great theologian as Rudolf Bultmann, for example, the question has an absurd irrelevance to his theological concerns. The only Jesus available to us is the Jesus presented to us by the New Testament. Antiquarians might try to get behind the Gospel narratives, but they cannot, by so doing, produce a figure who rivals the Christ of Faith in vividness or power.

This is the theologians' position; and it is one, paradoxically, where the ultra-orthodox and the modernists meet. The ultra-orthodox Christians – whether Catholic or Protestant – are so anxious to preserve their religious faith intact that they do not dare to confront the conclusions of the last two hundred years of New Testament scholarship. The religious modernist dares to confront them, but says that religion and religious practice matter more, or matter at some deeper level, than academic speculations. The ultra-orthodox continue to believe that God came down to earth in human disguise in order to found a Church, and/or to save the human race from its sins. The religious modernist recognises that

---

[1] D. F. Strauss: *The Life of Jesus Critically Examined* (translated into English by George Eliot, 1846).
[2] Ernest Renan: *La Vie de Jésus* (1863).
[3] Albert Schweitzer: *The Quest for the Historical Jesus, a Critical Study of its Progress from Reimarus to Wrede* (ET London 1910).

the New Testament is mythology, but would want to say that we can only hope to make sense of the New Testament if we submit to its own vision of things, and fail to apply to it our own crass historical or scientific assumptions. What does it matter, by such a standard, if Jesus instituted the Eucharist, or even whether he existed at all? The important thing is that Christians are sustained now, today, by the body and blood of Christ.

Like the majority of Christians, I swayed uneasily between these two positions for a number of years until they both came to seem dishonest. This is not a spiritual autobiography, it aims to be a dispassionate account of Jesus. But it is only fair, at the outset of such a bold enterprise, to admit my own position. For many years, I was a practising Christian, and tried to avoid facing the implications of what I had studied when I read theology at university. As the years went by, however, and as I read more, and reflected more deeply on what I had read, this would not quite do. I had to admit that I found it impossible to believe that a first-century Galilean holy man had at any time of his life believed himself to be the Second Person of the Trinity. It was such an inherently improbable thing for a monotheistic Jew to believe. Nor, having learnt how to read the New Testament critically, could I find the smallest evidence that Jesus had ever entertained such beliefs about himself; nor that he had preached them. Once I began to understand more about Paul, and the audience for whom he wrote his letters, and the nature of the Gospels, I saw how important it was to study the 'situation in life', the *Sitz im Leben*, as the German theologians called it, of each of these New Testament writers. I began to see how it was possible that Paul might have invented the Christian religion – though this is too simple a way of putting it. It was a slow, and in my case, as it happens, painful process, to discard a belief in Christianity; and when I did so, I did not feel it was honest to continue to call myself a Christian, to attend churches which addressed Jesus as if he was alive, to recite creeds which acknowledged Jesus as Lord and Judge of the world. I knew that many of my fellow Christians shared my doubts and have continued somehow or another to reconcile the practice of the Christian faith with the knowledge that it is founded on a fundamental untruth; but I could not do this.

But nor could I entirely share the sceptics' view that we could know nothing about Jesus. I have been tremendously inspired and interested, over the years, by the writings of Geza Vermes, and in particular by his book *Jesus the Jew*. Professor Vermes is a scholar who has done more than any other to bring alive the first-century Jewish world. He is a leading authority on the Dead Sea Scrolls. He is deeply versed in the language and literature of the period. His writings have shown us that it is actually possible to find in the pages of the New Testament details which identify Jesus as belonging quite firmly to the great prophetic tradition of Israel. Jesus, if approached in this manner, remains a shadowy figure, but he remains much less shadowy than he was in the pages of the modernist German theologians like Bultmann. For Vermes, and those who think like him, Jesus comes alive again as a recognisable Jew of the first century. I may as well start by confessing that this is the Jesus in whom I have come to believe. I believe that Jesus was a Galilean *hasid* or holy man. A *hasid* was an heir of the prophetic tradition. He had peculiar insights into man's relationship with God, and he had charismatic powers of healing. We shall meet other *hasidim* in the pages which follow. I believe that Jesus was born in Galilee. A likely date for his birth is 4 BCE. Like other Galileans, he probably made sorties into the neighbouring province of Judaea, and it was here that he met his death, at the hands of the Romans, in about 30 CE. He wrote no books. No one has left us a physical description of what Jesus looked like. Nor do we possess any of the biographical information about him which would normally furnish a modern 'life'. We do not know, for example, whether Jesus was married. It would be surprising if he was unmarried, but it is simply not the sort of information with which the Gospels supply us. Nevertheless, I should maintain that the Gospels do furnish us with a number of very vivid pictures of Jesus, and a number of sayings and stories attributed to Jesus which are highly unlikely to have been invented. I have found that in seeking him as an historical being, he has been in some ways much more vivid to me than he ever was when I tried to approach him through the eyes of Christian belief.

I have mentioned my debt to Professor Vermes's books. He has also performed me the service of reading this book at a rudimentary stage of its development and offering profoundly helpful suggestions. Any errors it contains and all the opinions are my own, but I am very grateful to him, nonetheless. I should also like to record my gratitude to two men who taught me the New Testament at Oxford, Alan Stephenson and Cheslyn Jones. Both of them are now dead, and I do not think that either of them would have agreed with this book, or liked it much; but I could not have written it without their help. Further back in my biographical history, I should like to thank Messrs R. P. Wright and T. A. Buckney who first taught me Greek (after a very rocky start) and left me with an amateur enthusiasm for the language which is undiminished. Without their help, I could never have begun to read the New Testament in its original tongue, and to see it as I see it today. I should also like to thank Douglas Matthews for compiling the index, and his staff at the London Library for being so unfailingly helpful.

# I

## JESUS THE JEW

JESUS INHABITED A world which was utterly different from our own. There are many ways in which we can see the truth of this obvious fact, but every so often we should remind ourselves of it. It will save us much time-wasting. For example, what is the point of asking ourselves whether the Ascension of Jesus into Heaven took place after his demise? The story was told by writers who believed that the sky was like a dish. You could fly through it and enter Paradise. For a modern observer, of whatever religious beliefs, it is impossible not to know that a man ascending vertically from the Mount of Olives, by whatever means of miraculous propulsion, would pass into orbit.

Only dullards would need to be told this. But it is only by trying to feel ourselves back into the world of Jesus, and the common world-view entertained by his contemporaries, that we shall start to understand him and his place in the scheme of things. For instance, pagans and Jews were both agreed that it was a world populated by demons and spirits.

Today, we believe in our own forms of magic. We place vast credulity in medical science. For the Jews and Pagans and Christians of the first century CE it was axiomatic that an epileptic was possessed of demons, that the way to cure deafness or palsy was to drive the demons out. Their universe was of a different composition from ours. Copernican astronomy was unknown. Time was different; they believed that the world was of finite duration and that it would probably be coming to an end during their own lifetimes. 'Science' and 'history', as understood in a post-Enlightenment sense, did not exist.

If we wish to understand the New Testament, we must look at the world of Jesus, as well as at Jesus himself, with imaginative eyes. We do not need to dispute some of the claims by the New Testament writers that they 'saw' the things which they write about in their books. I do not see any necessity to suggest that these books must have been written decades after the event by people who never knew Jesus personally. The difficulty springs from our certain knowledge that if we, with modern and prosaically 'scientific' eyes had seen the things which were seen and heard by the disciples of Jesus, we should have seen quite different things. At his Baptism, for example, in the River Jordan, we should probably have seen merely a bedraggled young man emerging from the water; but the eyes of faith saw the heavens open, and the Holy Spirit of God descending on Jesus in the form of a dove. In the Fourth Gospel, Jesus is scorned by Nathanael because he comes from the nondescript small town of Nazareth. But when Nathanael actually meets Jesus, he is more impressed. Jesus remarks that he had seen Nathanael, before they met, sitting under a fig tree. For some reason which the narrative does not make clear, Nathanael regards this observation as preternaturally astute and proclaims, on the strength of it, that Jesus is the Son of God and the King of Israel. 'Jesus answered and said unto him, Because I said unto thee, I saw thee underneath the fig tree, believest thou? thou shalt see greater things than these. And he saith unto him, Verily, verily, I say unto you, Ye shall see the heaven opened, and the angels of god ascending and descending upon the Son of Man.'[1]

The strange fact is that the figure of Jesus remains, even in a world where institutional Christianity would appear to be on its last legs, and where religious belief itself, in the West at least, would appear to be rapidly on the decline. Jesus is a shadowy figure historically, but he remains doggedly there, and, in spite of what the clergymen may tell us, we remain aware of him, not as a mystical presence, but not as a figure of pure legend, either. He is more real than Robin Hood or King Arthur. 'Heaven and earth shall pass away, but my words shall not pass away,' he is reported to have said. It is a prophecy which has come true.

Scholars have been right to urge caution upon anyone who thinks it is possible to assess whether Jesus actually said any of the words attributed to him by the Gospels. He wrote no books, and his words have been reported by writers who demonstrably distort their accounts of things to persuade us of their own point of view. The chances, in such circumstances, of catching the *ipsissima verba* of Jesus

[1] John 1:50,51.

are slight. And yet, if Jesus did not say some of the words which are attributed to him in the New Testament, we find ourselves in the presence of a remarkable body of sayings, and feel like the critic who said that if Bacon did not write the plays of Shakespeare, then he missed the opportunity of a lifetime. The prayer which begins with the words 'Our Father'; the stories of the Good Samaritan and the Prodigal Son; the body of apothegms assembled by St Matthew and known as the Sermon on the Mount; the dozens of parables; questions, moral saws and arresting psychological inquiries which have been attributed to Jesus cannot be ignored. A Jewish scholar has written, 'In his ethical code there is a sublimity, a distinctiveness and originality in form unparalleled in any other Hebrew ethical code; neither is there any parallel to the remarkable art of his parables.'[1] It is easy for clever Christian scholars, or post-Christian, ex-Christian scholars, with their noses too close to the text, to take the words of Jesus for granted, and merely to delight in detecting characteristics of Matthew, Luke, or John. Such judgments have their place in the study; but they can distort. The words of Jesus have extraordinary power. They continue to change human lives.

The same is true of the life-story of Jesus, in the fragmentary form in which it exists in the Gospels. His preparedness to be identified with social outcasts and sinners, his compassion for the sick and the poor, his psychological penetration and insight, so that he could speak to a woman whom he had never met before and appear to know everything about the emotional chaos of her life – these are images which cannot be dispelled by scholars calling into question their historical plausibility. Their immediacy makes it unimportant whether they actually happened. The early hearers of these stories, and the majority of those who have heard them recited since in Christian groups and churches, have themselves become characters in the story. They 'come to Jesus' by placing themselves within these Gospel scenes.

> But warm, sweet tender, even yet
> A present help is he;
> And faith has still its Olivet
> And love its Galilee.[2]

[1] Joseph Klausner: *Jesus of Nazareth*, quoted in Geza Vermes, *Jesus the Jew* (1973).
[2] J. G. Whittier: 'Immortal love for ever full', *English Hymnal* No. 408.

Stronger still is the image of an innocent, silent man standing before the civil accusers and in his weakness appearing to be stronger than Caesar himself. We need to recollect, as we turn over these stories for historical clues, that they were not written as source-material for modern biographers.

After his death, Jesus was believed to have risen again. In this, he was not unique. The New Testament tells us that at the moment of Jesus's death, 'the tombs were opened and many bodies of the saints that had fallen asleep were raised'.[1] In his own lifetime, Jesus was credited with bringing back from the dead a young man in Nain, the daughter of a synagogue-ruler called Jairus, and his friend Lazarus of Bethany. After the death of John the Baptist, King Herod believed that he too had risen from the dead. Modern scepticism about such phenomena must be well-placed. Those Christians who insist upon the literal and historical truth of Jesus's Resurrection must ask themselves what happened to all these other resurrected bodies which walk the pages of the New Testament with such apparent natural-ness. Did they, like Jesus, ascend into heaven, or did they have their dying to do over again?

Jesus survived after his death as a cult figure, and the cult is to be found in three distinct strands of tradition: first, in the Jewish 'Church' of Jerusalem, which did not detach itself from the main-stream of Jewry, and presumably had no sense of Jesus having founded a new religion.

Secondly, the cult was propagated by the Apostle Paul, in a very different form, and for very different adherents. Third, and perhaps most mysterious of all, the cult of Jesus survives in the Fourth Gospel.

The first of these traditions, the purely Jewish remembrance of Jesus as a great prophet or holy man, is only represented in the most shadowy form in the annals of the New Testament. We know that it existed. We know from the Acts of the Apostles that the Jewish followers of Jesus in Jerusalem reacted with scandalised incredulity to the idea of preaching 'Jesus the Messiah' to the uncircumcised Gentiles, and to Paul's idea of breaking away from Judaism and disregarding the ancient ritual and dietary observances of Israel. These early followers of Jesus were Jews and never stopped being Jews. But their witness more or less died with the Temple itself

[1] Matthew 27:52.

when the city of Jerusalem was sacked by the Romans in 70CE. They wrote no books about Jesus, which survive, though we perhaps catch some flavour of their religious attitudes in the Epistle of James and in a few passages quoted in Acts. We find fragmentary quotations from the so-called 'Gospel According to the Hebrews' in the writings of the early church fathers, Irenaeus and Clement, and above all in Jerome, who translated the Greek Bible into Latin. Irenaeus tell us that the Ebionites believed Paul to be a heretic, an apostate from the law.[1]

The gentile Church which grew up after the first generation of witnesses had died would have had no understanding of these first-generation Jewish followers of 'the Way', as they called their discipleship of Jesus. Still less would the Gentile Christians have had any desire to perpetuate the memory of these people who saw the very idea of Gentile Christians as a contradiction in terms. Paul won the argument. He took his mystic Christ to the ports of Asia Minor and Greece and finally to Rome itself, the capital of the Empire. The Gospels of Mark and Luke, and to a lesser extent that of Matthew, are written under the heavy influence of Paul's ideas.

The Fourth Gospel is of a different character. Again and again it reiterates not merely the religion of a mystic Christ, but the claim that it retains an authentic memory of Jesus as he actually lived on this earth as an historical personage. But from internal evidence of that Gospel it would seem likely that the 'Fourth Gospel Christians' felt themselves to be at variance not only with the Gentile mystics of Paul's Church but also with the 'Judaeans' of the Jerusalem Church.

We, the modern readers who search the figure of Jesus down the years of Christian history and through the tangles of Christian mythology, have a sentimental tendency to believe that if only we could have known members of this original Judaean Church, we should have a clearer picture of what the historical Jesus was actually like. I think that this is a yearning which, had it been granted, might have proved illusory. Their Jesus might well have seemed to us as peculiar and as 'mythological' as the Jesus of John and the Jesus of Paul.

Yet, while we must be wary of the attempt to reconstruct the historical Jesus, this is not a reason for saying that nothing is known or worth knowing about the subject. In the last few decades there

[1] M. R. James: *The Apocryphal New Testament*, 1.

have been a number of plausible attempts to get behind the Gospels by means of analogy with Jesus's contemporaries or near contemporaries.[1] Professor Vermes, for example, has shown us in his book *Jesus the Jew* that there are many aspects of Jesus, even as he comes filtered to us through the testimony of Christian evangelists, which are recognisably those of a first-century Galilean *hasid*. He is comparable to other *hasidim*, who also went about healing the sick, casting out devils, controlling the weather, and quarrelling with the religious hierarchy in Jerusalem. Like archaeologists, sorting through rubble, we can come across shards and fragments in the New Testament which, if we examine them with sufficient patience and learning, can provide us with clues of what we seek. By the standards of many ancient texts, the Gospels actually tell us rather a lot about their principal subject. The danger which faces any modern reader who is not used to reading old texts in this way is that we shall mistake the nature of the material; that is why it is necessary, before turning to the life and career of Jesus, to consider the witness of Paul and John. This I shall do in the chapters which follow.

But it is also necessary, before one starts, to empty the mind and to take nothing for granted. The centre of Jesus's teaching was his belief in God, and his belief in Judaism. And it is perhaps necessary to spell out the obvious and to remind ourselves of how extremely distinctive that belief actually was.

Men worship gods made in their own image; but these Gods in turn, once made, have a potency of their own to shape and enslave their devotees. The pagan gods of classical antiquity had no concern with ethics, which is why the Greek moralists, from Socrates and Plato onwards, viewed the activities of Mount Olympus with disdain, and stretched out to abstract concepts of Goodness and Justice of a kind which had been axiomatic to the monotheistic Jews for centuries before their pagan neighbours. The purity and abstractness of the Jewish theology, from the eighth century BCE onwards, is remarkable. While other nations were bowing down to images of wood and stone, the Jewish prophets were calling their people to a recognition that the will of God could only be fulfilled by a virtuous and neighbourly life; by making provision for the poor; by establishing a just society in which men and women could live with the

[1] See, for example, Geza Vermes: *Jesus the Jew*; J. D. M. Derrett: *Jesus's Audience*; John Bowker: *Jesus and the Pharisees*.

dignity of believing that they were the children of God. The Old Testament is the record of an evolving religious consciousness without equal in the literature of the world. Yahweh, from being one tribal God among many, from being a savage tutelary deity whose only interest appears to be in securing the victory of one semitic tribe in its battles with other semitic tribes, emerges as an inspirational force of ethical and spiritual power. In the Book of Joshua, when God is helping the Hebrews to lay waste the cities of the Hivites, the Perizzites, the Jebusites and the Canaanites, He seems to have no more interest in ethics than do Hera, Zeus or Pallas Athene in Homer, as they unfairly and capriciously devise military conquests for their mortal favourites. As the mythology came to be rehearsed and rewritten however, from, perhaps, the time of the Jewish exile in Babylon (597–538 BCE) that journey itself from Egypt (?1250 BCE) into the promised land came to be seen as a journey of ethical discovery; the setbacks the Hebrews suffered in their Exodus, the punishment of Moses for forsaking the Law which had been vouchsafed to him and his people on Mount Sinai, emphasise the importance of God's righteousness more than his favouritism. The Jews themselves, his chosen people, can only serve God if they revere His commandments; if they hold fast to the principle of monotheism; if they eschew idolatry; if they meditate in their inmost hearts on the nature of the Good, and if they pursue that Good in practical ways, in lives of sobriety, chastity and generosity to the poor.

Though a reverence for the Torah, the Law, is at the heart of Judaism, in time it came to be seen as only a part of the covenant which God had made with his chosen people. To Jeremiah at the time of the exile, God made the revelation (in 627 BCE) that he was accessible to the Jews not merely by some external ordinance, not merely in the Ten Commandments and the other provisions of the Law which had been declared on Sinai, but in a much more inward and mystical sense. 'I will put my law in their inward parts, and in their heart will I write it; and I will be their God, and they shall be my people: and they shall teach no more every man his neighbour, and every man his brother, saying, Know the Lord: for they shall all know me, from the least of them unto the greatest of them, saith the Lord.'[1] This is a far cry from the world of the Homeric gods, whose sexual antics, and whose bloodthirsty involvement in the

---

[1] Jeremiah 31:33,34.

affairs of mortals, are incalculable and opaque. Though they converse with mortals, they live apart from them. The ethical world which they inhabit is as chaotic as the morality of the human race itself, of which it is a grotesque parody. They have no morality to teach the human race, so they can scarcely direct its conscience.

But the Homeric theology has this advantage over the Jewish. It is more readily plausible as an explanation for the anguish and suffering of the human race. The *Iliad*, written perhaps a hundred years before the Jews were being taken into exile by the Babylonians, represents the universe as an infinitely suffering place without moral purpose. Heroism and virtue are possible in this universe in defiance of 'Nature, heartless witless Nature'. The dawn is rosy fingered and the sea is wine dark whether or not the heroes enjoy good fortune.

Lust, love, defeat, victory, physical pain, homesickness, anger, all go on against a background in which mortals can shake their fist at the Gods for their siding with one group of people rather than another; but the Homeric deities cannot be called to account for their lack of justice. That is because Justice was never part of the covenant. Priam can say that he blames no one for the conflict between the Greeks and the Trojans, for all the calamities which have befallen them are a result of the machinations of the gods.[1] That is the nature of things; and that explains why the *Iliad* has such cohesion, and why its heroes are heroes.

There are no 'heroes' as such in the Bible until the period of the Maccabees (166–160 BCE). There is only the naive certainty that God is on the side of his chosen race; God is right, God is just, and therefore the cause of the Jews is right and just. This simplicity of approach, which produces a bloodcurdling mythology in the book of Joshua, is tested to breaking point by the actual historical experience of the defeat of Israel in 597, when the Temple of Jerusalem was destroyed, and large numbers of the defeated Jews were taken into captivity in Babylon – present-day Iraq. This experience provoked in the Jewish prophets the anguished self-questioning which produced the finest books of the Old Testament. Since the righteousness of the Jews is something they themselves took for granted – were they not obeying the Torah which had been revealed to them by God himself? – and since the righteousness and power of God

---

[1] *Iliad* III:165–165. 'It is the Gods, I believe, who are to blame, who aroused against me the tear-soaked war of the Achaeans.'

were both axiomatic, how could He have allowed His chosen people to suffer this appalling national calamity? The simple answer – that they had not been righteous enough, not loyal enough to the Torah, too ready to intermarry with neighbouring semites, too lax in their dietary laws – could only satisfy the legalistic and simple minds which produced the books of Ezra and Nehemiah (350 BCE? describing the events of 538 BCE). For the prophets and Psalmists who meditated upon the problem, and for the later writer who composed the Book of Job (date unknown: 450 BCE?), it was a question much deeper than that, a question which urgently posed itself, but which could never be answered. It was the question of innocent suffering which seemed to call in question whether the Jewish idea of God, elevated and noble as it was, could truly be sustained in the face of all the evidence which seemed to contradict it.

There are many attempts in the later books of the Old Testament to resolve this question, a question which was destined to haunt the Jews until our own century, when unimaginable suffering was to be their destiny. But two figures stand out from those Scriptures which Jesus himself would have read and studied. One is the figure of Job, and the other is the figure of the Suffering Servant in Deutero-Isaiah[1].

The Book of Job is the most Homeric of the Biblical books in this sense only: it depicts two immortals, God and Satan, playing with a mortal, testing his mettle. The virtuous human being who is visited by financial ruin, and by plagues of boils, does so as a result of an almost playful debate between the celestial powers. But the response of the suffering man is the very reverse of Homeric, for he never ceases to believe in righteousness. The scholars have debated about how the Book of Job came to possess its present form. General readers of the book will decide whether either of the consoling resolutions to Job's problems are in fact consoling: first that he knows he has an Avenger[2] who at some future judgment will reward virtue

---

[1] i.e. Chapters 40–55 of the Book of Isaiah as it is printed in the Bible. Deutero-Isaiah preached to the people of Judah in their Babylonian exile, some time between 550 and 538 BCE.

[2] Job 19:25. Job, in his anger with his comforters, asserts that he knows that he has a Defender or Avenger, a *go'el*, who will eventually establish his innocence. Whether he refers to God, or to some Celestial demiurge, is a matter of debate among scholars. The mistranslation of the phrase in the Authorised Version of the Bible is 'I know that my redeemer liveth', a phrase which Christian piety has applied to Jesus in his Glorified and Resurrected form. It must, particularly when set to music by Handel, be the most inspired mistranslation in the history of literature.

– an early hint of the dawning Jewish belief in the immortality of the soul; secondly that God in his greatness and splendour and majesty is not to be put on trial by the puny questionings of a finite human mind: 'Where wast thou when I laid the foundations of the earth?'[1] Nevertheless, the Book of Job precisely because of its rhetoric does not really work. It is self-defeating; we can believe that it is intentionally self-defeating on the part of its author(s).

Job actually has more powerful arguments than his detractors, more powerful arguments than God himself. Against all odds, against the desertion and even the effectual enmity of God, Job will continue to believe in God, and continue to believe in righteousness. 'Yea, though he slay me, yet will I trust in him.' 'I despise my life. It is all one; therefore I say, He destroyeth the perfect and the wicked. If the scourge slay suddenly, He will mock at the trial of the innocent. The earth is given into the hands of the wicked. He covereth the faces of the judges thereof. If it be not he, then who is it?'[2]

This is not a disturbing question for a polytheist who takes it for granted that the gods dispose human destiny with sadistic malice; but it is profoundly disturbing for a believer in one true, good God who has expressed His love for His people, and His desire for them to be righteous. It remains to this day a nagging question at the heart of Judaism. For anyone as well-versed in the Scriptures as Jesus, it must have been of over-riding importance, not least because in his own day, a threat hung over the very existence of Judaism which was every bit as menacing as the old Babylonian exile. The Romans had already shown themselves to be ruthless in their governorship of their Jewish colony, ruthless in their suppression of rebellion, and coarsely insensitive to the religious sensibilities of the people. They would, as Jesus is reported to have foreseen, one day destroy the Temple itself, and bring into being, for the people of Israel, a nineteen-hundred-year exile from their spiritual home. Any man who spoke to Israel about Israel in the time of the Roman occupation would have the old questions from the Book of Job in his mind. It was a situation of grave spiritual crisis for an entire nation, not to be resolved by theory. For many of Jesus's contemporaries it was axiomatic that God would redeem Israel in some way or another: he would allow Jewish insurrectionists to overthrow their foreign

[1] Job 38:4.
[2] Job 9:21–24.

oppressors, as Judas Maccabeus had attempted to do, by military force; or he would send his Messiah to bring history to an end, and redeem the suffering of Israel by the inauguration of a Messianic age. Jesus himself almost certainly entertained either or both such hopes, but it would seem as though he did so in a highly idiosyncratic manner.

There is another figure in the Old Testament who embodies this conflict between the manifest injustice of the world, and the righteousness of God and His Israel. It is the figure of the Suffering Servant in Deutero-Isaiah. This extraordinary poetic creation, of a righteous man who has nothing to do in the heartless world except to suffer, and in that suffering somehow to redeem his nation, is again, like that of Job, a type most specifically of Jewry, and one who haunts the whole history of his race. The Servant has become like the old scapegoat on whom the sins of the people were ritually lain before he was driven out into the wilderness. The Servant is a reproach to God, but so intensely strong is the Jewish reverence for the righteousness of God that Deutero-Isaiah makes no bitter Aeschylean railing against destiny. It is rather as if the insoluble question of why the innocent suffer, of why the righteous seem to suffer more than the wicked, can only be confronted by mythology. To be a Jew is, potentially, to suffer. To uphold abstract and absolute standards of righteousness, in a universe which seems at war with those standards, is to suffer. To insist on the inviolability of the moral law which is defied by the gods themselves, is to risk an infinitude of suffering, but it is a necessary martyrdom if the Jewish race, and we can add the human race with it, is not to sink into moral anarchy. For Aristotle and the Greek moral philosophers, the question does not take on such dramatic form because, for all their belief in a First Cause and in Absolute Morality, the Greeks inhabited a world which was imaginatively speaking polytheistic. It is for the Jews to mythologise the predicament. So long as this One Righteous Man exists, holding on to righteousness though all the powers of anarchy and darkness are ranged against him, then righteousness itself retains its validity.

'Who hath believed our report? and to whom hath the arm of the Lord been revealed? For he grew up before him as a tender plant, and as a root out of a dry ground: he hath no form nor comeliness; and when we see him, there is no beauty that we should desire him. He was despised and rejected of men, a man of sorrows and acquainted with grief: and as one from whom men hide their face he was despised, and we esteemed him not. Surely he hath borne our griefs and carried our sorrows: yet we esteem him stricken, smitten of God, and afflicted. But he was wounded for our transgressions, he was bruised for our iniquities; the chastisement of our peace was upon him; and with his stripes, we are healed.'[1]

These were the religious images which formed the mind of Jesus, as they have formed the minds of all Jews. For later, Christian generations, it seemed appropriate to see the figure of the Suffering Servant as a foreshadowing of Jesus himself; in all probability, for his earliest Jewish disciples, who had no wish to separate themselves from the community of Israel, the analogy or imagery of this idea had a potency which was sufficient in itself. Whether Jesus saw himself as an embodiment of the Suffering Servant can never be known. It is interesting that the Synoptic Gospels hardly allude to the Suffering Servant at all, though it was an image which could be said to have haunted the two great religious imaginations – Paul and John – who interpreted Jesus to the Gentile world; and that was to have reverberations and consequences which Jesus could never have foreseen or desired.

[1] Isaiah 53:1–5.

# II

# PAUL

SOME TIME DURING the winter of 50–51 CE, a small group of religious devotees in the Greek port of Thessalonika assembled to listen to a remarkable document being read aloud. The fact that it is the earliest Christian document which we possess does not of course mean that it represents the oldest, or the most primitive Christian beliefs, but it is early – written about twenty years after the death of Jesus.

In this 'letter', the author urges those listening to abstain from sexual immorality, instructions which he gives on the authority of 'the Lord Jesus' himself.[1] The purpose of the chastity practised by the Thessalonians was to keep themselves in trim for the imminent arrival of Jesus from the sky. Jesus died, the Thessalonians are told, he rose, and he will return on the day of the Lord. Those who have already died 'in the Messiah' will rise first, and then those who are still alive will be 'taken up into the clouds . . . to meet the Lord in the air'.[2]

If we are to understand the history of the cult which grew up in the name of Jesus so soon after his death, we shall find several crucially important ideas buried in this, the oldest Christian document. We must ask ourselves what this word 'Christ' (the Greek for Messiah) means to the author of this document and to his hearers. Then we must ask how this particular set of beliefs survived to become a world religion. Since every single thing prophesied in the First Letter to the Thessalonians in 51 CE turned out to be untrue, and since Jesus did not return and hover over the clouds in that beautifully hilly Greek port, how is it that the author of this prediction enjoys such influence and respect among the Christian peoples of the world?

Ever since the Thessalonians were warned to keep a look-out in

[1] I Thess. 4:3.
[2] I Thess. 4:14–17.

– 17 –

the skies for the arrival of a Jew who had been dead for twenty years, Christians have been signing hymns expecting the return of Christ on the clouds. It forms part of the traditional Christian liturgy for a whole month each year before Christmas, and it is not a belief restricted to the crankier sects of Christendom. The answer to some of these questions can be found if we read more deeply in the other writings of the man who wrote that urgent but essentially false warning to the Thessalonians: the Apostle Paul.

First, we should examine the phrase which Paul uses so often, the 'Gospel of Christ', which means, 'Good News about the Messiah'. The words 'Christ' or 'Messiah' mean the Anointed One, and they refer to the Jewish belief that in the last days of this earth, a time of blessedness would occur. God would raise up and anoint a Chosen One, who would lead the people of Israel. The Gospel, or Good News, for Paul, is that this figure has come.

The hope that the Messiah would come is a recurrent feature of Jewish piety in the century before Jesus was born. The Messiah, of royal birth, and descended from King David, would come to save the Jews from their Gentile oppressors, the Romans. His triumph would be both military and mystical. The sect at Qumran, near the Dead Sea, prayed that God would bless the Messiah.

> May the Lord raise you up to everlasting heights. . . .
> May you ravage the earth with your sceptre.[1]

Like the rival minority groups known as the Sadducees and the Pharisees, these people at Qumran were preparing for the arrival of the Messiah with particular vigilance: a renewal of piety combined with a concern with the political fate of Israel, the Jewish race.

A key text for all those Jews awaiting the Messiah was the prophetic book of Daniel, a fictitious work, set in the Babylonian captivity, but probably written between 167 and 164 BCE, just before the rebellion of the Maccabees against the Seleucids. The book foresees the collapse of the Greek Empire and the triumph of a Jewish Superman who would overcome all the enemies of Judaism and establish a reign of righteous people, in which the government of this earth would be given to the saints, the holy ones who had kept faith.

'I saw in the night visions and, behold, there came with the clouds

---

[1] Geza Vermes: *Jesus the Jew*, 132.

of heaven one like unto a son of man, and he came even to the ancient of days, and they brought him near before him. And there was given him dominion, and glory, and a kingdom, that all the peoples, nations, and languages should serve him, which shall not pass away.'[1]

The apocalyptic Messiah, had, in the opinion of Paul, been raised up by God, and his name was Joshua, or Yeshu, or Jesus, which means, appropriately enough, Saviour.

Some of the Thessalonians who heard the words of Paul might have been Jews of the Diaspora, that is to say, Jews who did not live in the Promised Land. The Book of Daniel had been variously interpreted by the Jews, and many books have been written about the Son of Man. For many Jews, he was not to be identified with the Messiah at all; he was a symbolic figure, representing a purified and triumphant Jewry. Other Jews did identify him with the Messiah. Paul's language about the expected Messiah would, for such Jews, fit into a particular pattern of myths and expectations. But the majority of Paul's hearers would have been Greeks with very different ideas and assumptions about God and the gods.

For Gentiles of this period, who had no preconceived ideas about the Messiah, it would have been much easier to think, not in terms of Israel's Anointed One, but of a demigod, or a god incarnate. As soon as Paul had succeeded in implanting the essentially Jewish Messianic idea into alien Gentile soil, the Gentiles would have no difficulty in turning Jesus into a God; and not merely Jesus, of course, but also Paul, and the Caesars, and anyone else whom they happened to admire. In the Acts of the Apostles alone, we read of three instances of divine incarnation. God was thought to have been reborn as Simon Magus.[2] In the fourteenth chapter of Acts, Paul and Barnabas, preaching in Lycaonia, are recognised as divine beings. 'The gods are come down to us in the likeness of men,' shouted the crowds, and the priest of Zeus brings oxen to sacrifice to the two Jewish missionaries. Barnabas they believed to be Zeus and Paul, the messenger, they decided was Hermes.[3]

In such a world, it was hardly surprising that the Jewish Messiah should have been perceived as divine; nor is it surprising that in such a world, Jesus himself should have been spoken of as a god.

[1] Daniel 7:13–14.
[2] Acts 8:10.
[3] Acts 14:13.

Paul never specifically states that Jesus was God, though he told his converts in Colossae that Jesus was the 'image' or 'ikon' of the invisible God.[1] But in the years following his letter to the Thessalonians, we can see an advance in Paul's thinking to a point where Jesus has become all-but divine, and the discipline of monotheism seems to have been left behind. As Paul's initial prophecies about Jesus proved to be false, his language about Jesus became more and more hyperbolic. The Messiah had been raised up! His rising becomes more important than his arrival on the clouds. This word, anastasis, or resurrection, is central to Paul's teaching. He never actually states in his writings that Jesus left behind an empty tomb, but he says something much more beguiling. The anastasis of Jesus will enable his followers to conquer death itself.

Here was an offer of far more universal appeal than the essentially esoteric claim that a Jewish Messiah had been born, who would usher in a period of Jewish rule by Jewish saints. Here was something to which any credulous slave in the Mediterranean could respond: 'Behold, I tell you a mystery: we shall not all sleep, but we shall all be changed, in a moment, in the twinkling of an eye, at the last trump: for the trumpet shall sound, and the dead shall be raised incorruptible, and we shall all be changed. For this corruptible must put on incorruption, and this mortal shall put on immortality. . . . Then shall come to pass the saying that is written, Death is swallowed up in victory. O death, where is thy victory? O death, where is thy sting?'[2]

These words, which have been read countless times since at Christian funerals, are at the heart of Paul's message to the world. Jesus is risen, and in his rising, he brings the hope of everlasting life to all who believe. By the time Paul was writing this famous disquisition to the Corinthians, possibly in 57 CE, the mystic Messiah whom he preached was a figure 'with a life of his own'. The Messiah who is the Lord of Life and Conqueror of Death, who comes before us in Paul's first letter to Corinth, is a figure who has outsoared history. He is an invention of Paul's religious genius. But, he still bears the name of one who was historical: Jesus. So, the Corinthians are told that the Israelites in the time of Moses were led by the Mystic Messiah. They were all 'baptized' into Moses. And they all did 'eat the

[1] Col. 1:15.
[2] I Cor. 15:51–55.

same spiritual meat and did all drink the same spiritual drink; for they drank of a spiritual rock that followed them: and the rock was Christ'.[1]

At the same time, the First Letter to the Corinthians makes very specific references to the historic figure who is at the heart of the new cult: to Jesus himself. This is the only place in which Paul does refer to 'the historical Jesus'. He tells us that Jesus instituted the Christian Eucharist, and he tells us that Jesus rose from the dead.

'For the tradition I received from the Lord' – it is noteworthy that Paul does not claim to have received this tradition from the Church, or from the friends of Jesus who were with him on the night before he died, but direct from the Lord – 'is that the night he was betrayed, the Lord Jesus took some bread, and after he had given thanks, he broke it, and he said, 'This is my body which is for you; do this in remembrance of me. And in the same way, with the cup after supper, saying, This cup is the new covenant in my blood. Whenever you drink it, do this as a memorial of me.'[2]

As we shall see when we come to the chapter of this story which deals with the last night of Jesus's life, it is highly unlikely that he ever 'instituted the Eucharist'. It is even less likely that, at a Passover meal, a devout Jew such as Jesus would have handed around a chalice of wine and told his friends that if they drank from it, they would be drinking his blood. This smacks strongly of the mystery cults of the Mediterranean, and has little in common with Judaism. 'Whenever you eat this bread, then, and drink this cup, you are proclaiming the Lord's death until he comes,' Paul tells the Corinthians.[3]

It is the death of Jesus which matters to Paul. The Eucharist is a symbol of that death, a symbol for Paul of that fateful night when Jesus was arrested, and taken away to die on the Cross. Paul does not commend Jesus to his followers as an admirable moral teacher, nor as a storyteller, nor as a famed healer and miracle-worker. He commends him in purely mythological terms. Jesus is the Messiah; Jesus is the Rock in the desert from which the people of Israel drank pure water; Jesus, like Mithras, God of the Morning, can be drunk from an uplifted cup of blood; Jesus, the dying demigod who comes to life again, is the conqueror of death itself.

'The tradition I handed on to you in the first place, a tradition

[1] I Cor. 10:3–4.
[2] I Cor. 11:24–26 (Jerusalem Bible).
[3] I Cor. 11:26.

which I had myself received, was that Christ died for our sins, in accordance with the Scriptures, and that he was buried; and that on the third day, he was raised to life, in accordance with the Scriptures; and that he appeared to Cephas, and later to the Twelve; and next he appeared to more than five hundred of the brothers at the same time, most of whom are still with us, though some have fallen asleep; then he appeared to James, and then to all the apostles. Last of all, he appeared to me too, as though I was a child born abnormally.'[1] It is a curious phrase; by suggesting that he is the runt of the litter, the child who has nothing in common with his siblings, Paul seems to be tacitly admitting that his Gospel is quite different from the beliefs and practices of Jesus's own friends and family who were at this period chiefly located in Jerusalem.

For Paul, the Resurrection of Jesus is the great sign that death itself has been defeated. To his converts, he offered the hope that if they were baptised into the death of Jesus they would rise again with Jesus to life immortal. Lest they should believe him to be lying, he assures them that at least five hundred people beside himself had seen the risen Lord.

It is a curious number, this five hundred. None of the Gospels suggest that the risen Jesus appeared to anything like this number of people. You might have supposed, if a man had truly risen from the tomb and appeared to five hundred people at the same time, that this would have attracted some notice on the part of the authorities. Yet we read of no such occurrence in the contemporary history of the Jews by Josephus. No Roman historian makes any mention of it, and nor does any other Christian writer. Corinth was a considerable distance from Jerusalem, and not many of those who first read Paul's account of Jesus's miraculous appearances after death would have had the chance to visit Jerusalem, and ask to meet any members of this highly favoured crowd of five hundred.

But with Paul, the essence of Catholic Christianity is born. We have the claim that the rites of his particular mystery-cult – the offering of the body and blood of Christ – was the invention of Jesus. We have the story that Jesus rose from the grave, and that there were many witnesses to this event. Paul may be said to be the inventor or founder of the Christian religion. The title certainly fits Paul much better than it fits Jesus, to whom it is sometimes applied.

[1] I Cor. 15:3–8 (Jerusalem Bible).

Since Paul is so influential a figure in our story, it is necessary to consider his history and character, and attempt some explanation, however tendentious this may seem, for his developing religious consciousness. Moreover, such an exercise is necessary if we are to understand Jesus himself.

Paul is popularly supposed to have been remote from the historical Jesus, the Jesus who lived. The first three Gospels, it is often supposed, tell us all that we can hope to know about the man Jesus; the rest of the New Testament writings are mere glosses, interpretations, embellishments. The truth is actually stranger than that. All the texts, and especially the gospel narratives, are interpretative, and this is as true of the Gospel of Mark as it is of Paul's Letter to Thessalonika. But equally, Paul's letters show more signs than is commonly supposed of a personal knowledge of Jesus and his teaching. He is, in his own strange way, a witness.

Paul is unique as a figure in the New Testament: a large part of what we know about him comes from his own pen. Jesus, Peter, John the Baptist, Mary Magdalen – they all come before us as figures depicted by others. Paul is the only New Testament autobiographer. Apart from many factual details about himself with which he peppers his writings – such matters as his place of birth, his educational and medical history and so forth – he is one of those writers who are incapable of anonymity. His personality breathes through every sentence which he wrote: volatile, tempestuous, mystical, prickly, ecstatic, quarrelsome, changeable. To say that he was self-contradictory is an understatement. He was a man who was fighting himself and quarrelling with himself all the time; and he managed to project the warfare in his own breast on to the Cosmos itself. The moral, religious and psychological contradictions within Paul become, in his writings, a grand principle about human nature itself, a vision of mankind which in almost every generation since Paul lived has had the power to unsettle and change his readers.

Given the fact that Paul was responsible, more or less single-handedly, for wresting the religion of Jesus from the Jews and making it available to the Gentile world, it is remarkable that so few scholars have ever asked themselves: Why? Why was Paul so obsessed by Jesus? Both in the first half of his life when he was a persecutor of Jesus's followers, and in the second half of his life when he was the most inventive and inspired Christian apologist who has ever lived, Paul seems unable to have left the idea of Jesus alone. Is it conceivable that the two never met? Nearly all Christian scholars take it for granted that they did not do so and that Paul somehow or another 'became a Christian' or invented Christianity more or less off his own bat after his conversion on the road to Damascus. But this does not explain why.

Paul could have continued a devout Jew to the end of his day; or he could have joined up with some mystery religion in the Mediterranean regions of Asia Minor. Or he could have invented a God for people to worship in Ephesus, Corinth and in Rome. But he did not quite do any of those things. He continued to tell them about Jesus.

Paul was a native of Tarsus in Cilicia, Asia Minor – a city in modern-day Turkey. He was a citizen of the Roman Empire. Strabo, the Greek geographer, sometimes mentions Tarsus in the same breath as Athens. [1] It was a highly cosmopolitan place, and the Judaism of its Jews was sophisticated and Hellenized. The Greek-speaking Jews of the Diaspora, like Philo of Alexandria, delighted in finding points of comparison between the Jewish conception of God, and the Greeks' idea of the Good. Proselytising was common. Philo probably exaggerates when he tells his readers that the laws of the Jewish people attract and win the attention of all, of barbarians and Greeks, of dwellers on mainland and islands, of nations of the east and the west, of Europe, Asia and of the whole inhabited world from end to end. [2] Such Judaism did, however, make an appeal, and it was rather different from the various forms of Judaism which flourished in Galilee or Jerusalem in this period. There was something genial and expansive about the Jewish world into which the cosmopolitan Paul was born.

But this, from a Jewish point of view, was potentially dangerous. How can a Jew continue to be a Jew, unless, as Nehemiah and Ezra had insisted after the Exile, he continues to keep himself unspotted by the Gentile world? For those who are not Jews, the rigour, and the detail of the Jewish Law – its apparent pettinesses – seem strangely at variance with its grand conceptions of God and Man, its high ethical view, its sublime vision of the human destiny. This critical view of the Jewish Law fails to take into account one of the functions of Law in the Jewish world: and that is to keep Jews separate from Gentiles. Do the rabbis really believe, and did they ever believe, that

[1] Strabo XIV, 673.
[2] Philo: *De Vita Mosis* I:20.

it was morally culpable – of the same order of sinfulness as stealing or lying or depriving the poor of food – to eat a shrimp, or to have butter on the table while you ate a lamb chop? No, of course not. But they believed that it was a sin to break a covenant which had been made everlastingly with God, and these petty little regulations were a good way of keeping religion in the family, of making it difficult, if not actually impossible, for Jews and Gentiles to socialise.

But these are, of course, modern Jewish preoccupations, relating to a time when the Jews lived chiefly among the Gentiles. A version of the debate must have existed, in the life of a Hellenized, civilised Jew of the empire, such as Paul. But this is where we reach one of the difficulties of making sense of Paul as an interpreter of Jesus. Paul lived and worked in the Gentile world. Jesus lived in a completely Jewish world. Paul, who was really a great religious poet more than he was a thinker, was able to project the conflicts in his own mind and soul on to the Cosmos. For someone who, like Jesus, mixed only with Jews, the grand question of whether the Gentile could know God, and His Law, was one which would scarcely have arisen. But for a Jew of the Diaspora, there was always a tension between knowing of the pious aspirations of the Hellenized world, the inbuilt thirst of the human race for God, and knowing that the Covenant had been made exclusively on Sinai with one God-bearing people.

At some point in his youth, Paul rejected the broad-based Hellenism of his upbringing and tells us that he became a Pharisee. He came to distrust the notion that human beings born outside the Covenant could approach God or be loved by Him. In his autobiographical Letter to the Galatians, he tells his readers that 'I outstripped most of my Jewish contemporaries in my limitless enthusiasm for the traditions of my ancestors'. [1] To the Philippians, he wrote, 'I was born of the race of Israel, of the tribe of Benjamin, a Hebrew born of Hebrew parents. In the matter of the Law, I was a Pharisee.' [2]

Writing to the Corinthians about the Jews, he exclaimed, 'Are they Hebrews? So am I. Are they Israelites? So am I. Are they descendants of Abraham? So am I.' [3]

---

[1] Gal. 1:14.
[2] Phil. 3:5–6.
[3] 2 Cor. 11:22, 23.

German scholars such as G. Bornkamm[1] have pointed out that there is a fundamental inconsistency between the account given by Paul of his own life in his autobiographical writings, and the narrative of the Acts of the Apostles, which deliberately underplays the fundamental conflict between Paul and the Christians of Jerusalem. Acts tells us that Paul put himself in charge of persecuting the Hellenizing Christians such as Stephen. It tells us that Paul was sent to Damascus, in Syria, with a mandate from the High Priest in Jerusalem to arrest any Christians there.

This cannot possibly be true since Damascus was outside the confines of Judaea, and the Jewish judicial assembly, the Sanhedrin, lacked any jurisdiction in this region. Outside the pages of the New Testament, there is no evidence that the Jews have ever been guilty of religious persecutions. The Jews have been notably disputatious among themselves, free with harsh words about one another, and ready to break into sects at seemingly small provocation. But this is different from persecuting zeal. There has never been a Jewish 'inquisition'. The story of such an 'inquisition' in Acts therefore needs to be treated with some circumspection. Paul tells the Galatians that at the time of his conversion, he had not met any members of the Jerusalem Church,[2] which sits oddly beside the account in Acts that he was a sort of religious police-sergeant, in charge of interrogating figures like Stephen. Later on in the story, when Paul had come to the view that Christianity was a new religion for Gentiles, and that there was no necessity for Christians to be bound by the Jewish Torah, we know that there was a great dispute between Paul and Peter (Cephas), who had been a disciple of Jesus, and who was the leader of the Christian Church at Antioch. 'When Cephas came to Antioch,' Paul bluntly tells us, 'then I did oppose him to his face since he was manifestly in the wrong.'[3] This quarrel is not mentioned in Acts. Presumably, at the time, the Jewish Christians went on doing things in their way, and Paul stubbornly took no notice of their desire to remain within the fold of Judaism. In Acts the quarrel is written up as a great Apostolic Assembly at Jerusalem which was amicably resolved, and which led to the acceptance by the Jewish Church of Gentile membership.

The scholars are almost certainly right to regard Acts as a late

[1] G. Bornkamm: *Paul* (1969).
[2] Gal. 1:16 (Jerusalem Bible).
[3] Gal. 2:11 (Jerusalem Bible).

work, perhaps dating (like its companion-volume the Gospel of Luke) from forty years after the Letters of Paul. Like Luke, it is a book designed to reassure any Roman official who might be reading it first that Christianity was no threat to the imperial authority, and secondly that it was quite distinct from Judaism. After 70 CE when the Romans had destroyed the Temple at Jerusalem, the Jews were regarded in Rome as dangerous malcontents. Tacitus, in his *Annals*, cannot have been alone, among the civilised Romans, in having only a vague sense of the difference between Jews and Christians. Describing the persecution of Christians by Nero in 64, when they were blamed for the fire which destroyed much of Rome, the historian wrote, 'Nero fastened the guilt and inflicted the most exquisite tortures on a class hated for their abominations, called Christians by the populace. Christus, from whom the name had its origin, suffered the extreme penalty during the reign of Tiberius at the hands of one of our procurators, Pontius Pilate; and a most mischievous superstition, thus checked for the moment, again broke out, not only in Judaea, the first source of the evil, but even in Rome, where all things hideous and shameful from every part of the world find their centre and become popular.'[1] It was to safeguard Christians against this sort of bad press that Luke wrote his accounts of Roman soldiers being commended by Christ for their faithfulness, of a centurion standing at the foot of the Cross and exclaiming that Jesus was the son of God, and of Paul, the Roman citizen, travelling about the empire, completely in harmony with the rest of the Christian community, though much at odds with the troublesome synagogues. The Roman persecution of religious minorities, the Jews included, inspires the author of Acts to invent the fiction of Jews as the great persecutors; a persecution for which Christendom felt itself entitled to take revenge for many centuries afterwards.

So, scholars have been right to warn us not to place too much reliance upon Acts as an historical source. On the other hand, buried beneath its untruths, and its distortions, there are clues as to what might actually have been the case. Paul tells us himself that he was a persecutor of Christians, and that it was a confrontation, not with the Christians, but with Jesus himself, which changed his mind. A hypothesis which might make sense of this claim is that Paul did actually come face to face with Jesus during his lifetime.

[1] Tacitus: *Annals* XV:44.

A way in to the matter might be found in Paul's curious use of the word 'boast', *kauchesis*. Paul's 'boast' to have been a Pharisee when he was a young man takes us to the heart of his paradox, the paradox of his religion and of his personality. 'Boast' is a word highly characteristic of Paul. In two of his letters, 2 Corinthians and Philippians, he makes a boast of being a Pharisee, but this boast, *kauchesis*, has been transformed into a Christian affirmation. The Christians, taught by Paul, are *kauchomenoi en Christo*, boasters in Christ. 'As Christ's truth is in me, this boast of mine is not going to be silenced,' he wrote to the Corinthians. [1] The same word is used in his most startlingly paradoxical boast to the Galatians. 'As for me, it is out of the question that I should boast [*kauchasthai*] except of the cross of our Lord Jesus Christ.' [2]

Now, the tradition preserved in the Gospels is that the Pharisees were the sect within Judaism singled out by Jesus for particular censure. In almost all the clashes between Jesus and the Jewish authorities which we read about in the Gospels, his particular quarrel is with the Pharisees. This is most noticeable in the Gospel of Luke, [3] the Gospel which purports to have been penned by Paul's companion on his missionary journeys; and while we must make the allowances which I have set out earlier about the plausibility of Luke and Acts, in their finished form, there is no reason to suppose that those passages of first-person narrative in Acts, which describe the author travelling with Paul on his missionary journeys, do not contain a kernel of historical memory.

Later, when we try to investigate the earthly life of Jesus, we can ask ourselves whether these supposed conflicts between Jesus and the Pharisees were very likely to have taken place. For the time being, it is enough to notice that Paul certainly believed that there was a conflict between Jesus and the Pharisees, and that in the Gospel attributed to Paul's companion Luke, Jesus expresses inveterate hostility to the Pharisees, the very religious group to which Paul 'boasts' of belonging.

Is there any resemblance between the actual Pharisees of history, and the Pharisees buzzing about in the poetic mind of the Apostle

[1] 2 Cor. 11:10 (Jerusalem Bible).
[2] Gal. 6:14 (Jerusalem Bible).
[3] There are thirteen distinct references to the Pharisees in Luke, against eight in Matthew and one in Mark and six in John. The references in Luke are 11:37, 18:10, 18:11, 12:1, 11:42, 11:43, 11:44, 5:30, 15:12, 6:7, 7:30, 11:39, 16:14.

Paul? The Pharisees were among those Jews who believed that the Messiah could not come, nor with him the redemption of Israel, until the Jews had purified themselves. They were therefore anxious to sanctify the whole of daily life with a multiplication and extension of trivial rules governing such matters as how cooking pots and eating vessels should be cleaned. In Luke's Gospel, Jesus exclaims, 'You Pharisees! You clean the outside of cup and plate, while inside yourselves you are filled with extortion and wickedness.'[1] The same author in Acts makes Paul boast, 'I am a Pharisee and the son of Pharisees.'[2]

That a Hellenized Jew of Tarsus was the son of Pharisees we can take leave to doubt. That Paul regarded himself as the spiritual child of Pharisees in his early manhood we can believe. There is some internal evidence from Luke's Gospel that the author did not really understand the basis of Jesus's quarrel with the Pharisees. Some scholars have even wondered whether Jesus in fact had any quarrel with the Pharisees, since the teaching of the actual Pharisees and those of Jesus would seem to have been quite similar. But if we understand the word 'Pharisee' to mean the religious bigotry of Paul, then we can say that there was a conflict between Paul's earlier rigid legalism and his later, liberated sense of Jesus redeeming the world from sin. In this internalised sense, the quarrel between Jesus and the Pharisees, as Paul conceived it, was the most important thing in his entire religious experience of the world. He makes it, in fact, the theme of his Letter to the Romans, his most sustained piece of theological writing, which has been called 'The Gospel according to Paul'. For Luke, the Pharisees are hypocrites, empty vessels, men who seem to be virtuous while concealing an inner wickedness. Paul, who claims to have been a Pharisee, must have known that this was not true. The Pharisees were among the most virtuous men who had ever lived. They may have been occasionally petty in their application of the Law of Moses, but they did not shrink from keeping that Law. They believed it to come from God, and the point of their apparently absurd religious observations was not a love of the Law for its own sake; it was a belief that if the Jews returned faithfully and dutifully to the Law, the Messiah would come, and there would dawn the promised time of blessedness on earth when men could live in harmony with God.

[1] Luke 11:38.
[2] Acts 23:6.

Such men would have found the Parable in Luke's Gospel about the Pharisee and the Publican (tax collector) both going up to the Temple to pray profoundly abhorrent. Luke's simple-minded introduction to the story shows that he does not himself begin to understand it, and that he has not meditated, as Paul has done, on its metaphysically explosive potential. He says that it is told to people 'who prided themselves on being upright and despised everyone else'[1] but that is not really the point of the story: Two men went up into the temple to pray; the one a Pharisee, and the other a publican. The Pharisee stood and prayed thus with himself, 'God, I thank thee, that I am not as the rest of men, extortioners, unjust, adulterers, or even as this publican. I fast twice in the week; I give tithes of all that I get. But the publican, standing afar off, would not lift up so much as his eyes to heaven, but smote his breast, saying, God, be merciful to me a sinner. I say unto you, This man went down to his house justified rather than the other.'[2]

The parable is not, as Luke says, a warning against self-righteousness or spiritual pride. It is a much more fundamental and devastating thing than that. About half the Psalms, the hymn-book of Judaism, would, if reduced to a précis, be an echo of the Pharisee's prayer. The Jewish Scriptures see nothing wrong with respecting virtue, and being aware of virtue for its own sake. But, if it is God who forgives sin, what part does virtue play in the scheme of things? The Pharisees believed with most rational beings, religious or irreligious, that virtue was its own reward, that it was worth pursuing for itself. Like Plato and his followers, like the Stoics, and certainly like most Jews, the Pharisees believed that God smiled on virtue and frowned upon vice. In so far as the Pharisees belonged to that group within Judaism who believed in the immortality of the soul, they would have taken the simple view that those who led good lives would be rewarded with future blessedness.

The story of the Publican and the Pharisee denies this common-sense love of virtue absolutely. It denies it root and branch. It is a shocking, morally anarchic story. All that matters in the story appears to be God's capacity to forgive. Since the Pharisee has no sin, he cannot get into touch with God. It is the sinner who goes home 'justified', because for him, the test of a good life is not virtue

---

[1] Luke 18:9 (Jerusalem Bible).
[2] Luke 18: 10–14.

but a childlike dependence on the mercy of God. This is not a moral fable to put us on our guard against excessive self-righteousness. It is a nihilist's charter.

And we are bound to ask, where does it come from? Clearly Luke, or the final reviser or redactor of Luke, can be discounted as the originator of the story since he obviously failed to understand it. One explanation could be that the story does in fact go back to Jesus himself. If it is anything like representative of the kind of thing which Jesus thought, and believed, and preached, then we can understand why Paul the Pharisee reacted so violently to the idea of Jesus.

The life-story of Paul can then start to make sense, against the background of his written work. First, we have Paul the Hellenized Jew of Tarsus – wide-ranging and with a knowledge of Greek literature, and non-Jewish culture. He then comes to Jerusalem, where, by his account of himself quoted in Acts, he becomes a Pharisee, and the disciple of a famous Pharisee called Gamaliel. This revered old figure is quoted in Acts as urging caution upon the Sanhedrin. 'Men of Israel, be careful how you deal with these people. Some time ago, there arose Theudas. He claimed to be someone important, and collected about four hundred followers, but when he was killed, all his followers scattered, and that was the end of them. And then there was Judas the Galilean, at the time of the census, who attracted crowds of supporters, but he was killed too, and all his followers dispersed. What I suggest, therefore, is that you leave these men alone.'[1]

Gamaliel had every reason to be sympathetic to these Galilean *hasidim*, of whom Jesus was one. Another of them, famous in his day, was a healer called Hanina ben Dosa. Gamaliel, head of the Pharisees in Jerusalem, had a son who was sick of a fever, and seemed as if he was going to die. Gamaliel sent two of his disciples to visit Hanina who retired to an upper room, and then emerged to tell the disciples: 'Go home, the fever has departed from him.' When they returned home, they found that the boy had been cured at the self-same hour that Hanina had offered up his prayer.[2]

It is likely that this speech of Gamaliel's from Acts is roughly speaking authentic, since it departs from Luke's stereotype of Pharisees being all stiff-necked hypocrites. Here was one who saw

---

[1] Acts 5:35–38 (Jerusalem Bible).
[2] Quoted Vermes, op. cit., 75.

no virtue in religious persecution. Nor would it have been necessarily thought blasphemous if, either before or after his death, Jesus was regarded as the Messiah. 'Even before Jesus's day, considerable bodies of peoples had regarded now one, now the other "prophet" as the Messiah without laying themselves open to the risk of persecution by the Jews and excommunication.'[1]

But picture this scene. Paul, having feared the universalism and breadth of Hellenized Judaism, flees to the spiritual haven of Jerusalem as a young man, and finds himself mentally at home with a religiously observant group, the Pharisees. The conflicts within Palestinian Judaism were different from the conflicts in the mind of Paul. In the Gospels, which are written from a Gentile perspective, the Pharisees seem petty and conservative. In their actual habitat, the Pharisees were not conservative, but radical. Whereas the conservative Sadducees were content to regard the revelation of God through the Torah as a fixed and finished thing, laid down in the Scriptures, the Pharisees sought ways of applying the Scriptural regulations to every detail of contemporary life. To a Hellenized Jew like Paul, the Pharisees must have seemed like men who were hanging on to salvation by a profoundly attractive legalism. To old legalists like the Sadducees, the Pharisees seemed like moderns, trying to alter the nature and basis by which the Law was understood. What Paul's encounter with Pharisaism taught him was something which was a little different from its real aim and purposes. The Pharisees believed that the will of God could be discerned in every detail of everyday life, and it was for this reason that they were prepared to interpret it, and reinterpret it. But this idea, that God's will can be worked out not by minimalist religious observance but by a contemporary reassessment of what is and is not right, leads in Paul's mind to a searching analysis of the deepest questions of moral philosophy. He approaches these problems, however, not as a philosopher but as a mystic, and the investigation led to a profound personal crisis. In the course of this journey, he found a threat to Judaism far more devastating than anything which the most eclectic Greek philosopher could have devised back home in Tarsus. It is a question with a sort of village-idiot simplicity. If God forgives us our sins anyway, why should we think that he loves righteous men more than sinners? Does sin actually matter that much? Is God really to be found in the

[1] Bornkamm, op. cit., 15.

Torah, or can he not also be found in the repentance of a corrupt government quisling, or in the penitent tears of a whore?

From everything we know of Paul from his epistles, this strand in the teaching of Jesus would be very nearly literally maddening. It could have reduced the Pharisaic moralist in Paul to despair, to murderous despair. If he was a young Pharisee, as he says he was, would not his time of Pharisaical fervour have coincided with the time of Jesus's ministry? What was there to have stopped Paul having heard Jesus speak, and being totally horrified by what he heard: fascinated, but horrified?

The simple answer would be to ask another question. If Paul knew Jesus, or at least heard him preach, why does he say nothing about it? There is a phrase in 2 Corinthians 5:16 where Paul says 'even though we have known Christ after the flesh, yet now we know him so no more', which could imply that he did, as a matter of fact, at least set eyes on Jesus. The important thing now, he says, is that we should contemplate the mystic Christ, and not dwell upon the earthly Jesus. And an explanation for this could lie in his curious 'boasting' about his Pharisaic past, coupled with his 'boasting' in the Cross, the hideous method of torture by which Jesus met his end.

Paul's most distinctive teaching – one could almost call it his theological invention if one could be totally sure that it owed nothing to Jesus himself – is the idea of Grace. Paul expounds it briefly in his letter to the Galatians, and much more fully in his letter to the Romans. It is precisely the same idea as lies at the centre of the story of the Publican and the Pharisee: that is, that God's forgiveness is not dependent upon human virtue at all, but rather on a free outpouring of divine love for the human race, regardless of their moral rectitude or turpitude. To the Galatians he makes it clear that he did not hear the Gospel from any of Jesus's friends. 'It was not from any human being that I received it, but it came to me through a revelation of Jesus Christ.'[1] He explains in the same letter why, having been the strictest and most bigoted young Pharisee, he now believes that God's grace has been poured out, not merely to the Chosen Race, but to all mankind: 'If I now rebuild everything I once demolished, I prove I was wrong before. In fact through the Law I am dead to the Law so that I can be alive to God. I have been crucified with Christ and yet I am alive; and yet it is no longer I, but Christ living

[1] Gal. 1:12.

– 33 –

in me.'[1] Possibly the most remarkable metaphor in the whole of Paul's oeuvre is his claim to have been crucified himself, along with Christ. Pious interpreters of Paul's claim that he bore in his own body the marks of the Lord Jesus have even wondered whether Paul did not, like St Francis of Assisi and so many others who have devoted their fixed attention to Christ's wounds, receive the stigmata, that is the very wounds of Christ reproduced in hands and feet and side.

Later in this book, another explanation for this stigmata will be suggested. We observe, for the moment, the Paul who emerges in his letters, and the unfolding picture of Jesus which they provide. Paul's interpretations of who Jesus was, and what his significance might be to the rest of us, is one which is in a state of violent flux. Urgent dialectic is mixed with flights of ecstatic or visionary apostrophe, with moral admonition (frequently self-contradictory) and beautiful poetry. In his early letters, such as I Thessalonians, he seems to draw chiefly on the tradition of Jesus as the Promised Messiah, the man raised up by God for a Messianic destiny who will very shortly return to earth on the clouds to lift up his followers in glory. Later on, Paul's language about Jesus suggests a kinship with the theology of the Fourth Gospel,[2] and it is almost as if Paul believes that Christ existed in his divine being before his birth,[3] or that he played some part in the creation of the universe.[4] It could never be proved that Paul had been in contact with what we might call Fourth Gospel Christians or with others who believed in the divinity of Jesus (however this divinity might have been understood). Perhaps he reached similar conclusions on his own – though never going so far actually as to say that Jesus was God.

Paul, as he often likes us to remember, was a Pharisee of the Pharisees. That is, he had believed that God's will was enshrined in the Torah, the Jewish Law. As a devout Pharisee he would, like the Pharisee in Jesus's story, have believed that he was closer than most men to fulfilling God's will. If, like most Pharisees, he looked for the coming of the Messiah, he could not fail to have been scandalised by Jesus's reported laxity in his view of the Law, and in particular

[1] Gal. 2:20 (Jerusalem Bible).
[2] See Michael Goulder: 'The Two Roots of Christian Myth' in *The Myth of God Incarnate* (SCM 1977), 80.
[3] 2 Cor. 8:9.
[4] 1 Cor. 10:4.

of ritual observance. Jesus was reported to have said that 'the Sabbath was made for man and not man for the Sabbath'. [1] There is nothing here which would have shocked the real Pharisees. In fact, we find very similar thoughts in the Rabbinic literature. Seen in the context of a debate among Jews, there is nothing so revolutionary about this idea. But as Paul saw it, this idea of Jesus's was extremely dangerous. With the part of his mind which regarded himself as a 'Pharisee of the Pharisees', Paul saw the Torah as representing what Kant was later to call the categorical imperative. [2] It was something given, not something invented for man's convenience. The story of the Pharisee and the Publican does not suggest a mild difference of emphasis between Jesus and the Pharisees. It suggests a complete gulf, an absolute and violent division. The man who told that story was opposed to everything which the Pharisees held sacred. (To every-thing the Stoics held sacred, too, and the Platonists, and the Aristot-elians; to everything which most moral philosophers have ever held to be true.) How could a man who preached a doctrine so dangerous, so heedless of the God-given nature of moral teaching, make any claim to be the Messiah? If (as we shall discover) there were those who proclaimed Jesus to be the Messiah in his own lifetime, they must have been, by Paul's standards, sinfully wrong. 'And if any man shall say unto you, Lo here is the Christ; or Lo, there; believe it not; for there shall arise false Christs and false prophets and shall shew signs and wonders that they may lead astray, if possible, the elect.' [3] Jesus himself is reported to have said these words in the last week of his life. How the Pharisees could have echoed them! And how satisfying it must have been to them, from a purely religious point of view, when this false Messiah, Jesus, was done away with by the Roman method of execution, crucifixion. This is not to say that they were sadists, but this method of execution would make it clear that by the strict standards of Jewish Law, Jesus could not have been the Messiah. 'Christ redeemed us from the curse of the law by being cursed for our sake since scripture says: Anyone hanged is accursed,' Paul wrote to the Gentiles of Galatia. [4] That was not how

---

[1] Mark 2:27.

[2] Kant had little time for the evangelical notion of grace and saw the Kingdom of God, in the New Testament, as 'a People of God according to the moral law' or 'a Republic under the moral law'. See Die Religion innerhalb der Grenzen der blossen Vernuft, quoted by Anders Nygren, Agape and Eros, 102.

[3] Mark 13:21, 22.

[4] Gal. 3:13.

it seemed to him at the time of the Crucifixion. The Law was not a 'curse' for the young Pharisee; it was a blessing, for it is written again and again in the Psalms that no greater blessing can fall upon a Jew than when he rehearses the Law, recites the Law, meditates on the Law, and of course obeys the Law. Such a one will be 'like a tree planted near streams; it bears fruit in season and its leaves never wither'. [1]

Paul of Tarsus, however was never much like a tree, rooted, stable and firm. We cannot know, and we could never prove that he was in Jerusalem on the day that Jesus died, but it would seem to me highly likely. I should guess that he was some minor servant of the High Priest, who perhaps even had a hand in the arrest of Jesus and the handing over of the false Messiah to the Roman authorities. This might go some way to explain why Paul, more than any other New Testament writer, is so much preoccupied with the Cross. It entered his soul, to the point where he himself can 'boast' that he was crucified with Christ. No other writer makes such a claim.

We have already alluded to Paul's assertion to the Galatians that he did not know any of the early Christians assembled in Jerusalem at the time of his conversion. The Acts of the Apostles tells us that Paul was responsible for the prosecution of Stephen, the first Christian martyr, for blasphemy; but this is very unlikely to have been historically correct. If Paul was actually concerned with the condemnation, not of Stephen, but of Jesus himself, this would have been a fact with which his conscious mind, in the Christian phase of his life, was unable to come to terms. The Synoptic Gospels and the Acts of the Apostles both draw on Christian traditions which are heavily influenced by Paul's interpretation and version of events. Their historical suppression or distortion of the truth would, if my theory is correct, correspond to the psychological suppression of the truth within Paul's own person. Further, if, as Galatians makes plain, Paul held strongly divergent views from Peter, if would be natural that in the Pauline tradition, we should read accounts of Peter's denial of Jesus rather than Paul's actual condemnation of the Lord to death.

Stephen's martyrdom by stoning, even in the account in Acts, reads like an echo of Jesus's own death on the Cross. Both Stephen and Jesus die with the same prayer on their lips – 'Lay not this sin

[1] Psalm 1:3, 4.

to their charge' and 'Father, forgive them, for they know not what they do'.

Acts tells us that after the stoning of Stephen, Paul set out to Damascus, 'breathing and threatening slaughter against the disciples of the Lord'. [1] There are no fewer than four accounts of Paul's conversion in the New Testament, three in Acts, and one in Galatians. [2] The accounts all make it clear that Saul, as he was called at this date, is in a state of considerable mental turmoil. Why? Because, presumably, the conflicts which rage through every para-graph of his letters were churning about in his mind: the conflict between the idea of God's justice, demanding righteousness from the Jews, and offering punishment to the unrighteous, and on the other hand, the free mercy of God, a mercy so full, a love so abund-ant, that it could hear and forgive the prayer of the sinful Publican, while taking no interest in the formal religious observance of the Pharisee. It is at this point that the anguished, guilt-ridden Saul sees a binding light in the heavens, and he hears a voice speaking to him in Hebrew. It is not the voice of Stephen. 'Saul, Saul, why are you persecuting me? It is hard for you, kicking against the goad. Then I said, who are you Lord? And the Lord answered, I am Jesus whom you are persecuting.' [3] Not 'Stephen whom you are persecuting', but 'Jesus whom you are persecuting'. Having confronted the hard truth about himself, and about what he had been doing, Saul collapsed.

After a period of recuperation in Damascus, Saul, now renamed as Paul, took off to Arabia for three years before going anywhere near Jerusalem. It is only after his Christian faith has already formed itself in his head that he went to the capital, and met Cephas (Peter), though he did not meet any other members of the chosen band of twelve followers whom Jesus left behind. He did, however, meet Jesus's brother James. In his characteristically self-centred manner, Paul says that Cephas and James gave Glory to God for him, [4] though this is distinctly not the impression given by other parts of the New Testament, such as the Epistle of James – which does not merely repudiate, but actually satirises Paul's doctrine of Justification by Faith.

The faith of Paul is not the faith of the Galileans who had been

[1] Acts 9:1.
[2] Gal. 1:11–24; Acts 9:1–30; Acts 22:1–21; Acts 26:4–23.
[3] Acts 26:15–16.
[4] Gal. 1:24.

Jesus's close personal friends. It grew out of a hatred, a fascination, in the end a possessive love for one strand in Jesus's teaching which they seem to have missed: that is the strand contained in the parable of the Publican and the Pharisee. For Peter, James and the other followers of 'the Way', as they called Jesus's particular brand of Judaism, Jesus was the last great Jewish prophet, misunderstood like all his predecessors, but speaking quite centrally within the main body of Judaism. It was out of Paul's confrontation with Jesus that there dawned the idea that Judaism itself had to be overturned.

The full realisation of this took a long time to mature in Paul's mind; it was never a fixed or finished idea. Since he believed that the *parousia*, the coming of Jesus on the clouds, was going to happen at any minute, it was no part of Paul's ambition to draw up a formalised new religion, of the kind which was established by the Prophet when he founded Islam. Many have believed, from Paul's day to our own, that he essentially distorted the message of Jesus, and that he conjured up a strange new cult, 'Cross-tianity', as it has been called, out of his own teemingly energetic imagination. But if this were wholly true, it would be hard to explain why he focussed on Jesus as the object of his interest, rather than merely proclaiming his own visions. Hard as it is to make sense of Paul, it must be the case that he thought he was telling his followers the truth about Jesus. He was coming to grips with Jesus himself, with the death of Jesus, but also with his message. He discerned in both a meaning which was inchoate or invisible to other Christians who had known Jesus, but we find in his most extended piece of theological writing, the Epistle to the Romans, a picture of man's relationship with God which is not incompatible with some of the most troubling of Jesus's reported sayings in the Gospels.

Romans is one of the most influential books which was ever written. It had a profound and life-changing effect on such figures as Augustine of Hippo, Luther and Calvin, and could therefore be said to be one of the key books to understanding the intellectual and social development of the Western world. It expounds the great theory of original sin. God is good, and righteous and just. This righteousness is expressed in what men call Law. But since the human race is neither righteous nor just, the existence of Law merely highlights the sinful condition of mankind. Even those such as the Jews, with whom God has drawn up a special covenant, merely had their sins spelt out to them when the Law was graven in tablets of stone on Mount Sinai. For how can God, who is all righteous, set aside sin, pardon sin, without appearing to suggest that sin is of no importance? A price had to be paid for sin. That price is death. The human race itself has been condemned to misery and death through its own sinfulness. Men can only be saved through faith. It is faith in the mercy of God which enables us to approach him and call him Father, as Jesus taught us that we could. But of course, no one could do so, unless that heavy price had been paid, if the wages of the sin had not been attributed to Jesus's account.

Since Jesus died for sinners, a tremendous hope has come into the world. The love of God is poured out unconditionally through the death of Jesus. 'God commendeth his own love toward us, that while we were yet sinners, Christ died for us.' [1] The Epistle to the Romans is not a great work of argument or reason. In a passionate and poetic manner it offers an incomparable gift to its readers: the vision of God cancelling out sin through love. Centuries before Freud discovered the crippling effect of guilt on human lives, and offered them comparably powerful myths by which to unload their guilt, Paul offered his converts the much deeper mystery of forgiveness through Christ.

Paul is a man of conflicts, and his dialectic grows from a violent inner turmoil: the conflict between Law and Grace, between God's righteousness and Man's fallen nature, between Sinai and Golgotha. Seven years after he had written to the Thessalonians, Paul found himself in Achaia (of which Corinth was the chief city) for a space of three months; and it is probably here that he found the leisure to write to the Roman church, which he had not yet visited.

No one knows how or why there came to be a group of Christians in Rome at this date. Certainly the new faith had not been taken there by Peter, since he was still the leader of the Christian Church in Antioch, and no mention is made in the New Testament of his ever visiting the capital of the empire. [2] The decree of Claudius banished the Jews from Rome because they were 'continually raising tumults at the instigation of Chrestus', [3] and this would suggest that a high proportion of the more vociferous Jews there had returned from Jerusalem as converts to 'the Way'. Juvenal's sixth *Satire* suggests that many Romans were attracted to Jewish ideas and Seneca,

---

[1] Romans 5:8.
[2] Nor is there any mention in the Acts of the Apostles of Peter being the Bishop of Rome.
[3] Suetonius: *Claudius* xxv.

in a lost fragment quoted by St Augustine, stated that 'the conquered gave laws to the conquerors'.[1] Possibly a dispute had arisen in the synagogue at Rome between the tumultuous followers of 'Chrestus' and the more orthodox Jews. The people in Rome to whom Paul wrote his Epistle are expected to understand Jewish concepts of the Law, and it is assumed that they have an acquaintance with the Scriptures; but he makes it plain that a significant proportion of them are not of Jewish extraction. The numbers in any case must have been tiny. A hundred years later, in the time of Irenaeus (*c.*130–*c.*200 CE), the Church of Rome still did not number more than a hundred or a hundred and fifty people.

'The whole purpose and intention of the apostle in this letter is to break down all righteousness and wisdom of our own . . . and to show that for breaking them down, Christ and his righteousness are needed for us.' So wrote Luther, for whom the Epistle was a life-changing, inspirational document.

Romans represents a remarkable development in Paul's religious awareness. Only five years earlier, his mind was still full of the death of Jesus. This letter makes no reference to the Cross of Jesus. In relation to Jesus, there are three phases in Paul's life. First, there is the period of bitter hostility, when he was breathing out fire and murderous threats. Then, as we must believe, as a result of a profound and intolerable guilt that he had been persecuting Jesus, Paul suffers the collapse known as his conversion. Thereafter, he 'boasts' in the Cross, repressing the thing of which he is most guilty, and making out of it a means of release. In his final, more expansive phase, he has internalised Jesus altogether. He sees the conflicts between Christ and Satan which are going on in his own self as being a universal phenomenon. 'For the good which I would I do not; but the evil which I would not, that I practise.'[2] In Romans, the predicament is seen not as a specifically Jewish thing, but as a universal problem. The mere existence of moral imperatives cannot 'save' us, since we are all, whether Jews or Gentiles, exiles from our true homeland with God. Paul is not saying that no human being is capable of morality. He knows that there are virtuous men, like the Stoics and the Pharisees. But it is possible to keep the Law without the existence of God. Man's true destiny is to be able to call Abba,

---

[1] Augustine: *De Civitate Dei* vii: chapter ii.
[2] Romans 7:20 (Jerusalem Bible).

Father.[1] Some of the more alarming teachings of Jesus would suggest that righteousness is not enough. We can abstain from murder, but we all carry about within ourselves the destructive impulses of anger. The Law of Moses can tell us to be chaste, in negative terms. That does not banish the ever-present demons of lust. Jesus, as recorded in the Gospels, taught that morality was not enough; he was even accused by his enemies of believing that it was not important. Life, for Jesus, began with the reconciliation of Man and God – God in his absolute righteousness, Man in his absolute earthiness and sinfulness. This yawning gulf between the perfection of God and the imperfection of man could never be bridged by a mere religious observance of rules.

Paul, in meditating upon these profundities, felt that the whole creation itself had been groaning and travailing in pain until that moment in history when Jesus appeared. Jesus offered his followers not the chance to be morally better, but a new freedom, the glorious liberty of the sons of God[2]. I find it impossible to believe that this liberating and extraordinary idea does not derive from some confrontation with Jesus himself, 'Jesus whom thou persecutest'. Paul's writings do enshrine ideas which could very well have been those of Jesus himself – the life-transforming effect of being able to say 'Abba' to God.

Whether or not Paul knew the historical Jesus could never be proved; and it perhaps does not matter very much, since his Jesus became, in Paul's writings, an internalised redeemer, offering him love. 'For I am persuaded that neither death nor life, nor angels, nor principalities, nor things present, nor things to come, nor powers, nor height, nor depth, nor any other creature, shall be able to separate us from the love of God, which is in Christ Jesus Our Lord.'[3] Paul's religious discovery touches the human soul at the deepest level, which is perhaps why Samuel Taylor Coleridge said that the Epistle to the Romans is the 'most profound book ever written'. The claim that it makes for Jesus takes Jesus out of the sphere of history and places him in a position which is unique, as the one reconciler between God and man. The 'unsearchable riches of Christ',[4] which Paul found in his own communings with the Absolute, are poured

---

[1] Romans 8:15. (Jerusalem Bible).
[2] Romans 8:21, 22.
[3] Romans 8:39.
[4] The phrase is actually from Ephesians 3:8; probably not written by Paul himself.

out to his hungry converts, offering a remedy for the deepest level of human guilt, and a salve for the deepest human fears: of failure, of inadequacy, and of death itself. He found in Jesus his personal saviour, the one who makes communion with God possible. His own writings, and his overpoweringly energetic life can all be read as a commentary on Jesus's parable of the Pharisee and the Publican. Paul's epistles are the story of the Pharisee who longed to be in the position of that Publican, able, without the paraphernalia of organised religion, to open his heart in penitence to Absolute Love. 'Protestants have always felt their affinity with this institutionalist, mystics with this disciplinarian. The reason, put shortly, is that St Paul understood what most Christians never realise, namely that the Gospel of Christ is not *a* religion, but religion itself, in its most universal and deepest significance.'[1] The first three Gospels in the New Testament were written by men who had learnt to look at things in Paul's way. They are not in that sense history. They are lenses, focussed on the person of Jesus through the eyes of Paul of Tarsus. In a series of extraordinary images, Paul focussed on Jesus and saw him as a man in whom God Himself was at work. 'God was in Christ reconciling the world to Himself.'[2]

Jesus was, for Paul, a new being, who heralds into existence a new type of humanity. Paul's great hymn to *agape* in the thirteenth chapter of I Corinthians is a meditation upon the significance of Jesus in his life and in his death. Scholars have debated whether the Love or Charity celebrated by Paul in this famous passage is the Love of God to Man, or the Love which Man should display towards his neighbour.[3] But anyone who has followed Paul in his wrestling with Jesus will know that the distinction has become meaningless. Jesus, in such stories as the Prodigal Son, shows what he believes about God's love for man. But more, in the belief of Paul and the Synoptic Gospellers, Jesus exemplified a God-like love in his own person. He exemplified and set forth a principle of the universe: that is, that in defiance of all the cruelty of men and the indifference of nature, the principle of life itself was love. To live without this *agape* makes morality itself a sham. It even deprives religious observance of its meaning. In Paul's great sentences about love, we can believe that he, and the Christian Church since, would willingly

[1] W. R. Inge: *Outspoken Essays* (1927), 229.
[2] 2 Cor. 5:18.
[3] For a discussion of these views, see Nygren: op. cit., 133–144.

have substituted the word 'Jesus' for wherever the word 'Love' appeared. 'Love suffereth long and is kind; love envieth not; love vaunteth not itself, is not puffed up, doth not behave itself unseemly, seeketh not its own, is not provoked, taketh not account of evil, rejoiceth not in unrighteousness, but rejoiceth with the truth.'[1]

For the modern reader there is an alarming discrepancy between how we should perceive 'the truth' and how Paul would have perceived it. In that great hymn to love, he reminds us that his own way of looking at the person of Jesus was purely mystical and visionary. What he saw 'according to the flesh' is of no importance. The events of Jesus, and of his life, only take shape long after they have been seen through the eyes of faith; and the same is true, probably, of all human lives. 'For now we see in a mirror, darkly, but then face to face.'[2] In his mystical enthusiasm, Paul has forgotten that normally, when we look into mirrors, we see no face but our own. As in some Surrealist canvas by Magritte, he looks into the glass and sees Another.

[1] I Cor. 13: 4–6.
[2] I Cor. 13:12.

# III

## THE COOKED FISH, or HOW TO READ A GOSPEL

NEARLY EVERYTHING WE know about Jesus comes from the Four Gospels printed in the New Testament. But, before we plunder them for 'evidence', are we sure that we know how to read them? What is a Gospel? The word in Greek means 'Good News', but a 'Gospel' is not a known literary form. You could go to a library in the ancient world and find histories, letters, biographies (of a sort), prose fiction, epic verse, drama, philosophy, philosophical dialogues, mathematics, magic and medicine. But you could not find any other 'Gospels'. They are a unique literary genre. They are designed to teach us theology, but they do so very largely by narrative means. They are not dispassionate histories, but they are crammed with information. In fact, they would appear to contain more biographical information than many ancient biographies. But can we trust the information which they contain?

The first three Gospels are all related to one another. They use much of the same material, and if they are looked at together (Greek *synopsis*) it may be seen that they all draw on common witnesses. Since they can be usefully analysed together by *synopsis*, they are generally referred to as the Synoptic Gospels. Most New Testament scholars have concluded that the oldest Gospel is Mark, and that Matthew and Luke both based their Gospels on a combination of sources – Mark, and their own distinctive traditions. Some scholars have posited the previous existence of some lost source (German *Quelle*), usually referred to as Q.[1] B. H. Streeter suggested nearly seventy years ago that Mark was written in Rome *c.*60 CE; Matthew in Antioch *c.*85 CE, and Luke in Corinth *c.*80 CE. Other scholars

[1] The literature is enormous. B. H. Streeter: *The Four Gospels: A Study of Origins* (1927) gives a full account of the theory recounted in the last sentence. See also F. C. Grant: *The Gospels: Their Origin and Growth* (1957); Vincent Taylor: *The Formation of the Gospel Tradition* (1953); Wilfrid Knox: *Sources of the Synoptic Gospels* (1959); E. P. Sanders and Margaret Davies: *Studying the Synoptic Gospels* (1989).

have differed from this approach; and there have been some notable defenders of the priority of Matthew's Gospel.[1] More recently, the comparatively late dating of the Gospels has been questioned.[2] One of the most curious features of the whole of New Testament scholarship is the fact that, though learned men have pored over these documents for centuries, they have never managed to establish beyond doubt such simple questions as where the Gospels were written, or when they were written, still less, by whom they were written. Intelligent guesswork is all that they have managed to produce. Probably, all the Gospels evolved through at least two stages: oral tradition about Jesus being eventually written down, and then reshaped by the evangelists for their own particular audiences.

The Fourth Gospel stands apart from the first three in matters of style, and provenance and theology. Because it had a 'high' Christology, a belief that Jesus was the pre-existent Logos, who had taken flesh and dwelt among us, concealing his true nature from all but those who saw him with the eyes of faith, it has been assumed that this was the last Gospel to be written, perhaps as late as 100 CE. But even this judgment is questionable, and the truth about the matter will probably never be known. There is no logical necessity which compels us to place a late date upon the Fourth Gospel, though it is obviously different in character from the first three. And if we forget about dating and provenance, and concentrate upon the texts themselves as they appear on the page, we see that the Fourth Gospel does present as much 'evidence' about Jesus as the other Gospels – 'evidence', in fact, of a more concrete kind, in the matter of dates, and places and people.[3] Scholars have disputed whether any of this 'evidence' can be understood historically, since the Fourth Gospel so obviously writes from a 'theological' point of view.

But the problem of the Fourth Gospel is not an isolated problem: it is the problem of the Synoptic Gospels as well. Only if we are straining to read the Synoptics in the wrong way will we fail to see that problem. We, the historical investigators, the detached inquirers, and the majority of modern Christians, naturally want to see how much in these strange books may be taken as 'literal' or useful, or plausible historical material. An unbeliever might decide,

---

[1] See e.g. B. C. Butler: *The Originality of St Matthew* (1951).

[2] See J. A. T. Robinson: *Redating the New Testament* (1976).

[3] See Fergus Millar: 'Reflections on the Trial of Jesus' in *A Tribute to Geza Vermes* (1990), 355–80.

having read one of the Gospels that it was all 'untrue', whereas a believer might wish to say, 'No! I believe that Jesus did change water into wine, was able to walk on water, and did, in a quite literal sense, rise from the tomb.' But both sorts of reader, the believer and the unbeliever, if they approach the New Testament in this spirit are readers, in Paul's phrase, 'according to the flesh' and will never begin to understand it. They are in a foreign country and yet they have not noticed that they are abroad.

Like the other three Gospels in the New Testament, the Fourth Gospel presents us with a number of historical statements which appear to be verifiable by means of modern historical analysis. Depending upon our own religious beliefs or upon the extent of our desire to extract historical details from such stories as the Gospels relate, we can decide whether these details are 'authentic' or not. In the Fourth Gospel's account of the Feeding of the Five Thousand, for example, we find that the fish eaten at that miraculous meal is not *ichthus*, the normal Greek word for fish, used by the other evangelists, but *opsarion*. This is a diminutive of the word *opson*, which means cooked food. *Opsarion* probably meant 'pickled fish'; it is a word a bit like 'kipper' or 'bloater', that is to say, fish that had been prepared for the customers by a tradesman. It is not a word which Matthew, Mark or Luke would use, remote as they were from the fish trade, and the events which they relate in their Gospels. The use of such a 'trade' term as *opsarion* suggests that the author might well have been drawing on traditions which go back to actual fishermen, actual trade. For John Robinson, the *opsarion* is an authentication of 'the Gospel of the Nazaraeans'. It helps Robinson believe that the author of the Fourth Gospel was actually John the fisherman, the friend and disciple of Jesus, who, by virtue of his position as an important fishmonger had an *entrée* through the tradesman's entrance into the High Priestly household, and was therefore able to witness the interrogation of Jesus during the night before his death.[1]

Like much in the Fourth Gospel, the *opsarion* seems like a tiny chink through which we see plain historical light. And there are many details like this in the New Testament; for instance, in the Fourth Gospel's account of Jesus's arrest. There is a scuffle, and one of the High Priest's servants gets his ear cut in a sword-fight with

[1] J. A. T. Robinson: *The Priority of John* (1985), 117.

Peter. The other Gospels record this scene, but only the Fourth Gospel gives the high priest's servant a name: Malchus.[1]

Such details, so realistic and so apparently verifiable, can actually confuse the modern reader into thinking he is reading one sort of narrative whereas he is actually reading another. It can confuse him into thinking of himself as a 'prospector' wading down the river with a sieve in search of 'facts', like some Forty-Niner in search of gold nuggets. Amid all the dross and the 'mythology', such a reader might suppose, we can find the occasional nugget – a piece of pickled fish, a servant with a name. So, a sceptical 'prospector' might point out that the Fourth Gospel believed that the office of High Priest circulated on an annual basis,[2] whereas in historical fact, the Jewish High Priest did not have to stand down after only one year in office. The 'believer', by contrast, will think that the Fourth Gospel is full of authenticating small details – the descriptions of darkness falling, the more-or-less plausible chronology, the fish, the servant. Then can follow apparently well-based discussions about whether the Fourth Gospel was 'right', historically, to offer a chronology of Jesus's death which is so radically different from the Synoptics. The Synoptics say that Jesus instituted the Eucharist before he died (no mention of that in the Fourth Gospel) and that he was crucified after the Passover. The Fourth Gospel (which knows, for instance that Jews were/are forbidden to carry swords during Passover) places the arrest and condemnation of Jesus before the festival. The Crucifixion in the Fourth Gospel happens at about the time that the Passover lambs are being slain in the Temple.

But such details as the servant's name, when we investigate them, rebound against us if we try to view them as 'nuggets' of fact, like the pickled fish. 'Did St John in fact believe that the servant was called Malchus?' asks one New Testament scholar, Aileen Guilding.[3] She believes that the author of the Fourth Gospel *did* so believe, but she demonstrates most convincingly the processes by which he might have reached this belief. He did not do so by asking those present at the arrest of Jesus. Nor was he very likely to have done so by searching his own memory. In her book, *The Fourth Gospel and Jewish Worship*, Dr Guilding demonstrates how this author wished to establish that Christianity is the New Israel, a replacement for the old

[1] John 18:10.
[2] John 18:13.
[3] Aileen Guilding: *The Fourth Gospel and Jewish Worship* (1960), 232.

Israel, the old religion of Judaism. He does so by arranging the stories about Jesus in patterns which reflect and echo the readings assigned in the Synagogue Lectionaries for the various feasts of the Jewish year. In the first half of his Gospel, the episodes follow the feasts of Passover, New Year, Tabernacles, Dedication and Purim. In the second half of the Gospel, with the account of the supper and Jesus's discourses to his disciples, followed by his arrest and Crucifixion, all these feasts, and in the same order, are absorbed into the narrative, to emphasise that Jesus, in his last hours, re-formed and re-established Israel as a new religion, that of Christianity. So, in his washing of the disciples' feet, Jesus echoes the Synagogue Lections for Passover from the Book of Numbers in which the Israelites are told to sprinkle the Levites, the sacerdotal class, with water, 'that they may do the service of the Lord'. (Numbers 8:1 ff.)

Such Scriptural echoes may be discovered in all the final chapters of the Gospel. The readings for the Jewish New Year, for example, conclude with Deuteronomy 2:13: 'Now then, arise'; and Exodus 33:1: 'Depart – go up hence!' In the middle of his last great discourse, the Fourth Gospel Jesus makes the contextually baffling comment, 'Arise, let us go hence'. If we see that he has here come to the end of his 'New Year discourse', corresponding directly to the Synagogue readings for New Year, then these words of Jesus make sense. In ordinary narrative terms, they are incomprehensible, since the disciples do not, at this juncture, arise or go hence. Similarly, in the readings for Tebeth, we find I Kings 2:37: 'On the day thou passest over the brook Kidron, know thou for certain that thou shalt surely die.' In the apparently 'straight' narrative of John 18:1, we read 'When Jesus had spoken these words, he went forth with his disciples over the brook Kidron'.

The readings for the Feast of Dedication in the Jewish calendar speak of God as the Shepherd-King. The Messiah will come to gather in the true Israel, the elect of God, when wicked men have dispersed the flock. 'Thus saith the Lord my God: Feed the flock of slaughter, whose buyers slay them, and hold themselves not guilty: and they that sell them shall say, Blessed be the Lord for I am rich. For I will no more pity the inhabitants of the land, saith the Lord; but lo! I will deliver the men every one into his neighbour's hand, and into the hand of his king [Hebrew *Malko*] and out of their hand I will not deliver them.'[1] It would seem from at least one of the manuscript

[1] Zechariah 11:4 ff.

traditions in which this Gospel survives (in Syriac)[1] as if John's Greek *Malchos* were a mere transcription of this Semitic form.

Now that is a long preamble, but to many modern readers, whether they are sceptics or Christian believers, it will come as a surprise. We can believe, with Dr Guilding, that the servant really was called Malchus, or anyway that the evangelist genuinely thought this was the man's name. But he did so purely 'on the authority of holy Scripture'.[2] We know from other Gospels that the tradition that Jesus himself applied the passage of Zechariah just quoted – 'Smite the shepherd and the sheep shall be scattered' – to the moment of his own arrest. The prophecy of Zechariah is conveniently fulfilled in every particular for the Fourth Gospel, on that last night of Jesus's life. The shepherd is smitten. The betrayer, Judas, is enriched. The followers are delivered into the hands of Malcho, Malko, Malchus, a word which originally means 'the King'.[3] 'The fact that St John took this, and many other such details, from the Synagogue Lections is of some importance, for, since Lections were inspired Scripture, they had for him an authority which far outweighed that of any human testimony, however well attested. Every part of the Scriptures – the Law, the Prophets, and the Writings – spoke beforehand of Christ. Indeed, an injunction in the Torah about the preparation of the Passover Lamb ("neither shall ye break a bone thereof") is regarded as literally fulfilled in the events of the Crucifixion.'[4]

The question facing the reader of the Fourth Gospel today is: which came first? Did the event find an echo in Scripture – was Scripture indeed 'fulfilled' – or did the Scriptural reference 'suggest' the event? It is absolutely essential at the outset that this should be grasped and understood; otherwise the reader of the New Testament, and in particular of its narratives, is going to be beguiled into thinking that the evangelists are writers or historians in a modern, post-Enlightenment sense of the word, that their statements can be tested by references to other historians, or to neutral events exterior to the Gospel-narratives themselves. The truth is odder. The evangelists' way of putting together a narrative so as to interpret events in terms of other written traditions would seem alien to a modern writer.

[1] F. C. Burkitt: *The Syriac Forms of New Testament Proper Names*.
[2] Guilding: op. cit., 165.
[3] And the first King of Israel was called Saul. But see chapter ten for a development of this speculation.
[4] Guilding: op. cit., 232.

Matthew, for example, makes Jesus into a new Moses, delivering a New Law to his people from a mountain-top. For Mark, Jesus/Joshua, like his namesake in the Old Testament, is leading a band of followers on a trek through the wilderness to a promised goal. He is also, and at the same time, an echo of Joseph, betrayed by Judah/Judas into the hands of wicked men, but finding new life as a leader of Gentiles. It is rather as if a modern biographer of President Kennedy chose to write his story by opening a life of Abraham Lincoln and building up his narrative by an endless series of reflections and echoes between the one and the other. The Gospel writers did not go to a modern research library and spread out all the 'facts' in order to tell a dispassionate story. They started with a set of theological beliefs about Jesus, and they fitted their narratives into these beliefs; not the other way around. It is not impossible that the Fourth Gospel contains strands of tradition and memory of the historical Jesus which go back to his contemporaries. But even if we supposed for the sake of argument that the Fourth Gospel was actually written by John the son of Zebedee, drawing on his actual memories of Jesus of Nazareth, we should still need to approach his book in the knowledge that what he called memory was not the same as what a modern journalist or historian would call memory. The evangelist would have understood the assertion of Lewis Carroll's White Queen: 'It's a poor sort of memory that only works backwards.'[1] The most urgently meaningless disputes have taken place between modern persons about whether or not the Gospels are 'true', and all such disputes have been based upon the assumption that 'truth' would mean the same to the Fourth Evangelist as it would to ourselves. Pilate's question to Christ during his trial in this Gospel[2] is not answered, either by Jesus or by the evangelist, but it is important that it should be embedded in the narrative. We have to answer it, though they would not: *'Ti estin aletheia?'* – 'What is truth?' How we answer the question will determine how we read the Gospel. Supposing there were such a thing as dispassionate memory, colourless memory, memory which made no interpretation of facts! If there were such a transparent camera-brain in a human head, it was not in the head which conceived of the Fourth Gospel. He was not 'remembering' a 'straight' version of Jesus's life and death, and then

---

[1] Lewis Carroll: *Through the Looking Glass*, chapter five.
[2] John 18:38.

reading the Hebrew Scriptures, and then exclaiming – 'Look at this! How amazing! The prophecies have been fulfilled! It says here in the Book of Zechariah that the scattered flock will fall into the hands of Malko, the King. Now, what was the name of that man in the garden – the one who had a fight with Peter on the night of the Lord's arrest? Malchus, wasn't it? Malcho? Something like that. Well, isn't that a coincidence!'

On the contrary. Our author was *starting out* with the assumption that his story had parallels in the Scriptures. He was not making a 'straight' story into a myth. He was starting with a myth. [1] The myth is that in the beginning was the Word, the creative energy of God, who was both with God and who was God, and without whom nothing was made that was made. And this Word, the pre-existent Godhead, enters His creation. For those to whom he grants *gnosis* or knowledge, he reveals his glory – by means of 'signs'. To the stubborn and unregenerate people among whom he moved, however, this glory was not revealed. Such people are shut out as much by ignorance as by sin – indeed, in the Fourth Gospel the two things are more or less indistinguishable. It is a book which is scathingly harsh about the *kosmos*, the 'world'. For though God loved the *kosmos*, and gave himself for it, the ignorant *kosmos* continues to reject God. It is a place of darkness. Its natural inhabitants are blind. Only to those who have received the revelation of glory is given the power 'to become the sons of God' [2] like Jesus himself. Like the Community at Qumran, whose religious ideas have been revealed to us so fully in the Scrolls unearthed in 1947, the Fourth Gospel sees life as a perpetual conflict between light and darkness, with the darkness never able to 'master' the light, never able to understand it or to conquer it. The *kosmos* hates Jesus. He does not need to judge or condemn it, for it condemns itself by its own ignorance. The 'love' which God shows to the *kosmos* in this Gospel is, to say the least, limited. In his mythological way of looking at things, benighted humanity is represented by the 'Judaeans' who failed to

---

[1] By saying 'he', rather than 'they', I do not mean to imply a theory of authorship about this Gospel. Many scholars believe that the Preface is a separate piece of mythologising which does not originally belong to the 'story' or narrative part of the Gospel. Other scholars have posited the theory that there are at least two 'authors' or traditions behind the final redaction of this Gospel as we read it today – if indeed what we read *is* a final redaction. Similarly, by using the word 'myth', I do not wish to suggest that the Fourth Gospel is either 'true' or 'false' – *vide supra* my comment on Pilate's question.
[2] John 1:12.

see the glory of Galileean Jesus even when he performed signs among them. These *Ioudaioi*, or Jews, are represented as urging the death of Jesus upon Pilate.

No doubt, modern readers are right to find in this the seeds of later Christian anti-Semitism. But there is also in the Fourth Gospel a strongly anti-Christian vein – or at least anti-Christianity-according - to-Paul-or-*Mark*- or-*Luke*. There is much less emphasis in the Fourth Gospel than in other parts of the New Testament on the Church, on the gathering together of the people of God. Such an idea would have been repellent to this writer, perhaps. Believers in the Fourth Gospel are born again as individuals into the Light of Jesus. They do not find Jesus in the Communion of Saints. There is no Eucharist. The faith of Jesus's followers who read this Gospel is precisely that, faith: it is not based on knowledge or seeing, though this Gospel is written to reassure those who have not seen with their bodily eyes the glory which was once revealed to the friends and disciples of Jesus himself.

Strangely enough, though millions of words have been written about the Fourth Gospel, no one has ever managed to locate it in time or place. Its date and its authorship and its provenance, like the date and authorship and provenance of all the other Gospels, is quite unknown. If I had to speculate about the community from which the Fourth Gospel emerged, I should say that it was a sect based somewhere in or near Samaria: anti-Jerusalem, anti-Paul, and with a distinct set of memories and traditions relating to Jesus and his family, traditions which were unknown to those who wrote down the Synoptic Gospels. It would not be in the least surprising if this group had some kinship with the sons of Zebedee.

But whether it comes from Samaria, or from Ephesus (as some ancient sources suggest), the point about this Gospel is that it can only be read as a testimony, not as a neutral history. It is the story of the Divine Logos (which is not quite the same thing as God – the Fourth Gospel does not state that Jesus was God, still less that he was the Second Person of the Trinity) moving about in an ignorant world, and only revealing signs of himself to the Chosen, a new Israel. The 'facts' in the story – such as that, on the night of his arrest, he crossed the brook Kidron, or that he and his disciples had a sword-fight with a man named Malchus, were not arrived at by historical 'research'. All these 'facts' derive from the evangelist's mythological presuppositions. Demolish the myth and the 'facts' go with it. You demolish the Temple with no hope of rebuilding it.

But that is not to say that there is nothing at all in the Gospels upon which an historian may fruitfully meditate. Of course, much the cleanest and easiest approach to the New Testament is the one adopted by Rudolf Bultmann and his followers. It is much easier to say that the Fourth Gospel, and indeed the whole of the New Testament, is purely self-referential. It is impossible to extract from them kinds of 'reality' which were not interesting or available to the New Testament world-view. Therefore, says Bultmann, accept that it is ALL mythology! An attractive idea, not least because of its sweepingness and its neatness. Then you do not need to ask the question whether there is any historical reality behind these stories. All you have to do is to establish what these stories are doing in their context, what they tell us about the community of belief from which they come. Did Jesus institute the Eucharist, for example? A foolish question, by Bultmann's standards. You have New Testament books which say that he did. You have others, such as the Fourth Gospel, which make no mention of it, but which regard Jesus himself as the Bread of Life, who 'feeds' believers with the gift of himself when they come to him in faith. The Fourth Gospel puts all this teaching into the mouth of Jesus at the time of the Feeding of the Five Thousand. But whether the Feeding of the Five Thousand, or the Last Supper, or indeed anything else in the life of Jesus 'actually happened' could not possibly be proved, and therefore cannot be of interest. All that the books of the New Testament show us, according to Bultmann, is the belief and practice of particular sets of people. The 'quest for the historical Jesus' can thus conveniently be put on one side as the occupation of sentimentalists and methodological illiterates.

The stubborn fact remains, however, that nothing is ever as simple as scholars would wish it to be. However chaotically antiquarian and unmethodological it might seem, historians are entitled to ask 'What was the real Jesus actually like? What did he teach? Can that be recaptured at all, however tentatively, from the documents in our possession?' The Gospels, after all, start out with some presuppositions which are alien to our way of viewing the world; but that does not mean that they only contain 'mythological' truth, and no 'facts'. Given the mythological framework of the Fourth Gospel, for example, it still purports to be a story with an actual historical setting. Even if we allow that the book went through several stages of composition and is not in the modern sense the work of a single 'author', it is a book which claims, in its final redaction, to be the memory of an actual individual. After the description of the Crucifixion, it tells us how the soldiers came to break the legs of Jesus and of the men crucified alongside him. The purpose, if we are reading this as a literal narrative, was to cause the victims to die of asphyxiation, since by breaking their legs they would hang solely by their arms and the pressure on heart and lungs would overpower them. A different reading would point out that in Exodus (12:46) we read that the bones of the Passover Lamb should not be broken before they were consumed – so this is Jesus the Lamb of God, dying to take away the sin of the world. But it is not one or the other; it is both. It is not a narrative made up entirely of Scriptural echoes; nor is it straight 'history'. Yet, there is the sentence, worryingly challenging, describing this gruesome scene at the foot of the Cross: 'he that saw it bare record, and his record is true, and he knoweth that he saith true, that ye might believe'. [1]

Those who believe that Jesus was an invented character, that he did not exist at all, are in a very small minority of New Testament scholars. We are not obliged to believe that the evangelists had the same purposes as modern historians. They wrote, as the Fourth Gospel says, 'that ye might believe'. But it is eccentric to deny that they are describing actual people, actual places, even on occasion actual events, of which the Crucifixion of Jesus was surely one. We can discount the idea that Jesus ever claimed to be the Second Person of the Trinity, or that he ever claimed to be God, since the New Testament never states that he made any such claim. We can even discount that Jesus ever thought of himself as the Pre-existent Logos, sent from the Father to 'reveal' God to the enlightened few, as the Fourth Gospel would maintain. The passages where the Jesus of the Fourth Gospel makes these claims for himself are so unlike the Jesus of the Synoptic Gospels that it is impossible to imagine that they are 'historical'. But it strains belief to suppose that there was not an actual Galilean preacher, exorcist and miracle-worker who died on a cross in or around the year 30 CE.

A comparatively recent book on the Fourth Gospel[2] has shown that it is possible, without total absurdity, to reconstruct a chron-

---

[1] John 19:35.
[2] J. A. T. Robinson: *The Priority of John*.

ology of the last three years of Jesus's life from that Gospel. This is not to say that the ordering of events in it is not highly symbolic. This is not to say that the 'signs' and Jewish feasts, and the sayings of Jesus, are not here arranged in a highly artificial way. But it is to say that the Fourth Gospel (unlike the other three) provides us with a chronology and there is no reason *per se* to suppose that this was not *something like* an accurate timetable of events.

| | | |
|---|---|---|
| 27 CE | (autumn?) | Appearance of John the Baptist. |
| 28 CE | March (?) | Baptism of Jesus. |
| | | Jesus in Cana and at Capernaum. |
| | | In Jerusalem before and during Passover and the Feast of Unleavened Bread. (28 April–5 May). |
| | May | In Judaea baptising. |
| | | Arrest of John the Baptist. |
| | June–October | In Galilee. |
| | 23–31 October | In Jerusalem for Tabernacles. |
| | November–April | In Galilee. |
| 29 CE | (early?) | Death of John the Baptist. |
| | April | Desert Feeding, before Passover (18 April). |
| | May–September | In Phoenicia, Ituraea and Galilee. |
| | 15 October | In Jerusalem for Tabernacles (12–19 October). |
| | November–December | In Judaea and Peraea. |
| | 20–27 December | In Jerusalem for Dedication. |
| | January–February | In Bethany beyond Jordan. |
| 30 CE | February (?) | In Bethany in Judaea. |
| | March | In Ephraim. |
| | 2–6 April | In Bethany and Jerusalem. |
| | 7 April | Crucifixion. |

I can vividly remember when John Robinson's book, *The Priority of John*, was first aired, as some posthumous lectures (the 1984 Bampton Lectures), read aloud by another New Testament scholar, Charles Moule, to the congregation of St Mary's Church in Oxford. The New Testament scholars were all shaking their heads and thinking that poor Bishop Robinson had gone off the rails before he died. No longer the firebrand who had made himself famous in the 1960s by writing a short book called *Honest to God*, which seemed to call into question Christian orthodoxy, he had devoted what turned out to be the last years of his life to establishing cranky theories about the Fourth Gospel.

I believe that the scholars missed the point when they shook their heads. Robinson wrote his book, I am convinced, partly as a donnish tease. He intended to give us pause. He asked the theologians to suspend their prejudices and to look afresh at the New Testament. Supposing that we had not been told by most scholars since the last century that the earliest Gospel was that of Mark, and that Matthew used Mark and some material of his own; and that Luke used Mark and some material of his own; and that they might both have drawn on a mysterious common source known as *Quelle* or Q. Supposing that no one had ever told you that the Fourth Gospel was a very late composition. Supposing that it was actually, whatever happened to it in later redactions, the work of one of Jesus's own disciples, John the son of Zebedee. (The ascription is first given by Theophilus of Antioch in about 170 CE, and about ten years after that, Irenaeus said that the Gospel was 'written by John the disciple of the Lord, the same who leant on his breast'.) [1]

Bishop Robinson did not prove that the Fourth Gospel was the work of John the son of Zebedee. No one could ever do that. But if, merely as an imaginative exercise, we try to read the Fourth Gospel in Robinson's way – as if it was in fact a treasure-hoard of plausible historical details – we discover many such details, which make sense on an historical level but which have no immediately discernible parabolic significance. Hence the importance of the word *opsarion*, the 'trade' word for fish, the word which only a dealer in cooked fish might think of using. When, at the end of the Gospel, the disciples are fishing in the Lake, both words for fish are used. On Jesus's advice, the disciples throw their net over the right hand side of the boat, and catch a miraculous draught of 153 fish. While the fish are live in the net, they are described as *ichthues*; Robinson notes, incidentally, that it is a professional touch, in our evangelist, to notice that 'for all there were so many, the net was not rent'. [2] But when they bring the fish to land, and the fish has become a comestible, Jesus says to Peter, 'Bring of the fish which ye have now taken', using the word *opsarion*. [3] Why should anyone who was not in the fishing business make such distinctions?

[1] Eusebius: *Ecclesiastical History* 3:23 ff.; 5:8.4.
[2] John 21:11.
[3] John 21:10.

The servant's name was Malchus. This seems suspiciously useful for the evangelist's purpose. He has, surely, started with the old Scriptural text and made up his story to fit the 'prophecy'. 'Bring of the *opsarion* which ye have now taken': we are at once in a world of real fishermen. At the very least, it seems like oral tradition; we could even be tempted to believe that this is the actual memory of an old man who, as the Gospel claims, witnessed the events which it describes.

So, in these two words – the name of the servant, Malchus, and the word for a piece of fish – we can observe in microcosm what makes it so difficult to read the Gospels. On the one hand, we must always remember that the New Testament is not unbiased history. There is not one word of it which is not written to instruct the faithful. Moreover, its way of viewing the universe – history, geography, the truth itself – is entirely unlike our own. On the other hand, it is choc-a-bloc with details, details which seem immensely beguiling to a modern historian.

The one thing which you can never do is to disentangle the threads and say, 'We recognise that this particular event is being told by someone who knew first-century Palestine at first hand: the chronology just about fits, the geography is more or less right, the details could all be true – and therefore we are going to read this narrative as something which it isn't: post-Enlightenment historical narrative.' We cannot say that we are prepared to take some bits of the narrative and throw away the supernaturalist wrapper in which they are contained. (We want to say it; we will say it, but we are not entitled to treat these texts in this way.) We cannot say, 'Jesus and his disciples once had a picnic by the Lake. They caught an unusually large amount of fish; but I refuse to accept that there is any supernatural explanation for what happened on that day.' The reason that you cannot, as it were, take the cooked fish and leave behind the miracle is contained in the discussion which we had about the name of Malchus. Why is the evangelist telling us this story about a huge catch of fish? Why this story, and not another? After all, as he himself says, 'if they should be written every one, I suppose that the world itself could not contain the books which should be written'[1] about Jesus. Thus, with consummate and teasing elegance, the book ends. It had begun with a solitary Word. It ends with the prospect of a

[1] John 21:25.

deluge of words. It begins with some disciples of John the Baptist standing by the bank of a river. It ends with Jesus standing by the edge of a lake, and those same disciples struggling with a net full of fish. The miraculous draught is a symbol. The number is a symbol – nobody quite knows of what, but presumably it is symbolic of the number of converts to Christianity. [1]

But nor can you read the story as pure parable or symbol. This book refuses to be read either as 'literal' history (whatever that would be) or as mere 'symbolism'; for the meaning of all the 'signs' is contained in every detail, in every multi-layered texture of the events. The numerological mystery of the 153 fishes is contained in a narrative which is supposed to be plausible; the parable is in the actual – the fish, the coal fire, the figure by the shore; earlier, in the very wounds in the body of Jesus. Blessed are they that have not seen and yet have believed. [2] And here you approach another facet of the Fourth Gospel, another layer in its endless layers, another ingredient in its inexhaustible richness and fascination as a literary text: that is, that we ourselves, who read it, or hear it read, are meant to be characters within the story. It is not trying to be history of the sort written by Tacitus or Livy, where we can weigh the evidence of the ancient historians against other sources, against the evidence of archaeology or numismatics. The story of what Jesus said and did is, in the Fourth Gospel, inseparable from who he was – who he was in the mind of the narrator.

Because the literary processes of this strange book are, as it were, flaunted, and because its style, theology, mannerisms differ so markedly from those of the Synoptic Gospels, we might be tempted to think that the difficulty resided solely in our encounters with the Fourth Evangelist. For a 'simpler' version of events, we could always turn to Mark, or Matthew, or Luke. But that would be a mistake. It is true that the Fourth Gospel has this strange habit of making the doings of Jesus into 'signs', his actions, so to say, into parables. So, for example, at Cana of Galilee, Jesus turns water into wine; and the water is contained in stone jars 'for the Jewish rites of purification'; [3] and this story is told not to entertain us with Jesus's party tricks, but to tell us something. The Jewish pots are the old Israel, and they

[1] See J. A. Emerton: 'The Hundred and Fifty-Three Fishes in John XXI:11', *Journal of Theological Studies*, April 1958, 86–9.
[2] John 20:29.
[3] John 2:6.

contained something which was refreshing and nourishing, water, and cleansing too, but not intoxicating. Jesus himself is the new wine, filling the jars. God is making a new Israel. What had been a merely empty ritual – cleansing with water before eating, washing the specified cooking vessels at the specified time and in the specified manner – becomes something quite new: an intoxication with the living God! The Synoptic Gospels make the same point – but they do so by making Jesus utter one of his pithy remarks: 'new wine into fresh wineskins'.[1] But it would be wrong to suppose that the symbolism so much loved by the Fourth Gospel was absent from the first three. In Matthew, for example, the disciples accompany Jesus on a boat trip during which there is a storm. Jesus sleeps through the storm until they wake him with the plea, 'Save Lord, we perish'. Jesus awakes, rebukes the winds and the waves, and there follows a great calm. The boat is a parable for the Church. The disciples are the early Church, distressed by the storms of persecution. They cry out to Christ and he appears to be sleeping; but when he awakes, there is a great calm.

Matthew no doubt believed that there literally was an occasion in which Jesus demonstrated his ability to control the weather, but he tells the story in order to instruct the Church in times of hardship. Like John, he believes that all the things which occurred in the life of Jesus took place to 'fulfil' the Scriptures. That is to say, he has been through the Scriptures cheerfully lifting details, and then inventing the 'facts' to fit the 'prophecies'. Micah said that the Messiah would be born in Bethlehem, so Jesus finds himself, most improbably for a Galilean, being born in Bethlehem. If John fits the life of Jesus into a 'grid' of which the Synagogue Lectionary is the model, Matthew chooses the Pentateuch, the first five books of the Jewish Bible. Jesus is Moses, delivering his law on the mountain-top and leading his people to redemption, feeding them in the wilderness, and so forth. Mark has equally ingenious ways of making history interpret prophecy, rather than the other way around; one of his models being the story of Joseph and his brethren; another being Joshua/Jesus (same name) conquering the land of Promise.

In such strange ways, the Gospels creep up on us. They are not history so much as they are tracts. But they are also works of a high imaginative order. I use the word 'imaginative' in the sense in which

---

[1] Mark 2:21.

it was used by the Romantic poets and painters – William Blake, Samuel Taylor Coleridge and others – not to mean 'fanciful' or dishonest, but possessed with a capacity to remake the world. William Blake understood this when he wrote – '"What", it will be Question'd, "When the Sun rises, do you not see a round disk of fire somewhat like a Guinea?" O no, no, I see an Innumerable company of the Heavenly host crying, "Holy, Holy, Holy is the Lord God Almighty".'[1] It would be cumbersome to spell these things out were it not for the fact that so many readers of the New Testament approach it with a carnal (to use Paul's word) vision, rather than with imagination. 'Why is the Bible more Entertaining & Instructive than any other book?' William Blake asked a correspondent; giving the reply, 'is it not because [it is] addressed to the Imagination, which is Spiritual Sensation, and but mediately to the Understanding or Reason?'[2] Many New Testament scholars have compiled 'theologies', and commentaries, and textual and historical analyses of the Gospels with a plodding disregard for this truth.

The attentive reader of the New Testament must give himself up to the world-view which it represents, and look at the nature of things through the eyes of men and women whose hopes, beliefs and preoccupations, not merely about Jesus, but about God and about everything are wholly at variance with those of post-Enlightenment 'modern man', and subtly at variance with those of their 'Hellenistic' contemporaries. Rudolf Bultmann, who was one of the greatest of twentieth-century theologians, and who did understand the necessity to read these books imaginatively, contrasts the Hellenistic concept of the world (*kosmos*) with the uses of the word in the Fourth Gospel. For Greek writers as different as Aeschylus and Plato, it was axiomatic that man was part of the natural order. To this degree, contemporary man is closer to Socrates than he is to St John. 'The sages say that heaven and earth, the gods and men, are held together by fellowship (*koinonia*) and friendship and harmony (*kosmiotes*) and self-limitation and righteousness. So, they call the universe as a whole order (*kosmos*) not, as we say, disorder, or want of discipline – perhaps the fact escaped you that the mathematical relationship has power among gods and men.' Bultmann quotes this passage from Plato's *Gorgias* to demonstrate that in the Hellenistic

[1] William Blake: 'A Vision of the Last Judgment'.
[2] William Blake: Letter to the Revd. Dr Trusler, 23 August 1799.

concept of *kosmos* the Gods and men are all part of the same thing, the same harmonious whole. From the time of Homer to the time of Jesus it was still axiomatic in the ancient world that immortals and mortals, angels, and animals, and matter itself were all bound together in the same chain of desire, sadness and decay. There is a law, *nomos*, of nature, expressed in its purest form in mathematics, but also discernible in the sphere of ethics and of what we would call natural science from which none could escape, even though the Platonist would wish to escape from the bonds of the physical and ascend to the spiritual, to discard the world of nature, which is merely a shadow of that heavenly reality which can be discovered by intense thought, asceticism and prayer.

For the Fourth Evangelist, and for the other New Testament writers, however, the *kosmos* is not the ultimate reality. The New Testament is not even remotely interested (as purportedly 'other-wordly' Plato was) in concepts of mind, of mathematics, of politics, of law. The New Testament posits a quite different way of viewing the *kosmos*, a way which we find in the pages of the Old Testament and in the Dead Sea Scrolls, but not among the Greeks. The closest analogy in the non-theological sphere is the 'imagination' as it was conceived by the Romantics, who, of course, derived their concept of Imagination as much from the Scriptures as from Kant. 'Belief,' Bultmann insisted, 'is not a *Weltanschauung*. A *Weltanschauung* seeks to make even my destiny comprehensible on the basis of a general understanding of man and the world, as an instance of what happens generally. According to the view of the New Testament, in that way I am running away from my real existence. I do not attain to my existence in the sphere of what happens generally, but rather in a concrete situation, in the here and now, in my individual responsibility and decision, where as I hazard myself I can gain or lose myself. That is, I stand as an individual in the presence of God.'[1] It is in this light that we are to understand the Fourth Gospel's perpetually dismissive attitude to what it calls the *kosmos*, dismissive, yet profoundly paradoxical. 'I am come not to judge the world but to save the world.'[2] 'In the world ye shall have tribulation; but be of good cheer. I have overcome the world.'[3] For the Fourth Gospel, Jesus, the Eternal Logos, is the point at which, unseen and misunderstood

[1] Bultmann: *Essays*, 78.
[2] John 12:47.
[3] John 16:33.

by the world, the Godhead can be apprehended; not by mankind in general, and not by the Church, but by the individual – by you, by me. 'My kingdom is not of this world,' says Johannine Jesus to Pilate at his trial. [1] It means that the reader who is still 'of this world', still looking at the sun and seeing 'a round disk of fire somewhat like a Guinea', will be simply unable to 'see' what the book is about. The reader who does understand, or who is prepared to understand, will be like Nicodemus who comes to Jesus by night, with all the rich symbolism of the darkness which surrounds him. The darkness is the darkness of a corporeal, as opposed to an imaginative vision. Nicodemus is a 'ruler of the Jews' and in this Gospel, the 'Jews' are not so much the actual adherents to Judaism (Jesus and his disciples are that); more, they are the people who inhabit the kosmos, who have Weltanschauung not faith, for whom God and Man and Law are part of the same clockwork game. In order to escape this system, the 'ruler of the Jews' must be reborn. He can not inhabit the old womb any more, nor can he worship in the old Temple. He is confronted with the rebirth of spiritual crisis. [2]

We, too, the readers or hearers of the Gospel come to Jesus by night; that is to say, blinkered with the desire to make sense of things, bounded by common sense, decency, and by ethical and scientific notions which are containable within the kosmos rather than being wholly outside it. Clutching our text from Wittgenstein, we believe that 'the world is that which is the case', and we want to know whether the Gospel is, in this sense, 'the case', whether the stories which it relates are in any sense or in any small particle, verifiable. That is the nature of our coming by night. The Gospels themselves would appear to invite us to test their evidence by just such a scale of 'realistic' values. Take the story of Doubting Thomas. A Jesuit priest once said to me that if he did not believe this story to be literally true, he would renounce his religious calling. Many thousands, millions, of readers of that story must have been comparably arrested by it, challenged by it; and in precisely this way. It makes no sense if, by the end, you cannot, with Thomas, be kneeling before Jesus and saying, 'My Lord and my God' as he offers to show you the scars of his Sacred Passion. [3] Perhaps, of all the stories which this supremely skilful writer tells in his short book, this one has the

[1] John 18:36.
[2] John 3:3.
[3] John 20:28.

greatest power. It is the supreme example of the self-fulfilling story, the literary artefact which becomes for the reader an imaginative fact in his or her imaginative scale of things. My Lord and my God! Blessed are those – that is, the readers – who have not seen and yet have believed. 'And many other signs truly did Jesus in the presence of his disciples which are not written in this book. But these are written that ye might believe.'[1]

The scholars have created stupendous mountains over the Fourth Gospel: speculations about its origins, provenance, relationship to Gnosticism, analogues in the Dead Sea Scrolls, debts to Hellenistic Judaism, originality, or lack of it. But the modern, benighted, *kosmos*-inhabiting reader ultimately wants to know: Is it true? Did the story of Doubting Thomas take place in the circumstances which the Fourth Gospel describes? Were the disciples, as a matter of historical fact, sitting in a house together after the Crucifixion of Jesus; and did he, in the evening of that Sunday, appear to them? Did he, as a matter of actual, observable, verifiable historical fact return a week later and offer Thomas the chance to put his hands into that wounded side?

If your answer to these questions is 'Yes', then you have beheld the glory of Jesus, and you have become as one of the Sons of God. The world will be transformed. As Paul said, 'If any man be in Christ, he is a new creature; old things are passed away.'[2] How quickly, though, the believer comes to dislike bobbing about in the sea of faith, and wishes to swim back for his life-belt of plausible historical reassurance. How quickly he believes not out of faith, not from a position of unseeing, but because he imagines himself there in that scene with Doubting Thomas, and tries to persuade himself that it is a narrative such as a contemporary observer might have written about the Battle of Jutland! And it is not like that at all.

The unbeliever in the story can be puzzled on another level. Since the story is untrue, palpably and obviously untrue – bodies do not, in our *kosmos*, resurrect themselves – how do we reconcile ourselves to the paradox that the New Testament is patently the work of men striving to be good? How can we reconcile ourselves to the idea that the Fourth Gospel, with its great injunctions to love one another as Jesus loved his disciples, should concoct such a whopping lie as the story of Jesus's resurrection?

[1] John 20:31.
[2] 2 Cor. 5:17.

William Blake was a very good man. Sincerely and with no intent to deceive, he would tell his friends that he had been conversing with angels, or that he had been visited, that very week towards the close of the eighteenth century in his house in London, by Julius Caesar or the prophet Isaiah. If his friends protested, or asked where these august personages from the past were to be seen, Blake would tap the side of his head.

Human beings have such a boundless capacity to fantasise, particularly in the area of religious experience, that we need not question the sincerity of the evangelists when they describe the reappearance of Jesus from the tomb. In our own day, many people have seen the Blessed Virgin Mary, either over the rooftops of Cairo, or in the skies of Yugoslavia. This is not the place to examine the veracity or otherwise of individual Gospel stories. It is the point, merely, to admit the kind of books which the New Testament contains. Anyone so ignorant, or so innocent, as to open the New Testament in the hope of finding a neutral historical source will be knocked back by a hurricane. Open it, and you will find a Pandora's box of personal challenges and ethical commands. By the end, the last thing you are worrying about is whether it is true, because you yourself have become a character in the story.

And yet, and yet. There remains that figure at its centre who haunts us. Sometimes, like the fishermen in the last chapter of the Fourth Gospel, we see him in the distance, barely in focus, and we are not sure whether we have seen him or not. Sometimes, as in the great discourses in the Fourth Gospel (chapters 14–17), we lose his accents completely. He has been replaced by a different being altogether; he is pure Word. But even in the Fourth Gospel, which composes speeches for Jesus which are quite unlike the sayings in the Synoptics, we overhear little exchanges which are at variance with the generally high tone which is supposedly being maintained. The sudden, rather snappy exchange with his mother at a wedding (his own?): 'Woman, what have I to do with thee?'; the (jocular?) savagery with which he teases Nicodemus: 'Art thou a ruler of Israel and knowest not these things?'; the unconventionality (indeed by the strictest Jewish standards, the illegality) of talking to a Samaritan woman at Jacob's Well: 'The woman answered and said, I have no husband. Jesus said unto her: Thou hast well said, I have no husband: for thou hast had five husbands; and he whom thou now hast is not thy husband.' Does not this have the mercilessness and directness which we meet in other dialogues in other Gospels? And then again, like the tiniest clue in a detective story there is that verbal mannerism, which the Christ of the Fourth Gospel shares with the Jesus of the Synoptics: '*Amen, amen, lego soi*', 'Verily, verily, I say unto you . . .' It is not an idiom, it is an idiolect. We do not find it anywhere else in Greek, nor its equivalent anywhere else in Hebrew or Aramaic.

For all that the evangelists have done to Jesus, like creative artists fashioning a painting or an icon of a figure to the point where it is all but impossible to guess the true appearance of the original sitter, they cannot quite obscure the figure of Jesus himself within their pages. He is more than their creation. In spite of them, he fascinates us, as a figure independent of their fantastical visions. And, inevitably, like the disciples in Matthew's Gospel, we ask ourselves the unanswerable question: 'What manner of man is this?' Granted the human capacity to mythologise anything and anyone, to make immortal gods out of such unpromising material as Julius Caesar or Elvis Presley, what was it about the figure of Jesus which so inflamed the imaginations of his early followers? Scholarship urges us to steer clear of such a question because it is so fraught with pitfalls and hazards. But it would be unnatural not to ask it. We are inspired by more than the retrospective argument, which says that because he inspired such devotion, he must have been worthy of it. That is not necessarily the case. What leads us back to the 'blind alley' pursuit of the Jesus of History is the power of his recorded utterance, and the fascination of the figure the different evangelists have drawn. Though the New Testament writers seem to have done their best to obscure Jesus altogether in an encrustation of fantasy, he won't quite be pinned down. He struggles free of the evangelists sometimes. 'Heaven and earth shall pass away, but my words shall not pass away.'

Of course no one can prove that Jesus said that, but the cumulative effect of reading his words is to be confronted by a wholly distinctive view and voice – distinctively Jewish, distinctively of its time, but distinctive. But it is more than the teachings of Jesus which make us blink our eyes and wish that we could adjust the focus a little more clearly on that figure who is one moment transfigured in glory on a mountainside, and the next is squatting on the ground frying some fish.

It is the fish which lures us on. It is those little details – a man irrationally losing his temper with a tree. It is someone remembering that a little girl, when she recovers from a fever, will be extremely hungry. It is the man who, after his arrest, can turn to look at one of his best friends, and make that man weep with the knowledge that he has not been loyal to the end. These little novelistic details could all, of course, have been fabricated, though it is hard to see what purpose would have been served in inventing them. Often, as when he is quarrelling with his family, or insulting them behind their backs, or making cleverly cruel debating points, these details seem to clash with the 'sinless' Jesus of theology. No one could write a biography, in the modern sense, of a figure who is seen so fitfully, and seen through such strange lenses as the books of the New Testament. Nor, however, can we ignore his power. I am speaking neither of the power of the Christian Church, nor of the New Testament writings, great as they both are. I am speaking of those moments when imagination and instinct are shocked into recognition, and he stands before us. 'Then came Jesus forth, wearing the crown of thorns and the purple robe, and Pilate saith unto them, Behold the man!'

# IV

## HIS WONDROUS CHILDHOOD

JESUS PROCLAIMED HIS godhead in the cradle, as one of the apocryphal Gospels attests.[1] The truly orthodox Christian believer, holding that the Christ-child was the Godhead veiled in flesh, believes that all knowledge and all power and all dominion were invested in that baby boy. As he lay in the manger, Jesus knew the entire future history of the world, until the moment when he would announce that it was time for the Last Judgment. He understood all the mysteries of creation. He understood, as no ancient scientist or mathematician could have done, the mysteries of astro-physics which are as yet unknown in the most advanced laboratories of the twentieth century. He had the capacity, merely by blinking an eyelid, to bring all creation to a stop, just as it was by the will of Jesus, true God and true Man, that creation had come into being in the first place.

It is this belief which inspired the imagination of Christendom for 1800 years. Nearly all the images and pictures of the baby Jesus which come down to us are cloaked in this idea. It would be an impossible and hopeless task to divest the Christ-child of his divinity. It would be rather like trying to discuss Aphrodite and Artemis as two ordinary mortal women, or 'Apollo, his human side'. The infant Jesus is a divinity, and it is not surprising that in some quarters he should actually be worshipped almost as if he were a deity who was in some ways different from the suffering figure on Calvary. (I am

[1] See M. R. James: *The Apocryphal New Testament* (1924), 80. Gospels continued to be written after the pioneering work of Mark. Some of the Gospels which failed to be included in the canon of the New Testament were still regarded as authoritative by the churches from which they sprang. A fuller account than M. R. James may be found in Edgar Hennecke, *New Testament Apocrypha, Vol. 1: Gospels and Related Writings*, edited by William Schneemelcher, English translation by R. McL. Wilson (1963). In the last thirty years, various Coptic Gospels have been discovered in Egypt of whose existence the scholarly world was previously ignorant. See Jean Doresse: *The Secret Books of the Egyptian Gnostics*, English translation by Philip Marret (1960). There is a useful brief survey of the non-canonical Gospel literature in Floyd V. Filson's *A New Testament History* (1965), 68–70.

thinking of such devotions as the Infant of Prague in the Roman Catholic Church.)

On the other hand, it has to be said that there is no logical justification for dividing the infancy narratives of the New Testament from the rest. Many Christian scholars have wished to do so, suggesting that the legendary character of the birth and childhood of Jesus in Matthew and Luke is obvious. It is only later on, they imply, that you come to the solid facts. But the miraculous birth at Bethlehem, hymned by choirs of angels thronging the skies is just as 'historical' as the walk taken by the adult Jesus across the surface of Lake Galilee. We cannot say that one was any more legendary than the other.

The story of Christ invades history, but this does not mean that it is 'historical'. We shall never lay it bare by modern historical techniques; we can merely dismantle it beyond hope of restoration. The Gospel of Luke, for example, might seem to the uninformed eye like a piece of historical narrative, capable of adjustment by scholarly apparatus. Luke places the birth of Jesus in a particular year, in the reign of Herod, and at the time of the universal census commanded by Caesar Augustus. Historians might wish to say that Luke had got his dates right or wrong. Christians continue to say that their faith was an historical faith. The Incarnation, they would say, is something which happened in history, just as the Siege of Paris happened in 1870, or the Second World War ended in 1945. It was an 'event', which could be checked against the testimony of other historians. Luke is partly responsible for this belief. He tells us that the angel Gabriel flew from heaven to Nazareth at a particular date to announce to Mary that, though she was a virgin, she would bear God's child, just as Semele bore the offspring of Zeus. Then, just before the time of her *accouchement*, her betrothed, Joseph, was obliged to leave Galilee and go to Bethlehem in Judaea, the city of his ancestors, to take part in the Roman census. And so it came about that Jesus was born in Bethlehem of Judaea, the 'city of David'. Jesus was, in fact, of royal stock, being the son of Joseph, who was the son of Heli, who was the son of Matthat, who was the son of Levi, and so on, stretching back in a long genealogy through King David, and eventually back to Adam the son of God.

Either way, Jesus was the son of God, it would seem. Luke keeps both options open, by informing us that Jesus was miraculously conceived in a virgin womb by a process of parthenogenesis, and/or, if we do not like that idea, that he was lineally descended from

Adam and Eve *via* the Jewish Royal Family of David. The Roman census happened, by Luke's reckoning, when Quirinius was governor of Syria and when Herod was King of Judaea. Herod's reign lasted from 37 BCE until 4 BCE, and Quirinius was never the Governor of Syria during this period. To debate the historical probability or otherwise of Jesus having been born in Bethlehem is as useful, or pointless, as debating the historical probability of his having been divine. We can note that the Fourth Gospel very specifically states that Jesus was not born in Bethlehem, and that he was not born of David's line.[1] The crowds in that Gospel discount the possibility of his being the Messiah because he came from Galilee, rather than from Bethlehem. This does not mean, however, that the Fourth Gospel is more historical than Luke, only that they tell different stories, both without any of the purpose which might take hold of a 'dispassionate' historian, if there ever were such a being. The birth of Jesus may be said not to have happened according to 'real' history, but only within its own story, whose historical authenticity it would be fruitless to investigate. There are no referents to which appeal might be made which could link the birth of Christ to 'actual' history. No ancient historian, for example, ever made the slightest reference to this universal census supposedly conducted by the Emperor Augustus. Josephus, in his *Antiquities*, mentions a census in Judaea in 6 CE, and says that its purpose was to count heads before the imposition of a poll tax. The unpopularity of the tax, and of the census, led to the insurrection led by one Judas of Gamala (mentioned by Luke himself in the Acts of the Apostles).[2] The purpose of this census was purely statistical. There is no reason to suppose that anyone who took part in it would have been required to return to a village where some putative ancestor had lived more than a thousand years previously.

Luke's Gospel looks like history, and liberal Christian scholars, when they first came to work on it, thought that all they needed to do was to correct a few inessential errors in the matter of dates. It is only when you go a little deeper beneath the surface that you realise that it is not history at all. The figures of 'Caesar', 'Herod' and 'Quirinius', who so confusingly make Luke's narrative look as if it is at least *trying* to be historical in a modern sense of the term, in fact have no more or less reality than 'Richard the Lionheart', or 'The

---

[1] John 7:42.
[2] Acts 5:37. *Vide supra*, 26.

Sheriff of Nottingham' in the stories and ballads of Robin Hood. The narratives of the Gospels concern the supernatural. In the New Testament canon, Jesus is a very special being, chosen by God, sent forth by God, and raised up by God. He is never quite God himself, but he is invested with quasi-divine properties. In the non-canonical Gospels, he is actually God Himself, but whether we read of his divine birth in the New Testament or in the later Apocryphal Gospels, we find that the stories have far more in common with the icons of the Eastern Orthodox Church, with folk traditions, carols and nativity plays, with sculpted or painted scenes of the Annunciation or the Nativity, than they do with what a post-eighteenth century mind would call history. There is no historical method in existence which could possibly establish where Jesus was born, or who his parents were, or how his mother came to be pregnant.

It is probably true to say that the story of the Virginal conception of Jesus was unknown to the earliest Christian communities. It is noticeable, for instance, that no mention of it occurs in Mark's Gospel, nor in the Epistles of St Paul. All the New Testament Gospels agree that Jesus was brought up in Nazareth, and it would seem surprising if he had not been born there, rather than being born in the Judaean hill-village of Bethlehem during a non-existent census at a non-existent date. If we wish to believe that he was born during the reign of King Herod, then it must have been before 4 BCE, when Herod died.

The pagan philosopher Celsus, whose 'True Discourse' attacked Christianity in about 178 CE,[1] knew the rumour that Jesus was the illegitimate son of Mary and a Roman legionary.[2] Some scholars believe that there was an extremely early Jewish tradition, surviving in the Talmud, that Yeshu, or Jesus, was the son of a Roman soldier named Panthera, Pantera or Pandera. If the figure of 'Yeshu' who survives in these texts is the same Jesus as the figure in the New Testament, then it is of interest that he is sometimes called Yeshu ben-Pantera, that is Jesus, the son of Pantera. But the name Jesus was very common in first-century Judaea – as common as the name

[1] Origen, the great Christian Platonist of Alexandria, tried, in the middle of the third century CE, to write a refutation of Celsus called 'Contra Celsum'.
[2] For a good survey of hostile Rabbinic views of Jesus see Joseph Klausner: *Jesus of Nazareth* (English translation 1925), 18–47. M. Goldstein: *Jesus in the Jewish Tradition* (New York 1950) is also useful. See also Shlomo Pines: *An Arabic Version of the Testimonium Flavianum and its Implications* (Israel Academy of Science and Humanities, Jerusalem 1971) and Ian Wilson: *Jesus the Evidence* (1984), 62.

Joshua in the West today. A glance at the index to Josephus reveals a number of Jesuses. The rabbis have been unable to prove that Yeshu ben-Pantera is the same as the Galilean holy man. These texts, like those of the New Testament, yield evidence more freely to prejudiced scholars than to whose who approach them with a dispassionate mind.

The Book of James, believed by Origen (c.185–c.254 CE) to have been the composition of Jesus's brother, describes how Mary was one of seven Temple Virgins, kept by the High Priest in Jerusalem. In this book, as in the Gospel according to Matthew, it is Mary, rather than Joseph, who claims royal descent from the line of David. The angel of the Lord – not named here as Gabriel – announces her destiny when she is sixteen years old. She is six months advanced in pregnancy before Joseph meets her. To his consternation at the nature of her condition is added the embarrassment of discovering that the Temple priests hold him responsible for defiling one of their virgins. When 'Augustus the king' summons everyone from Bethlehem to be recorded in his census, the difficulties of Mary and Joseph have not been resolved. Joseph wonders what to do about his young fiancée. In the tradition known to the Book of James, Joseph had been married before,[1] since he says in a soliloquy, 'I will record my sons [in the census] but this child [i.e. Mary], what shall I do with her? How shall I record her? As my wife? Nay, I am ashamed. Or as my daughter? But all the children of Israel know that she is not my daughter.'

Joseph resolved the problem by saddling a she-ass and taking Mary to a hillside spot three miles outside Bethlehem. Sometimes, when he turned round to look at her, sitting on the ass, which he led on foot, he saw that she was laughing; sometimes, she looked sad; so he asked her why this should be. 'And Mary said: It is because I behold two people with mine eyes, the one weeping and lamenting, and the other rejoicing and exulting.' When the time of her confinement drew near, Joseph was still chiefly anxious to hide what he took to be Mary's 'shame'. He found a cave for her to lie in and, leaving her in the care of his sons, he went off in search of a midwife,

[1] See Filson: op. cit., 90 for an account of different traditional explanations for the existence of Jesus's brothers. One of the stories, followed by the Book of James, was that the 'brothers and sisters' of Jesus were Joseph's children by an earlier marriage. This was the view propagated by St Jerome, who translated the Scriptures into the Latin Vulgate, and it therefore obtained in the West until the time of the Reformation.

whom he conveniently found wandering the hillside. He explained to her that her services were required, not for his wife, but for his betrothed, who was a temple virgin who had been got with child by supernatural means. The midwife believed this story and came to the mouth of the cave where Mary lay. The cave was covered by a cloud of bright light, so bright that it strained the eyes of those who looked upon it. Little by little, however, the light diminished until the young child appeared, and took hold of the breast of his virgin mother.

A figure called Salome now enters the story. It is not clear whether she is in any way related to the Salome who danced before Herod and asked for the head of John the Baptist. She is evidently some sort of witch who performed cures. When she tried to approach the Virgin's body to examine it, however, her 'hand fell away from her in fire'. The narrative does not make it clear whether Salome was tortured by a burning sensation or whether her hand actually fell off; but it is only the first instance of many during the infancy of Jesus (in the apocryphal sources) where merely to approach his divine person was to court physical punishment and calamity. After Salome's hand had been injured, an angel appeared and suggested that she try to pick up the baby Jesus. The moment that she acted upon this advice, her hand was restored to its former health, and she praised God who had brought salvation to Israel.

The particular story of Salome and the midwife does not appear either in Matthew's Gospel nor in Luke's, which are the only books in the New Testament to treat of Jesus's birth and infancy. Matthew, who, wherever possible, links Jesus's life to the ancient Jewish prophecies, finds the nativity predicted in the book of Isaiah: 'The Lord himself shall give you a sign; a young woman will conceive and bear a son and shall call his name Immanuel – which means "God with us".'[1] The context of the original 'prophecy' was made to King Ahaz in the mid-eighth century BCE. It was an assurance that the line of Ahaz would be continued in spite of Assyrian threats to Israel's future. The suggestion that the king should call his son 'God with us' was propitious in time of war, since names were magic, names brought about the things they denominated. It would have been surprising if Isaiah, who lived some 740 years before Jesus, had been thinking of Mary and her first-born son when he made his prophecy

---

[1] Isaiah 7:14 (Jerusalem Bible).

to King Ahaz. Even if he had, by some extraordinary gift of fore-sight, been doing so, he never denoted that the 'young woman' would be a virgin. The word 'almah' means a young woman, and simply that. Yet, even today, one hears this text from Isaiah being used by Christians as a 'proof' that Jesus was born of a 'Virgin'.

In a rather similar way, the prophet Micah, living in Judaea some-where west of Hebron during the years 721–701 BCE, was not in a very good position to ascertain the provenance of Jesus's birth, seven centuries later. Micah's book came out of a series of bloody skir-mishes in the regions of Bethlehem, a hill-village a few miles south of Jerusalem. Micah predicted the destruction of Jerusalem and of the northern kingdom of Samaria, largely as a result of God's fury with their corrupt rulers. Micah asserted that, at the end of all these disasters, God would restore the fortunes of Judah. The Temple Mount in Jerusalem would rise up again in beauty and glory. A ruler would be born who would be able to conquer the Assyrians. With the help of seven other 'shepherds' he would 'shepherd' Assyria with the sword, the country of Nimrod with the naked blade.[1] This future guerrilla-leader would spare no foreign enemy in his ruthless protection of Judaean hill-villages. He would come from the village where King David himself had kept the sheep: Bethlehem.

Since the subject of the Gospel did not spend his life as a guerrilla-leader fighting Assyrians, it is not immediately apparent why Matthew should have seized on this particular text as an obvious reference to Jesus. He tells the story that some wizards came to Jerusalem 'from the east' and disturbed King Herod with the sugges-tion that this text from Micah proved that a rival king would be born in Bethlehem, and that they could prove this by means of astrology.

In Matthew, these 'wise men from the east' go to Bethlehem and find Mary and her baby in a house.[2] There is no mention of the cave, where we encountered Mary in the Book of James. The eastern mages are not three in number, as they are in so many Christmas plays, pageants and carols; nor are they kings; nor are we told their names. But they are astrologers, led by a star which hovers over the place where the young child lay.[3]

[1] Micah 5:4,5.
[2] Matthew 2:10.
[3] Matthew 2:10.

Luke's gospel makes no mention of these wizards, but it does contain the other delightful ingredient of the nativity tableau: shepherds. It was to the shepherds, keeping watch over their flocks by night, that the birth of Jesus was first proclaimed by angels. To Luke we owe the charming detail that when Jesus had been born, his mother laid him in a manger, though the idea that Jesus was born in a stable belongs to folk-tale rather than to the New Testament. Luke says that Mary laid her first-born son in a manger since here was no place (*topos*) in the *kataluma*. This is a Greek word which more often means 'room' than 'inn'. Luke never states that Mary and Joseph were staying at an inn, still less at an inn where there was no room for them, still less that they were therefore obliged to sleep that night in a stable. He merely says that the particular room in which Jesus was born did not have a cradle in it. One is presumably meant to understand that someone improvised, bringing a feeding-box for animals into the room, as a substitute for a cradle.

Folklore has built up a much more heart-rending and attractive picture, which is repeated each year at Christmas time.

> Enough for him, whom Cherubim
> Worship night and day,
> A breastful of milk,
> And a mangerful of hay;
> Enough for him, whom Angels
> Fall down before,
> The ox and ass and camel
> Which adore. [1]

The Saviour of the world entering his Creation as a helpless outcast, lying in straw, breathed upon by adoring cows, sheep, shepherds and three wise men, all in their kingly crowns, is one of the most poignant and haunting in the entire Christian story. It is the story which can still draw unbelievers to church once a year, and tears from their eyes as they behold the scene in the crib. But none of this delightful tableau is to be found in the pages of the New Testament.

Over the next period of Jesus's life – his early infancy – Matthew and Luke differ. Luke tells us that Jesus, like all Jewish boys, was circumcised on the eighth day. Then, after the statutory period, Mary went up to Jerusalem to be 'purified' by offering a sacrifice of

---

[1] Christina Rosetti: 'In the bleak midwinter', *English Hymnal* No. 25.

two turtle-doves – perhaps the origin of the curiously ornithological range of gifts presented to 'my true love' during the Twelve Days of Christmas in the old song. [1] It is at the Temple that the 'parents of Jesus', as Luke calls them, having forgotten about the Virginal Conception, of only a few hundred words earlier in his story, encounter the old man Simeon, who predicts that Jesus is 'set for the falling and rising up of many in Israel and for a sign which is spoken against; yea and a sword shall pierce through thine [i.e. Mary's] own soul; that thoughts out of many hearts may be revealed.' [2] Simeon recites his beautiful 'Nunc dimittis' – for he has seen the light which lights all the nations in this young child, and Mary and Joseph take the young child back to Nazareth where the child grew 'and waxed strong'. [3]

He had a considerably more eventful infancy in Matthew's account. Matthew tells the story of Herod's jealous fury when he heard that a rival king had been born in Bethlehem. He commanded that all the male children in Bethlehem of two years and under should be slain. We have no idea whether Harod actually conducted such a Massacre of the Innocents, though we know from Josephus that he was cruel: [4] he killed forty-five leading Jews for resisting his occupation of Jerusalem, and he was greatly hated for his tyrannical form of rule, his dissolute lifestyle (he had ten wives), his subservience to the Romans, and for the fact that he was not a good Jew. (He belonged to the race of Idumeans, who had been forcibly converted to Judaism by John Hyrcanus between 130 and 120 BCE. Herod himself was known to practise polytheism.)

In order to escape the Massacre of the Innocents, Matthew's Jesus was taken by Mary and Joseph into Egypt. As we should expect from Matthew, this fulfils an old prophecy, this time from Hosea – 'Out of Egypt did I call my son'. [5] We do not know whether Jesus ever in fact went to Egypt or whether this text of Hosea's 'suggested' the Flight into Egypt to Matthew. In any event, another potent range of stories was born, some of which found their way into the New

[1] On the second day of Christmas
My true love sent to me
Two turtle doves
And a partridge in a pear tree.
[2] Luke 2:34,35.
[3] Luke 2:40.
[4] *Antiquities* XIV: 11–16.
[5] Hosea 11:1.

Testament, and most of which did not. I remember on one of my early visits to Israel being shown a chalky rock, enclosed in a grotto, where the Blessed Virgin had sat down to suckle her holy child during the hazardous journey to Egypt. Because of her haste, a few drops of milk had fallen from her breasts, transforming the rock to white chalk in the process. Packets of chalk-dust, not dissimilar to powdered milk, were on sale at a nearby kiosk.

In Matthew's Gospel, all the boys in Bethlehem who are less than two years old are put to the sword. In the Book of James, Zacharias hides the infant John the Baptist with his mother Elizabeth in the hills; for his refusal to reveal the whereabouts of John, Zacharias is killed.

According to the Gospel of Thomas, a fourth-century Coptic Gospel, based on a second-century Greek Gospel, [1] Jesus was two years old by the time the Holy Family reached Egypt. The little boy happened to pick some ears of corn as they were walking through a sown field, and chewed them with his teeth. Thereafter, the field yielded 'the lord of the field so many measures of wheat as the number of grains he had taken from it'. [2] The Holy Family lodged with an Egyptian family for a year. Jesus was not without companionship of his own age but, on account of his divinity, he was able to play more interesting games than other children. For example, when he was three, he once came upon some boys playing with a basin of water. Jesus took a dried salt fish and placed it in the basin with the words, 'Cast out thy salt that is in thee and go to the water'. The salt fish came to life and the other children ran home to tell their parents. The notoriety which the incident attracted to the Holy Family had the unfortunate effect of making the landlady, the Egyptian widow, ask them to leave her house.

The Gospel of Thomas agrees with that of Matthew in stating that an angel informed Mary and Joseph of the death of Herod, an event which made it safe for them to return home. Thomas believed them to have settled at first in the town of Capernaum before living, as the canonical gospels suggest, in Nazareth, where tradition has it that Joseph pursued the carpenter's trade.

When, in grown-up life, Jesus started preaching at the synagogue in Nazareth, the local people asked themselves, 'Is not this the car-

---

[1] See Hennecke and Doresse: op. cit., and James op. cit., 14–16 and 49–70.
[2] James 59.

penter' or 'the carpenter's son'. [1] The Greek *ho tekton* is trying to render a word of Semitic origin. In the old Jewish writings, the word 'craftsman' or 'carpenter' had a metaphorical meaning: in the language which Joseph and Jesus would have spoken, Aramaic, the word is *naggar* and it could either mean a craftsman or a scholar, a learned man. There is no reason to suppose that Mark believed Joseph to have been a wood-worker or joiner. Just as Luke's one mention of a manger, used as an improvised cot for the baby Jesus, led to a whole folklore nativity scene fleshed out with a cast of adoring farm animals, so this one question – 'Is this the scholar?' or 'Isn't this Joseph the scholar's boy?' – has led to a whole mythology of the boy Jesus standing patiently in the carpenter's shop, as his foster father toiled with saw and adze. The Catholic Church, partly in order to steal a march on the Communist Party, and partly to express its keenly held belief in the sanctity of work, has instituted the feast of St Joseph the Worker on May Day. Like everyone who had a Christian upbringing, I have heard dozens of sermons about Jesus in that carpenter's shop – sermons about his humility, as the Incarnate God, doing work so humble, and sermons about the blessedness of work, and sermons about obedience, and sermons about the sacrament of the Present Moment. The image is enforced for us by paintings, such as Holman Hunt's *Shadow of the Cross*, which depict Jesus as an artisan. The Gospel of Thomas makes it clear that Jesus was an abnormally useful carpenter's apprentice. He was, for example, able to lengthen pieces of wood rather than make them shorter. [2]

Of Jesus's childhood itself, the canonical Gospels tell us almost nothing, but the apocryphal Gospels fill in this disappointing *lacuna*. When he was five years old, for example, Jesus made some clay sparrows on the Sabbath day. When his fellow Jews, Joseph among them, remonstrated with him for Sabbath-breaking, Jesus spread out his hands and commanded the sparrows, saying, 'Go forth into the height and fly; ye shall not meet death at any man's hands'. And, to everyone's consternation, the clay birds flew away. [3]

The education of such a child, who was fully aware of his own divinity, was not without difficulties. According to the Gospel of Thomas, a teacher called Zacheus was entrusted with the thankless

---

[1] Mark 6:3 and Matthew 13:55 respectively.
[2] James 63.
[3] James 55.

task of teaching Jesus his alphabet. He wrote out the first line of letters from A to T asking Jesus to repeat the letters after him. Jesus remained silent, so Zacheus hit him on the back of the head. Jesus insolently replied that he knew all his letters already, and that the teacher was an empty vessel. Thomas's vision of Jesus's childhood was as far removed as possible from that imagined by the Victorian hymn-writer Mrs C. F. Alexander, who wrote, 'Once in Royal David's City', the popular Christmas carol:

> And through all his wondrous childhood
> He would honour and obey
> Love, and watch the lowly Maiden
> In whose gentle arms he lay;
> Christian children all must be
> Mild, obedient, good as he. [1]

In Thomas's Gospel, the child Jesus reveals his power by sending people mad, or deaf, or blind, and then making them better again. He even strikes people dead, solely for the amusement value of bringing them back to life again. His teacher Zacheus, not unreasonably, supposes that Jesus is 'either a sorcerer, or a god, or an angel'. [2] One of the most remarkable tricks was recorded in the Arabic Gospel and the Syriac History but not in any Greek or Latin texts. It relates how Jesus tried to join in some children's games. They all run away from him into the cellar (or in some versions, the furnace) of a house. The woman of the house tries to protect the children from the little divine sorcerer as he pursues them. When Jesus asks her whether any children have run into her house, she says, 'No'. Jesus then inquires what beings they are, whom he can distinctly hear moving about in her cellar. She replies that they are goats. Jesus then answers, 'Let the goats out'. When the boy opens the door of the cellar, the woman discovers, to her horror, that he has turned all the children into goats.

The human mothers of these goats (formerly children) come to Mary and Joseph and implore them to use their influence with Jesus. He is very compliant, and transforms the goats back into children again. 'Come my playfellows,' he calls out, 'let us play together.' When they are fully human again, their mothers tell the children,

---

[1] *English Hymnal* No. 605.
[2] James: op. cit., 62.

'see that you do everything that Jesus the Son of Mary commandeth you to do'. [1]

While nineteenth- and twentieth-century Christians have rejoiced to see in the child Jesus 'our childhood's pattern', the earlier stories about him all chose to emphasise his inimitability and strangeness. There are very few surviving stories about the infant Jesus in which, by ordinary human standards, he is behaving well, or even being particularly pleasant. In Luke's Gospel, for instance, we read that Jesus accompanied his parents to Jerusalem for the Feast of the Passover when he was twelve years old. When the feast was over, his parents set off home to Nazareth, presumably in a big family gathering; Jesus, without informing them of his intentions, stayed behind in the city. They had assumed that he was somewhere in their party, and when they found that he was missing, they returned to the city to search for him. Three days later, they found him in the Temple sitting among teachers and rabbis and asking them questions.

When they discovered Jesus in the Temple, Mary – as any mother would – remonstrated with him. 'My child, why have you done this to us? See how worried your father and I have been, looking for you.' Jesus replied, 'Why are you looking for me? Did you not know that I must be in my Father's house?' [2] Another rendering of this abrupt rebuke might be, 'Did you not know that I must be busy with my Father's affairs?' If there were any continuity between the scrappy incidents in Luke's short book, it might be expected that Mary and Joseph would instantly have understood that Jesus had been set apart for a high purpose by God. Mary, after all, had been told by an angel that she was to bear a Saviour in her Virgin womb. Her cousin Elizabeth had called Mary, while the child was still in the womb, 'the mother of my Lord'. The birth of Jesus had been attended by a choir of angels appearing in the sky, and we are told that Mary pondered all these things in her heart. Nevertheless, only half a page later, she is completely baffled, when Jesus says that he must be busy with his Father's – i.e. God's – affairs. Presumably, like the author of the Gospel, she has momentarily forgotten that Jesus is supposed to be a quasi-divine being. Whether Luke considered Jesus's reply to his mother an admirable one, it is hard to tell. If he did not, why did he tell the story? If he did, what are we to make of his scale of moral values?

[1] James: op. cit., 68.
[2] Luke 2:48, 49 (Jerusalem Bible).

One of the more interesting facts about the canonical Gospels –
and the apocryphal ones also – is that nearly all references to Jesus's
family are ones of conflict. Jesus's mother is very understandably
worried that a twelve-year-old boy has been lost in the city. He
rebukes her. This is very much of a piece with his later references
to the virtues of leaving home, his disowning the family altogether,
or his rebutting what they say. He is always, in the Gospels, particularly rude to and about his mother. The family, for their part,
respond, at least in the Synoptic Gospels, by saying that Jesus is mad.
We could account for this by suggesting that there is some memory
here of actual quarrels between Jesus and his people. Or we could
say that those parts of the Church which produced the Gospels had
a quarrel with those who claimed kinship with Jesus. (There is some
evidence that there was a sect, quite early on, controlled by Jesus's
family. If this sect disdained any but 'founder's kin', it would not be
surprising if other parts of the Church, particularly the Gentiles,
liked telling stories about Jesus as a man who had no sympathy or
support from his family.) The composition of the Holy Family is
not a matter about which we could pronounce with certainty. We
have mentioned the possibility that Joseph had been married before
he married Mary, [1] but this is not mentioned anywhere in the Gospels. It was probably a story invented to accommodate those who,
like present-day Roman Catholics, were required to believe in the
Perpetual Virginity of Mary. Unless you believe in Joseph's previous
marriage, this is a difficult doctrine to sustain, since Mark's Gospel
tells us that Jesus came from a large family, with four brothers –
James, Joset, Simon and Jude, as well as some sisters. [2] Tradition
has it that one of Jesus's brothers, James, was the leader of the
first group of Christians in Jerusalem, which would rather point
to the idea that Jesus's family held an important position in the
Church before the destruction of Jerusalem. But the surviving
stories tell us nothing of Jesus's home life with James, or with
Simon or Jude. Since the two details of Jesus's childhood which
most haunt the imaginations of Christendom, western Christendom at least – the birth in the stable, and the years of honest toil
in the carpenter's shop – are not to be found in the New Testament,
we should perhaps be mistaken in searching the Gospels for too

[1] *Vide supra*, 4, n. 6.
[2] Mark 6:3.

many details of his home life. The unwritten stories and the legends about Jesus have, since earliest times, been just as influential as the written Scriptures.

One such legend, which haunted the imagination of William Blake and, through Blake's lyric 'Jerusalem', has passed into British national legend, is the story that Jesus visited Britain as a boy. Though written sources for this folk-tale are mediaeval, the oral sources on which the stories are based are probably much older. English metal-workers, before making a cast, used to murmur, 'Joseph was in the tin trade'. When questioned about this custom in the 1930s, a foreman in a tin works said, 'We workers in metal are a very old fraternity, and like other handicrafts we have our traditions amongst us. One of these, the memory of which is preserved in this invocation, is that Joseph of Arimathea, the rich man in the Gospels, and not to be confused with Joseph the husband of Mary, made his money in the tin trade in Cornwall. We also have the story that he made voyages to Cornwall in his own ships and that on one occasion, he brought with him the Christ-Child and His Mother and landed with them on St Michael's Mount.'[1]

The place in England most associated with Joseph of Arimathea is the Somerset town of Glastonbury. It is to Glastonbury, thirty years after the Passion of Jesus Christ and fifteen years after the Assumption of the Blessed Virgin into Heaven, that Joseph is traditionally supposed to have brought the Holy Grail for burial. Some other stories do speak of Jesus himself walking 'upon England's mountains green'. A letter from St Augustine of Canterbury to Pope Gregory in 597 CE speaks of the earliest missionaries, the Apostles Philip and James and Joseph of Arimathea himself, founding a church, 'constructed of human art, but by the Hands of Christ Himself for the salvation of His people'. Jesus himself is said to have built the church of St Mary's at Glastonbury in honour of his mother, when he visited the place in his teens.

Strangely enough, it is not merely in the English West Country that these tales survive. The admittedly eccentric E. V. Duff, 'Count of the Holy Roman Empire', found those in the Maronite and Catluei villages of Upper Galilee who told the tale of how Jesus as a youth 'came to Britain as a shipwright aboard a trading vessel of Tyre, and that He was storm-bound on the shores of the West of England

[1] Lionel Smithett Lewis: *St Joseph of Arimathea at Glastonbury* (Cambridge 1976).

throughout the winter'. [1] It may very easily be considered, once we start linking Jesus with Glastonbury, that we have placed him in the same realm as that other Glastonbury worthy, King Arthur. Historians of the Dark Ages consider it possible that there was once a '*dux bellorum*' who fought some battles against the Romans or against other invaders of Britain, some time in the fifth century, and whose last stand was at Mons Badonicus or Badon Hill. But this shadowy 'historical' character of an infinitely obscure Dark Ages warrior has far less substance than the figure of legend, Arthur of Camelot and his Round Table, and his court, and his Queen Guinevere, of his greatest friend Lancelot who cuckolds him, and so forth. Of him, we read in the old French romances and in Malory, a thousand years after he supposedly 'lived'. Since, in Malory, Lancelot is himself a cousin eight times removed of Jesus himself, the stories may be said to be linked.

Does the dispassionate historian have to make some such allowance for Jesus? Is the real Jesus as shadowy as the real Arthur? And are all the stories we know about him, like the stories of King Arthur and his Round Table, invented folk-tales, made up long after the event? Some writers, a minority it is true, but not an unintelligent minority, have surveyed the historical 'evidence' and concluded that no such person as Jesus ever existed; and it may be that, having read this chapter of stories about the conception, birth and childhood of Jesus, the reader will be tempted by this austere point of view. [2]

Very little documentary evidence about Jesus survives in non-Christian sources. What they have to say about Jesus could be written on the back of a post-card and does not prove that he actually existed. Tacitus in his *Annals* tells us that the ringleader of the Christians was 'condemned to death in the reign of Tiberius by the procurator Pontius Pilate'. [3] Pliny the Younger wrote to the Emperor Trajan and, while blandly recommending that the Christians should be persecuted, informs his emperor that 'they sing a hymn to Christ as to a god'. [4] This hardly proves that Christ existed. The Jewish historian Flavius Josephus (*c.*37–*c.*100 CE) refers to James as the leader of the Jerusalem Church, and says that he is the brother of Jesus who was

---

[1] Lionel Smithett Lewis: op. cit., 51–52.
[2] See, for example, G. A. Wells: *The Jesus of the Early Christians* (1971).
[3] Tacitus: *Annals* XV:44.
[4] Pliny: *Letters* X: 96–7.

called the Messiah. In another passage, Josephus speaks of Jesus as 'a wise man . . . a doer of wonderful works, a teacher of such men as receive the truth with pleasure . . . and the race of Christians, so named after him, are not extinct even now'. [1] It has been suggested that this passage was inserted into Josephus by Christians. This is not very likely. No Christian writer of the New Testament period refers to Jesus as a 'wise man'. It is possible that in this tantalisingly brief reference in Josephus we find an authentic near-contemporary record of what the Jews of Jesus's time actually thought of him: not a God, nor a heretic, but a wise man and a doer of wonderful deeds. [2]

Apart from such fragmentary glimpses, we have to accept the fact that all the documentary evidence comes to us filtered via Christian witnesses, and that Christians, after their religion became the official creed of the Roman Empire in the reign of Constantine (died 337 CE), busily set to work destroying or altering any evidence which might conflict with the Orthodox view of Jesus.

In the end, the reader must make up his or her own mind about the likelihood of Jesus having been invented by the myth-makers. For myself, I find such an idea inconceivable, and that is because of the nature and the variety of the stories which survive about him. Admittedly, a high proportion of these stories, which describe him turning children into goats, or water into wine, walking on water or turning clay sparrows into flying birds, do not seem immediately credible. But then, you come across a tiny detail which seems too strange to have been invented, such as a woman coming to pour ointment over the feet of Jesus and to wipe it with her hair, or another woman, a Canaanite, shrieking at Jesus and begging him to heal her daughter, and his replying that it is not worth throwing scraps from the Jewish table to dogs – that is, to Gentiles. The realistic details are too many, and too odd, for me to be able to accept that they were all invented by some unsung novelistic genius of the first century of our era; though they are so heavily outweighed by improbable stories, and so soaked in 'teaching' that I fully sympathise with any reader who has hitherto supposed that it was impossible to find a 'real' Jesus amid so much religion and folklore.

Our narrative has taken Jesus from his conception to his teens. We

[1] Josephus: op. cit., XVIII.III:3.
[2] See Geza Vermes: 'Josephus' Portrait of Jesus Reconsidered' in *Occident and Orient: A Tribute to the Memory of A. Scheiber* (Akademiai Kiado, Budapest, Brill, Leiden 1988), 373ff.

have noted that for this period of his life, there are absolutely no facts for us to rely upon and we could readily be forgiven for thinking that each incident, from the angelic salutation to Mary in Nazareth, to Jesus's appearance in Cornwall as a ship-wright, is as improbable as the last. Much more observable, and more dispiriting, than the proliferation of these folk-tales is their moral vacuity. It is hard to think of a body of stories which is less edifying. For sheer silliness, they are almost unrivalled. They circulated among people who believed that, as well as being divine, Jesus was also sinless. These stories are a wholesome reminder of the fact that ideas of wrong and right, like everything else in the human imagination, are capable of evolution and change. If you read the infancy narratives in Matthew, Luke and the Synoptic Gospels, and these narratives alone, and if you knew nothing of other Christian writings or teachings, it would not occur to you that the Christian religion had any claim to be morally serious.

Jesus, however, was morally serious, and we can say that because of the sayings which are attributed to him in the Gospels. Whether or not he said them all, whether or not he said the actual words, there is enough here to suggest a body of teaching which draws on the riches and conflicts of Judaism. In the middle years of the twentieth century, it was widely supposed that the Christ of Faith was all that mattered and that the Jesus of History was not merely irrecoverable, but somehow uninteresting. In various significant quarters, however, the scholarly balance has shifted in the last twenty or thirty years. Jewish, non-Christian and Christian scholars now recognise much more clearly than their predecessors the kind of documents which the New Testament contains. The astonishing discovery in 1945 near Nag Hammadi in Upper Egypt of a cache of Gnostic Christian writings – such as the Book of James from which I have already quoted, and the Apocalypse of Peter, the Apocalypse of Paul – was followed in 1947 onwards by the extraordinary discovery of the Dead Sea Scrolls, near Qumran. These were versions of the Scriptures, rules of religious life, works of astrology and messianic prophecy, apocalypse and moral teaching in great abundance, written by a monastic community more or less contemporaneous with Jesus and not twenty miles from Jerusalem. In the light that they throw upon the sectarianism of contemporary Judaism, on its messianic expectations, on contemporary ideas of God, on the everlasting warfare between Light and Dark, the Qumran documents offer many exciting parallels with the New Testament writings, particularly with the Fourth Gospel. To these discoveries were added the contributions of other scholars in the field of Semitic studies, who were able to offer us many parallels between Jesus as depicted in the Gospels, and his contemporary holy men, ecstatics, and exorcists. The cumulative effect of all this archaeology, and of all this recently discovered written material, and of contemplating the New Testament in the context of contemporary Judaism, has been to restore the hope that we might reconstruct, a little more accurately than our grandfathers could do, a portrait of the historical Jesus.

The world of Jesus has been more sharply focussed for our generation than for any previous generation since 70 CE, when his world was obliterated by the Romans, and the Catholic Faith, which had small interest in and less knowledge of Jesus's Semitic origins, pursued its own curious and in the end victorious course. Thanks to the work of modern scholars, we know far more than earlier generations about the way in which the contemporaries of Jesus thought and wrote. We are also weaned from any sentimental liberal Protestant idea that we might be able to find a 'primitive' account of Jesus which presented us with a portrait of the man detached from the theology. The theology must have been there from the beginning. We have also been weaned from the idea that, just because they attribute Jesus with miraculous properties, the Gospels must be of very late composition. Many of the ideas in the Fourth Gospel which earlier scholars confidently pronounced to be 'late' and 'Greek' are to be found echoed in the Qumran scrolls, written in all probability in the lifetime of Jesus.

There are some scholars now who would place the composition of Mark's Gospel as early as 55 CE, [1] and there are those who believe that the Fourth Gospel might have been composed in 30–50 CE, passing through a second revision by 65 CE. [2] Even if we are unable to accept such an early dating for the Gospels, it can no longer be taken as axiomatic that a Gospel is 'late' merely because it parades beliefs about Jesus which modern scepticism finds unacceptable. The New Testament could well be closer in time to Jesus than was once supposed.

We shall never recapture his features, his look, or the sound of

[1] J. D. M. Derrett: *The Making of Mark.*
[2] J. A. T. Robinson: *Redating the New Testament.*

his voice; but there are moments in the New Testament where one has the sensation of having only just missed the Presence. It is like walking into a room which a person has only just left, and seeing evidence of their presence – the impression of a head against a cushion, a glass half empty by the chair, a cigarette still smouldering in the ash-tray.

# V

# THE FORE-RUNNER

.

JESUS WAS BORN into a land of stupendous natural beauty and riotous political instability. Herod, who reigned from 37–4 BCE, and who had restored the Temple at Jerusalem in grandiose fashion, was a quisling tyrant universally hated by his subjects. Even as Herod lay dying, the rabbis, with unconcealed glee, were removing the busts and statuary with which he had – in their opinion idolatrously – adorned the Temple courts. As the Jews felt, Herod had sold out to the Romans, allowing his people them to be over-taxed and restricted in their religious freedoms.

It was not a confident phase in the history of Jewry. Folk memory lingered of the heroic wars of Judas Maccabeus in the second century BCE, when the Jewish religion had been 'abolished' and an image of Zeus blasphemously set up in the Temple. More recently, in 63 BCE, Pompey had profanely set foot in the Holy of Holies in the Temple, and been astonished by what he found there. On the one hand, he was amazed by its magnificence – the censers of solid gold, the spice cups, the libation cups and lamps, and the heaps of offertory money, none of which he touched. On the other hand, the Roman general was haunted by what was not in that sanctuary, as much as by what was. There was no visible god, no idol, no statue, no Delphic oracle, no inscription. The sanctuary was empty. At the end of a war in which the Jews had lost 12,000 men and the Romans had suffered almost no casualties at all, the Temple, and all the religion which it symbolised, was vulnerable to the step of the conqueror. Pompey had expected to find there a mighty God, some monstrous deity of the sort worshipped by the Cretans or the Egyptians. Instead, he found the secret of the Jews' vulnerability, and their indomitability: an empty sanctuary, a temple dedicated to the Unseen and Invisible God.[1]

[1] Josephus: *Jewish War*, 105.

The Jews had always been more interested in what other nations would call religion than they were in politics. Only, for them, to call it 'religion' would be to suggest that their destiny under God was a mere department of life, rather than what it was – the whole of life. Their national and ethnic identity was bound up in the belief which the empty sanctuary symbolised. Though they were willing to die in defence of their beliefs and their laws, these things – as tyrants have discovered to their fury over and over again since the Roman Empire vanished – are ultimately indestructible. You can destroy a graven image. You cannot so easily destroy an idea of God.

In the political ferment which followed the death of Herod, it was not surprising that religious feeling among the Jews should have been intense and confused. No one quisling monarch came forward in 4 BCE to take over Herod's position. Shortly before his own demise he had taken the trouble to murder his heir, and his successors were incompetent and divided. Such was the anarchy of the time, Josephus tells us, that 'a great and wild fury spread itself over the nation'. There were riots, reprisals, and the Romans killed the dissidents and the rebels whenever they appeared. In Jerusalem alone at this period, over two thousand Jews were crucified. It was the usual Roman method of executing criminals.

The ethnarch Archelaus, who presided over these horrors, was considered so tyrannical and unjust that the Jews even applied to Rome for his conduct to be investigated. He was recalled to Rome and exiled in Gaul. After Archelaus, Judaea was once more a Roman province, with Coponius as its first prefect from 6 to 9 CE. Pontius Pilate succeeded as the Prefect of Judaea in 26 CE. This province of Judaea did not include the regions of Batanaea and Gaulonitis – that is, the territory north east of the Sea of Galilee which is now part of modern Syria and Jordan. This, in Jesus's day, was ruled over by the tetrarch Philip, as a son of Herod the Great. Galilee was also a quasi-independent kingdom – not a province of the Roman Empire – and this was ruled over by Philip's half-brother Antipas. For the Romans in Judaea, the presence of these independent kingdoms on the borders of their province was uncomfortable. As in all comparable situations, before and since, those who wished to cause trouble for the Romans in Judaea could retreat into the hill country of Galilee and Gaulonitis when they wished to evade arrest.

There were repeated *coups*, guerrilla attacks and minor uprisings against the regime, invariably defeated, and usually defeated with great severity. All of them had a religious motivation or colouring. Meanwhile, the apocalyptic, mystic side of Judaism, which had begun to emerge during the Maccabean wars nearly two centuries earlier, flowered as it had never done before. Since the archaeologists opened the scroll jars at Qumran in the late 1940s, we have been able to study the ideas and doctrines of the religious community which flourished there during the lifetime of Jesus. They were a group of exclusive, monkish Jews who abstained from fleshly pursuits and who looked for the imminent End. They were obsessed by the Jewish calendar, and by the correct observance of the Feasts and Fasts of the liturgical year.[1] They believed that the Roman invasion, was a punishment for failing to keep these festivals correctly; and a punishment for laxity about some of the other commandments. They regarded themselves as the Elect, children of Light.[2] Many of the documents from Qumran, did not originate with the Qumran sect, but with other apocalyptic movements. One of the things which the Qumran discoveries makes us realise is that, at the time of Jesus, there must have been dozens of groupings within Jewry, all looking for the end of the world and its imminent destruction, all certain that God would avenge his saints by destroying the Roman Empire and bringing to pass, either on earth or in some new heavenly Kingdom, a place where the righteous could be happy for ever more.[3]

The Qumran community was probably of the sect known as Essenes. Other groups who shared these expectations were the Pharisees and the Sadducees. None of these groups numbered more than a few thousand adherents, and all of them believed that they were the authentic voice of Judaism. They sometimes expounded ideas which were radically different from one another. For example, the Sadducees, a priestly sect, based upon Jerusalem, did not, according to Josephus, believe in the survival of the soul beyond death. Like another Jewish writer, they would have been pleased to say, 'I do not have a body, I am a body'. The Sadducees' relationship with God, and their fulfilment of his word, was something which had to

---

[1] See Annie Jaubert: *La Date de la Cène* (Paris 1967), chapter 1.

[2] For a general introduction to the Dead Sea Scrolls and their significance, see Geza Vermes: *The Dead Sea Scrolls: Qumran in Perspective* (SCM 1962).

[3] See Geza Vermes: *The Dead Sea Scrolls in English* (Harmondsworth 1967); W. H. Brownlee: *The Meaning of the Qumran Scrolls for the Bible* (New York 1964).

be worked out in this world, and, like the huge majority of the Old Testament books, they did not believe in the resurrection of the body nor in the life everlasting. The Pharisees shared with the Sadducees and the Essenes a belief that everything done in this world by Jews, however trivial, was of interest to the Almighty. But they further believed that there would be a day of reckoning after death in which the wicked would be cast aside by God, while the righteous rose up to worship him in the heavenly Jerusalem.

The Essenes were ascetics.[1] Not much is known about them, but they were a priestly sect who came into being '390 years after the destruction of the First Temple'. For twenty years, they struggled towards the truth, and then they were instructed by a great Teacher of Righteousness. Like many religious groups, they soon broke into factions, and the Teacher of Righteousness was replaced by a 'Wicked Priest' or Teacher of Lies. To what historical incident, if any, this refers, the scholars are not agreed.

What all these Jews agreed, however, was that God was highly dissatisfied with the state of things in Israel, and that very soon, He would put things to rights. The Messiah would come to do this. It was widely believed that he would be preceded by the Prophet Elijah, *redivivus*. The political anarchy and religious dissolution of the country would be brought to an end by the arrival of a Deliverer, possibly born of the royal line of David.

'And when these things all come to pass,' states the Manual of Discipline at Qumran, 'in these moments, the Community of Isreal shall separate themselves from the habitations of perverse men to take to the wilderness to prepare there the Way of Him, as was written: "Prepare ye in the wilderness the Way of the Lord: make straight to the desert a highway for our God."' (Isaiah 40:3.)

If this was the attitude of the Qumran community, down below sea level near the Dead Sea, what was happening to the north of the country in the kingdom of Galilee? At this juncture in history, Galilee was effectively a separate entity, politically, geographically, and religiously. As any visitor to modern Israel knows, to leave Judaea in the springtime and to enter Galilee is to quit an arid, brown, rocky

---

[1] Geza Vermes: *Jesus and the World of Judaism*, 130–137.

country and to enter a green place. It is the most startlingly green place in the Mediterranean world: it feels like Wales or the Dordogne or Vermont at their lushest. It is agricultural country. Even before the arrival of clever modern Israeli settlers, it was extremely fertile. Fruit and vegetables grew there and in the centre of it all is the great inland lake or Sea of Galilee. There was a thriving fishing industry based on the Sea of Galilee which helped to feed the rest of the population, and the fish trade between Galilee and Jerusalem was plentiful and lucrative.

Because of the abundant agriculture and fisheries, Galilee was much the richest district of Palestine. It was also much the most independent province, having far less to do with Rome than either Jerusalem or Judaea did. Throughout the lifetime of Jesus, it was administered by the Herodian tetrarch Antipas (4 BCE–39 CE; thereafter by Agrippa, 39–44 CE). It had a measure of self-government in the religious as well as the political sphere. At sporadic intervals, it even convened its own religious Parliament or Sanhedrin. There were some Pharisees in Galilee, but fewer than there were in Judaea. There were some in Jerusalem who considered that the Judaism of Galilee was lax. 'Galilee, Galilee, you hate the Torah!' exclaimed one rabbi, Yohanan ben Zakkai, the man who was responsible for restoring Judaism after the destruction of the Temple in 70 CE. In the year 50 CE, tradition claims that he spent several years in a Galilean town, Arab, where he insisted that they be stricter in their observance of the Sabbath.

Galilee, at any rate the brigand-infested mountainous regions of Upper Galilee near and beyond Capernaum, was also a hotbed of political disturbance. The greater proportion of Jews who rose up against the Romans were Galileans. Insurrectionaries from this northern, semi-independent district were constantly urging the more passive Judaeans to throw off the Roman yoke. In the first seventy years of the Common Era, it was again and again the Galileans who plotted the uprisings. Judas the Galilean in 6 CE (his father had been executed by Herod for leading an anti-Roman agitation) incited the Jews to refuse to pay tribute to Caesar. His sons, Jacob and Simon, were destined to be crucified, some forty years later, for similar activities. At least twice during the procuratorship of Pontius Pilate, Galilean mobs descended on Jerusalem to incite the inhabitants to rise up and to assert their national and religious independence. All these attempts at rebellion were punished mercilessly and the ringleaders were usually crucified. Behind many such movements were the 'Galilean brigands' known as the Zealots.

As well as producing prosperous fishermen and political activists, Galilee would also seem to have been a fertile breeding-ground for holy men. The *hasidim* – types of charismatic healer and wonder-worker – are attested there. Unlike the Pharisees or the Temple priests in Jerusalem, these *hasidim* enjoyed very widespread popularity among ordinary people because of their spontaneous closeness to God and because of their ability to work miracles. They were more religiously fervent than the Temple hierarchy, but also more casual in their attitude to the minor points of ritual observance. One of the most famous of them, Honi, who flourished at the time of Pompey, had power over the winds and rain. So did the Galilean Hanina ben Dosa who lived about ten miles north of Nazareth. Hanina was so fervent in his devotions that he would not interrupt his prayer even when a snake curled itself around his ankles. Through prayer and the laying-on of hands, he could heal the sick, and he once, as we have already said, healed a boy without so much as having to visit him.[1] Like Honi, Hanina ben Dosa was able to make rain appear out of cloudless skies. As was the case with other holy men of the period, people supposed him to be a reincarnation of Elijah. Like that prophet, the *hasidim* led lives of the greatest simplicity. 'They hated their own money and even more the mammon of other peoples,' we read in the *Mekhilta*. They seem to have been especially close to God. No one thought they were divine, but one Hebrew source speaks of Honi as a 'son of God's household' and a heavenly voice alludes to Hanina as God's son.

It is out of this Galilee, of healers and shamans, of revolutionaries and freedom-fighters, of religiously independent northerners, of rich farmers and prosperous fishermen, that Jesus was to come.

As was made clear in the last chapter, history says nothing of the childhood and early life of Jesus. That period of his life is encrusted with legend, and we can no more imagine the reality which lies behind the tales of his childhood than we could envisage the original appearance of a Catholic saint by staring at a piece of his bone in some bejewelled reliquary which had been bathed in the devotion of centuries. Of Jesus's grown-up life, we can find out precious little, too, but we can guess and deduce, at precisely these moments when

[1] *Vide supra*, 31.

the Gospels drop their guard or contradict one another or give us information, which – because it seems to be unhelpful to their purposes – might be an echo of some early historical reality.

Even the Fourth Gospel, for so long regarded as a purely theological tract with no historical validity or purpose, in fact carries along with it, like barnacles accidentally clinging to a ship, accumulations of factual detail which there could have been no point in the evangelist inventing. In its story of the miracle of Cana of Galilee, for example, we are meant to be struck by the remarkable fact that Jesus turned some stone water-pots into vessels full of wine. As that Gospel says, it was by this 'sign' that Jesus first manifested his glory. As with every incident in the Fourth Gospel, the outward appearance of things conceals an inner spiritual truth, known only to the true believers who read or hear read the Good News. What the believers know, and the wedding guests did not know, is that the man who tells the servants to fill up the jars with water is the Eternal Logos. The believers know that the waterpots have a ritual significance 'after the Jews' manner of purifying';[1] they are symbols of the old religion, Judaism, out of which will spring a new faith – Christianity. But if we turn to the story itself, and try to ignore the sermon which it is preaching, we can ask some prosaic questions about it. Why did the servants come to Jesus when they realised that the wine at the wedding is about to run out? Why did the mother of Jesus tell the servants, 'Whatsoever he saith unto you, do it'? It is not for guests to arrange the catering at a wedding, though it might very well be for the bridegroom. Possibly – who knows? – the story of the wedding-feast at Cana contains a hazy memory of Jesus's own wedding. We are not told by any of the New Testament Books that Jesus was unmarried. When he told his disciples that some were made eunuchs for the sake of the Kingdom[2] there is no reason to suppose that he was describing himself. It would have been unusual at this date for a young Jewish male to have been unmarried. We can be fairly sure that he was not a member of the community at Qumran, and that he followed none of the stricter codes of the Essenes. He is described in the Gospels as a glutton and a wine-bibber – certainly no ascetic.

A modern biography would think it essential to tell us whether or not the subject of the book was married, but a Gospel is not the

---

[1] John 2:6.
[2] Matthew 19:12.

same as a modern biography. What did Jesus look like? What were the colour of Jesus's eyes? Did he have children? We will never know. Mark's Gospel and the Fourth Gospel do not even bother to tell us legends about the birth and childhood of Jesus. They tell us nothing, to start with, about his family background. They do not present the figure of Jesus at all until they have introduced us to the Fore-runner: a wild, shouting man in the Judaean wilderness, clad in goat's hair and feeding on locusts and wild honey. And his name was John.

If the John-the-Baptist religion (and we know there was one) had become the dominant cult of the Mediterranean rather than the Jesus-religion, we should probably feel that we knew more than we do about this arresting figure. His cult survived at least until the mid-50s, as the author of Acts is guileless enough to let on. When Paul arrived in Ephesus, he greeted the faithful there with the question, 'Did you receive the Holy Spirit when you became believers?'[1] This question is met with blank incomprehension. The Ephesian 'disciples' have never heard of the Holy Spirit, nor of the 'one who was to come' after John the Baptist: Jesus. [2]

This is one of those moments in the New Testament where the narrator of a particular book has been so clumsy in his arrangement of the material that we glimpse behind the scenes and discover a world which is wholly at variance with the traditional picture of things. Christian children in schools, tracing maps of Paul's mission-ary journeys and taught to believe that the 'Church' was founded on the Day of Pentecost, must always assume that when 'believers' or 'disciples' are mentioned in the Acts of the Apostles, this means believers in Jesus; possibly even believers in the divinity of Jesus. Yet, here in Acts, a book which is meant to describe how the Chris-tians taught a new religion to the Gentile world, we discover a community of believers who have never even heard Jesus's name. In Ephesus, they thought that 'the Way' (as the religion of these early believers was known) meant following 'the Baptism of John'. They had been told this on the authority of an Alexandrian Jew named Apollos[3] and he was clearly a missionary whose endeavours were seen as rivals to those of Paul. When Paul wrote to Corinth, he found that Apollos had been there too.

'From what Chloe's people have been telling me about you,

[1] Acts 19:2 (Jerusalem Bible).
[2] Acts 19:5.
[3] Acts 18:24.

brothers, it is clear that there are serious differences among you. What I mean is this. Everyone of you is declaring, "I belong to Paul" or "I belong to Apollos" or "I belong to Cephas" or "I belong to Christ". Has Christ been split up? Was it Paul that was crucified for you, or was it in Paul's name that you were baptized?'[1] A modern Christian, reading this passage from the point of view of faith, probably thinks it is laughable even to suggest that someone might be baptized in any name other than that of Jesus. Paul, however, makes it clear that Baptism was not necessarily in the name of Christ. For the Corinthian Christians, clearly, Paul, Apollos, Jesus, and Cephas were all interchangeable names, none more nor less divine than the rest. The Corinthians could not be expected to share Paul's obsession with the manner in which Jesus met his death. Until they read Paul's letters, there would have been no reason to suppose that their religion – the Baptism of Repentance – had anything to do with the Crucifixion. Like the Ephesians, the Corinthians would have been taught by Apollos, and the religion of Apollos, was 'the Baptism of John'.

From the New Testament, we learn that John had a following, though whether he sought it, we cannot tell. Like Jesus, he fell foul of the authorities and was arrested. Like Jesus, he was judicially murdered. Like Jesus, he was believed to have risen from the dead.[2] When Herod heard about Jesus and his popularity with his mob, his immediate reaction was to suppose that John had risen from the grave. This was a world where such wonders were conceived of as perfectly possible – together, oddly enough, with reincarnation, since the Gospels record the widespread belief in John's lifetime that he was a reincarnation of Elijah. Had Paul been a weaker personality than Apollos, or had he never written his epistles, it could easily have been the case that 'the Baptism of John' would have been the religion which captured the imagination of the ancient world, rather than the Baptism of Christ. Instead of the Sermon on the Mount, devotees would know all about the Sermon on the River-bank. Instead of stories about the heroic last hours of Jesus, they would have preserved stories of John the Baptist in prison, John the Baptist having his head chopped off, and, no doubt, John the Baptist appearing after his death to his chosen followers. The cult might even have developed to the point where present-day Johnites, or Baptists,

[1] I Cor. 1:10–12.
[2] Matthew. 14:1.

would have believed that the New Testament contained incontrovertible proof that John was divine.

This accident of history, however, was not to be. For all that, the New Testament cannot deny the importance of John. Jesus is quoted as saying, 'Among them that are born of women there is none greater than John', which sounds like high praise. Jesus then adds (or does the author of Luke add?), 'yet he that is but little in the kingdom of God is greater than he'. [1] Mark tells us that 'John came, who baptized in the wilderness and preached the baptism of repentance unto remission of sins. And there went out unto him all the country of Judaea, and all they of Jerusalem; and they were baptized of him in the River Jordan confessing their sins. And John was clothed with camel's hair, and had a leathern girdle about his loins, and did eat locusts and wild honey.' [2]

When the scrolls were discovered at Qumran, it was natural that scholars should have asked themselves whether John came from this ascetic community, that is, whether he was an Essene. If he had once belonged to the Qumran sect, or the Essenes, he did so no longer by the time he was preaching on the river-bank, since neither of these sects believed that salvation was on offer to all Israelites. They believed that God would save only an elect remnant of his people. John's universalism would not have been to their taste.

The language of washing, and indeed the practice of Baptism, are to be found in the Dead Sea Scrolls, however, and it has been plausibly suggested that John might once have been a member of this sect and then separated himself from his fellow sectarians in order to go into the desert – first as a solitary and then as a great, popular religious leader. 'And then (i.e. when the end is come, at the Day of Visitation) when the truth of the world will appear forever, God will purge by his truth all the deeds of men, refining for himself some of mankind in order to abolish every evil spirit from the midst of his flesh, and to cleanse him through a holy spirit from all wicked practices, sprinkling upon him a spirit of truth as purifying water.' [3]

John would seem to have been one of those Jews who imagined that the consummation of all things was at hand, that Israel was about to face a final judgment, and that there was about to arise a

[1] Luke 7:28.
[2] Mark 1:4–6.
[3] Quoted J. A. T. Robinson: *The Priority of John*, 175.

Messiah who would redeem the people and inaugurate an age of blessedness. Before this time could dawn, John knew from his reading of the Scriptures, the people must be purified. John saw this in straightforward and non-mystical terms. His message has much in common with the great prophets of the mid-eighth century BCE – Amos, Hosea and Isaiah. If, as the Gospels tell us, John had an enormous popular following, it was surely because his message was so accessible and simple.

'And the multitudes asked him, saying, What then must we do? And he answered and said unto them, He that hath two coats, let him impart to him that hath none; and he that hath food, let him do likewise. And there came also publicans to be baptized, and they said unto him, Master what must we do? And he said unto them, Extort no more than that which is appointed you. And soldiers also asked him, saying, And we, what must we do? And he said unto them, Do violence to no man, neither exact anything wrongfully; and be content with your wages.'[1]

Some commentators have questioned whether this was really what the Baptist preached, or whether Luke had put the words in his mouth to reassure any Roman readers of his book who might have heard that Christians were anarchic or anti-establishment. The coded message of the passage, as of other parts of Luke's books where Roman soldiers appear in a good light, is: 'Even in the days of its origins, our religion got on well with the Roman military'.

But there is no reason to suppose that the Baptist did not preach the simple message of repentance which Luke attributes to him. The simple message – repent of your evil ways, be good, be generous – lies at the heart of all 'the law and the Prophets' in the Jewish Scriptures. The great 'Hear, O Israel', recited to this day by any pious Jew, was, for Jesus, the essence of the Torah – 'Hear O Israel, the Lord our God is one Lord: and thou shalt love the Lord thy God with all thine heart, and with all thy soul, and with all thy might.'[2] Centrally important, too, was the message of the Book of Leviticus: Thou shalt love thy neighbour as thyself.[3] Jesus believed that 'on these two commandments hang all the law and the prophets, and

---

[1] Luke 3:10–14. 'Publicans' here translates the word which means 'tax-collectors', the hated collaborators with the Roman regime who collected the highly unpopular levies and polls for Caesar.
[2] Deut. 6:4.
[3] Lev. 19:18.

John would not have disagreed. [1] John taught that the Jews were to prepare for the Coming of the Kingdom, not by entering into some esoteric 'mystery' of the sort which flourished among the Gentiles; not by drinking the blood of Mithras; not by being 'reborn in the Spirit', like the Gnostics; but by trying to exercise virtue: by not being greedy, by not extorting the poor, by keeping decent and monogamous standards of behaviour at home. There never was, and never has been, any 'mystery' about the religion of Israel. 'And now, Israel, what doth the Lord thy God require of thee, but to fear the Lord thy God, to walk in his ways, and to love him, and to serve the Lord thy God with all thy heart and with all thy soul, to keep the commandments of the Lord, and his statutes which I command thee this day for thy good?' [2] That was how Israel believed that God had spoken to them in the wilderness on the occasion when the Torah was given to them. He spoke to them in that way also in the days of John the Baptist, and it was appropriate that they should have gone to hear the message in the wilderness.

The fringes of the Semitic deserts, wrote T. E. Lawrence, 'were strewn with broken faiths. It was significant that this wrack of fallen religions lay about the meeting of the desert and the sown. It pointed to the generation of all these creeds (Judaism, Christianity and Islam). They were assertions, not arguments; so they required a prophet to set them forth. The Arabs said that there had been forty thousand prophets: we had record of at least some hundreds. None of them had been of the wilderness; but their lives were after a pattern. Their birth set them in crowded places. An unintelligible passionate yearning drove them out into the desert. There they lived a greater or lesser time in meditation and physical abandonment; and thence they returned with their imagined message articulate, to preach it to their old and now doubting associates . . .' [3] John in the desert, and Jesus after him, did not dream up a new or radically altered Judaism. They are both cast, by themselves or by their disciples, in the roles of prophets like the prophets of old: men with a message, but also, like Jeremiah or Hosea, men who made their lives into that message. If one had to summarise their message in three words it would be, 'Be Better Jews'. That is the Law and the Prophets, as far as John and Jesus were concerned, though Jesus was

[1] Matthew 22:40.
[2] Deut. 10:12,13.
[3] T. E. Lawrence: *The Seven Pillars of Wisdom*, 39.

to ask some disturbing questions about what it meant to be a Jew, and perhaps what it meant to be 'good'.

Three interesting questions arise when we contemplate the figure of John. First, who did he think he was? Secondly, who did his contemporaries, including Jesus, think he was? And thirdly, who did John think Jesus was?

The New Testament was written, largely, by people who did believe that Jesus was the Messiah, so it is not surprising that they do not record any instance of John claiming to be the Messiah. Even making allowances, however, for the evangelists' bias, it would seem highly unlikely that John claimed to be the Messiah. My reason for saying this is because of one of those strange lapses in the Gospels, where the material presented is actually at variance with the message. This is the moment after John has been put into prison and he sends some of his followers to ask Jesus whether or not he was the one 'who is to come'.[1]

Pious Christians, when they read this passage from the Gospel, will assume that John, sitting in his prison cell, will be pleased to hear that Jesus has been healing the sick, raising the dead to life and preaching the Gospel to the poor – which is his answer to the imprisoned Prophet's question. But, of course, had John believed Jesus to be the Messiah, he would not have needed to ask the question. By asking the question, so anxiously, from a place where he must have known that he awaited death, he betrays the fact that he does not believe (or, more likely, that he no longer believes) Jesus to be the Christ. 'Go your way and tell John the things which ye do hear and see: the blind receive their sight, and the lame walk, the lepers are cleansed, and the deaf hear, and the dead are raised up, and the poor have good tidings preached to them. And blessed is he, whosoever shall find none occasion of stumbling in me.'[2] This range of activities, however impressive, is not what was expected of the Promised Saviour. It is entirely *sui generis*. John's message means, 'Are you the Messiah or aren't you?' Jesus's reply means, 'There are other ways of God showing himself – such as through my healing ministry and my preaching to the poor'. Jesus thought that John was 'a prophet and more than a prophet'. John sadly came to think the same of Jesus. He had hoped that he was something more. In the

[1] Matthew 11:3.
[2] Matthew 11:4–6.

Fourth Gospel, priests and Levites come down from Jerusalem to ask John in the desert whether he is the Christ and he denies it. He merely applies to himself the text from Isaiah, 'I am a voice that cries in the wilderness'.

So, we have answered our first two questions. John disclaimed his own Messiahship. He denied that he was 'that Prophet' who should precede the Messiah. When asked by the authorities who he thought he was, he answered them only in negatives, leaving them considerably baffled. This was a technique which Jesus learnt from John and was to use very effectively on occasions.

Jesus, during his own ministry, is frequently quoted as making allusion to John, usually for the purpose of annoying the authorities or for baffling his own followers. When the chief priests in Matthew's Gospel ask Jesus by what authority he behaves as he does, Jesus asks them, in reply, whether John's Baptism was of heavenly or of earthly origin. They are frightened to answer this question. If they say that John was inspired by God, they know that Jesus can ask them why they took no notice of John in his lifetime. If they say that he was not inspired by God, they would risk making themselves unpopular with the mob, who doted on the Baptist. 'And they answered Jesus, and said, We know not. He also said unto them, Neither tell I you by what authority I do these things.'[1] Perhaps it was no accident that it was with priests that Jesus had this acrimonious exchange. Luke tells us that John came from priestly stock himself, and that his father belonged to the Abijah section of the Temple priesthood.[2] John's ascetic manner of life – for example, his abstention from alcohol – was foretold by an angel when he was still in the womb of his mother Elizabeth.[3] Perhaps Luke was right to suggest that Elizabeth and Mary the Mother of Jesus were cousins. If John was Jesus's cousin, this might explain why Jesus left the north country in order to attach himself to the Baptist's entourage in the desert.

The Synoptic Gospels seek to emphasise that Jesus had a ministry entirely distinct from that of John, but it may be that the Fourth Gospel is closer to the truth in suggesting that Jesus and his first disciples came to know one another as fellow-disciples of John. The call for repentance, the summons into the wilderness, and the dra-

[1] Matthew 21:27.
[2] Luke 1:5.
[3] Luke 1:14.

matic and emotional effect of John's preaching are all recorded in the New Testament.

'What went ye out into the wilderness to behold? a reed shaken with the wind? But what went ye out for to see? a man clothed in soft raiment? Behold, they that wear soft raiment are in kings' houses. But wherefore went ye out?'[1]

These are questions which Jesus must have asked himself, as he went to follow his cousin's movement for spiritual renewal in the desert. The spiritual self-questioning, which the Gospels dramatise as 'The Temptations in the Wilderness', formed part of Jesus's experience at this time. What T. E. Lawrence discerned about the creed of desert people, whom he encountered 1900 years after John the Baptist, could have been said of the man in goatskin, and perhaps of his Galilean cousin. 'They were a people of primary colours, or rather of black and white, who saw the world always in contour. They were a dogmatic people, despising doubt, our modern crown of thorns . . . The common base of all the Semitic creeds . . . was the ever-present idea of world-worthlessness. Their profound reaction from matter led them to preach barrenness, renunciation, poverty.' And Lawrence makes the point that they sought the desert, not because they found God there but because 'in its solitude they heard more certainly the living word they brought with them'.[2] I have only spent a day and a night in the Negeb desert. An Arab driver abandoned me there, on my own, when I was a very young man, in the arid rocky territory south of Jerusalem where the wilderness begins. The extraordinary cold, and clarity of the night, the brightness of the stars above my head, the scorching heat of the day when the sun came up, the hunger and thirst which I felt until I was rescued by another Arab, who happened to be bowling along in a dilapidated car, all gave me a small insight into what other writers – T. E. Lawrence most notably – have said about the desert's capacity to simplify consciousness itself.

The profundity of Jesus's Temptations in the Wilderness is quite lost if we imagine that the Devil is whispering into the ear of a divine being. Though Dostoevsky makes magnificent mythological use of these temptations in *The Brothers Karamazov* as a comment upon institutional Christianity in general and on Roman Catholicism in

[1] Matthew 11:7–9.
[2] T. E. Lawrence: op. cit.

particular, this is not of course what the evangelists had in mind when they tell us that Jesus was 'tested' in the desert. By his persistent 'If-you-are-the-Son-of-God' questions in the Gospel accounts of the Temptations, Satan is not testing the idea of Jesus's divinity. He is testing the kind of *man* that Jesus is. He is not saying, 'If you are God – prove it!' The gospels of Matthew, Mark and Luke never state that Jesus claimed to be God.

The first temptation was to turn the stones of the desert into bread. It is a temptation to use his charismatic power for the benefit of others. It was a temptation which, we might suppose, haunted Jesus throughout his ministry. Though he is described as yielding to this temptation – as when he miraculously fed five thousand men in the wilderness, turned water into wine, or increased a poor night's fishing into a miraculously large netful of fish – the Gospels also represent him as chiding his followers for needing such 'signs'. 'Man does not live by bread alone, but by every word proceeding out of the mouth of God' is the text from the Scriptures with which he fights the impulse to earn popularity by means of giving his followers material benefits. [1] Jesus, rather, decides to live, and to teach his fellow Jews to live, as if he were a child of God, a son of God; one who could have such trust in Abba, his Heavenly Father, that he does not worry about what he will eat or drink or wherewithal he will be clothed.

He is imbued with the spirit of the 91st Psalm which speaks of God protecting those who love him:

> For he shall deliver thee from the snare of the fowler,
> And from the noisome pestilence . . .
> Thou shalt not be afraid for the terror by night,
> Nor for the arrow that flieth by the day. . .
> For he shall give his angels charge over thee,
> To keep thee in all thy ways.
> They shall bear thee up in their hands
> Lest thou dash thy foot against a stone. [2]

This poem, written hundreds of years before Jesus was born, was part of the Jewish Prayer Book. To recite it did not mean that the pious Jew believed himself to be divine. From some of the remarks attributed to Jesus, we can guess that he had a habit of hyperbolic

---

[1] Matthew 4:4, quoting Deut. 8:3.
[2] Psalm 91:3, 11, 12.

utterance. He is quoted as saying that a man with sufficient faith could move a mountain. It does not necessarily mean that he thought this was literally true, any more than that in this second quotation from the Scriptures, he genuinely believed that if he threw himself off a high pinnacle, the angels would come and hold him up. But the Gospel suggests that he was *tempted* so to believe. Jesus, in whom we read an almost perpetual tension between the harshness of the desert and the comedy of home (where a lost coin can turn into a disaster of world-shattering proportions, and rowdy neighbours wake you up in the middle of the night) rejects the option of lemming-like self-destruction, which any Jew of the time could see was a national option, an option which was being urged with some force by the crankier sects. He rejects the idea of throwing himself off the precipice: 'Do not put the Lord God to the test'. [1]

It is the third temptation which is the greatest, and which is the most important part of the myth of Jesus's encounter with the Devil in the desert. 'Again, the Devil taketh him unto an exceeding high mountain, and showeth him all the kingdoms of the world, and the glory of them; and he said unto him, All these things will I give unto thee if thou wilt fall down and worship me.'[2]

When Jesus rejects this temptation, he is, superficially at least, turning down the opportunity of political power. It would seem very likely that his career offered him the chances of political adventure, if not of actual power. We shall read of how the people tried to make him into a king, and he was to die with the cruel mockery of a crown on his head, and a royal inscription on his Cross. Jesus's distrust of kingship is deeply Jewish. The Jews had attempted to have kings in the time of Samuel, over a thousand years earlier than Jesus. The reigns of Saul and David had not been an undivided success. Ever since the internecine quarrels which grew up after the death of King Solomon, the Jews had maintained a healthy detachment from political concerns. Their obedience was the obedience of an individual toward God.

Had Jesus the Galilean *hasid* been able to look into the future when he stood in the wilderness, might he also have been tempted to extend his influence over the 'kingdoms of the world' in a more than political sense? Might he have felt the temptation to 'convert' Paul,

[1] Deut. 6:16.
[2] Matthew 4:8, 9.

to send dissension into the synagogues of Ephesus, Athens, Corinth, Rome; to establish a new 'world religion' which would one day become the religion of the empire? Would he have been tempted to found a church, or several churches, each accusing the other of heresy, and denouncing their fellow believers by the means of councils, papal bulls, inquisitions, and wars, until the capital of the empire stood thick with temples devoted to the worship of Jesus and altars where Gentile priests could, by repeating certain words, call down the very presence of Jesus into their midst? If he had foreseen such a thing, it is actually hard to suppose that the Jesus of the New Testament would have found it tempting, since it would have seemed to him so obviously like the work of the Devil.

In rejecting the third temptation, Jesus rejected the notion not merely of political power but also of the collective response to life. 'What is divine in man is elusive and impalpable, and he is easily tempted to embody it in concrete form. Yet those who set out for it alone will reach it together, and those who seek it in company will perish by themselves.'[1] In his stories and apothegms, Jesus was to exemplify this idea more devastatingly than any other 'thinker' or 'religious founder', though he was neither of these things. He refused to be called 'master'. He would have seen no meaning in the idea of founding a new religion, since for him there was only one religion, the religion of Israel, which enabled Jews to call God Father. It was a paradox that in rejecting the third temptation, he was also to overcome the world; not by the establishment of a world religion – with its popes and councils and theologians – but by his playful and yet passionately serious sense of the infinite worth of every individual in the fatherly protection of God. When the Gospels had been written down, and the teachings of Jesus could be propagated, they were to spread far beyond the confines of Jesus's own linguistic or ethnic group.

For John the Baptist, the desert, which enabled men to concentrate on their destiny with stark fierceness, was but the preliminary. It was 'training'. According to the Fourth Gospel, he believed that the Messiah would be one of his own followers.[2]

The Pharisees, and others from Jerusalem, came down to dispute with John. If he was not the incarnation of Elijah, or the Prophet

---

[1] Hugh Kingsmill: *The Poisoned Crown* (1944), 26.
[2] C. H. Dodd's reading of John 1:27. '*Ho opiso mou erchomenos*' means not 'he that cometh after me' but 'he that follows me', or 'my disciple'.

who foretold the Messiah, or the Messiah himself, who was he? His answer was that he baptised with water. One of his followers, one who stood among them even as he spoke, was the Messiah. This exchange took place at a village called Bethany, but it does not appear to have been the same Bethany which appears later in the story.

The Fourth Gospel records two very remarkable footnotes to this idea of John's that Jesus was the Messiah. The first is that other of John's disciples are convinced by it. The first is Andrew, a fisherman from Galilee, and he goes to his brother, Peter (otherwise known as Simon) and announces that, 'We have found the Messiah!' [1] Others are sceptical. 'From Nazareth?' inquires Nathanael scepti- cally. 'Can any good thing come out of Nazareth?' [2]

True, this is typical of the Fourth Gospel's irony. The readers have already been informed that Jesus is the Creative Demiurge who has come forth from the bosom of the Father; Nathanael is quibbling about which village he comes from. On the other hand, it suggests that from the first there were those who had their doubts about Jesus's Messiahship. He had the wrong credentials. To this day, the reason why the Jews resent the Christian claim that Jesus was the Jewish Messiah is that he did not inaugurate the Messianic Age as foretold in the prophecies. John clearly hoped or supposed that he would. Yet more remarkable than the sketched hints in the Fourth Gospel is the story in the Synoptic Gospels of Jesus's ministry developing alongside that of John's. John baptized Jesus, and the story tells that the heavens opened, and the Spirit descended upon Jesus in the form of a dove, and a voice spoke – either to Jesus himself or to those standing by – setting the seal of divine sonship upon him. If such a thing had actually happened, it is very strange that when John was thrown into prison by Herod Antipas, he should have sent messengers to Jesus asking, 'Art thou he that cometh, or look we for another?' [3] If John had heard the voice of God declaring from a cloud that Jesus was the Messiah, he would hardly have found it necessary to despatch messengers to confirm the fact. His question suggests bewilderment, if not an overwhelming disappointment in his follower.

John was destined to be killed by Herod Antipas, and to die as a martyr not for the Messianic dream so much as for the principle of

[1] John 1:41.
[2] John 1:46.
[3] Matthew 11:3.

monogamy. [1] Jesus was to share this fiercely monogamous view of marriage with John (and, incidentally, with the Qumran community). While he was in prison, John heard that Jesus had been preaching and performing miracles. Enough has been said already in this book to show that by first-century Jewish standards there was nothing unique about this. There were many preachers in John's day, and many miracle-workers. John, close to death, wanted to know if the Messianic Age was about to begin. If Jesus was the Messiah, he need only proclaim his God-given power and the people would rally behind him. John's question from prison is another version of the three Temptations in the Wilderness, goading Jesus to make a claim for himself which he always refused to make.

The exchange between the imprisoned John and Jesus, conducted by messengers, presupposes 'it to be historically conceivable that messengers were sent to Jesus by the imprisoned John with the attendant implications of a rather enlightened jail administration under Herod Antipas, visiting hours and an open line of communication with the outside world'. [2] But if it is a fiction, it is nonetheless an interesting emblem of a difference between John and his expectations, and Jesus himself.

Jesus, in the context of the exchange, pays the compliment to John that he is the greatest of all the children of men born to women, but then announces the inauguration of a new 'Kingdom' of his own. 'Yet the least in the Kingdom of Heaven is greater than he.' [3] A new age is about to begin, but it is not, quite, the Messianic Age which everyone had been expecting. A kingdom is to be inaugurated in which the first shall be last and the last shall be first, in which slaves and children will enter in before the wise and the holy.

John, like everyone else at the time, was looking for 'signs'. Jesus asks the messenger to return to the prison and tell John the things which he has seen and heard. The blind are given their sight, the lepers are cleansed and the lame can walk. But the most important part of the message – the phrase he leaves until last – is that the good news is proclaimed to the poor. These sayings are all allusions to the Prophets, particularly to the First Isaiah about the rule of God on earth, but they lack all the fire and mystery of the apocalyptic

---

[1] At least, according to the New Testament. According to Josephus (*Antiquities* XVII: 117—118), John was executed for his potentially dangerous eloquence.

[2] Geza Vermes: *Jesus the Jew*, 32.

[3] Matthew 11:11 (Jerusalem Bible).

prophecies of Daniel. You will know that God rules, Jesus seems to say, when the poor are treated with justice. Amos would have understood this, eight hundred years before. But John in prison is awaiting thunderbolts from heaven, and Jesus's words seem scarcely comprehensible. Jesus has been into the desert, and his own 'living word' has been simplified almost to the point of madness. What is more, Jesus appears at this early juncture to have abandoned all John's ascetic notions. 'What comparison can I find for this generation? It is like children shouting to each other as they sit in the market place. We played the pipes for you and you wouldn't dance; we sang dirges and you wouldn't be mourners. For John came, neither eating nor drinking, and they say, He is possessed. The Son of Man came, eating and drinking, and they say, Look, a glutton and a drunkard, a friend of tax collectors and sinners.'[1]

So, the boozy and strangely anarchic message goes back to the ascetic Baptist in the prison: 'The goods news is proclaimed to the poor'. John would have been as baffled by any of this as would have been anyone else who heard the words. He would certainly have been bitterly disappointed. Jesus is to establish a 'kingdom'; but his message is not one of apocalypse, but of inner virtue. There is to be no Messiah landing from outer space, but a man teaching sinners how to repent. As the Fourth Gospel has him say, 'The kingdom of God is within you'. It is a message of peculiar importance for the poor because, for the first time in history, perhaps, a teacher was to see the full, personal, political and religious consequences of regarding everyone as equal in the eyes of Almighty God. Jesus did not invent this idea. It is buried in the Psalms and the Prophets, but no one had made such startling use of it before. No one had started a 'kingdom' on the basis of it.

John, who had set such hopes on Jesus, was destined to die a violent death. He had consistently criticised Herod Antipas for marrying his brother Philip's wife. Herod, it would seem, was in awe of John and 'liked to listen to him'.[2] Not so Herodias, Herod's wife. There followed the famously gruesome birthday banquet at which Herodias's daughter Salome danced before Herod and so delighted him that he promised her anything she should desire. Salome (we know her name from Josephus, not from the Gospels) rushed to

[1] Matthew 11:16-19 (Jerusalem Bible).
[2] Mark 6:20 (Jerusalem Bible).

Herodias to ask what she should request from the king, who was offering her half his kingdom. When her mother had told the girl what to say, she returned to her uncle and asked for the head of John the Baptist on a dish – a request with which Herod reluctantly and with some terror complied.

Herod Antipas, it will be remembered, was the 'client' king of the Galilean region. John died not in the desert where he had preached, nor on the banks of the Jordan where he had baptized, but in a jail of the northern province. Presumably, he, like his cousin Jesus, was a Galilean. No sooner was he dead than the king found another preacher to listen to.

'I say unto you, that every one that putteth away his wife . . . maketh her an adulteress, and whosoever shall marry her when she is put away committeth adultery.'[1] Herod assumed that it was John, returned from the grave to torment him. Not for the last time in this story, a prophet who has caused trouble in the southern province of Judaea is seen – risen from the dead – in the northern province of Galilee.

[1] Matt. 5:32.

# VI
## GALILEE

ALL THE GOSPELS agree that Jesus came from Nazareth, a small hill town in the region of Galilee. They also tell us that he left Nazareth, and for a time took up residence at Capernaum, at the northern end of the Sea of Galilee.

Luke tells us that Jesus left Nazareth as the result of a quarrel. He had gone to the synagogue there on the Sabbath day, as was his custom, and read aloud the portion of Scripture appointed for the day – the passage in Isaiah where the prophet says, 'The Spirit of the Lord is upon me, Because he anointed me to preach good tidings to the poor'. When the reading was over, Jesus gave back the scroll to the attendant and said, 'Today hath this scripture been fulfilled in your ears'.[1] The people of Nazareth were so outraged that Jesus should be applying this prophecy to himself, that they 'rose up and cast him forth out of the city, and led him unto the brow of the hill whereon their city was built, that they might cast him down headlong'.[2] Thereafter, Luke says, he went to Capernaum.[3] The very different tradition of the Fourth Gospel would seem to agree with the Synoptics that Jesus fell out with those in his immediate locality, and was at odds with his family. It tells of his rough rebuke to his mother at the marriage in Cana, another Galilean town, after which he 'went down to Capernaum' – though in this tradition, his mother and brothers come with him,[4] We are told by this Gospel that Jesus's brothers did not believe in him[5] which coincides with the tradition known to Mark that the family tried to restrain Jesus

---

[1] Luke 4:21.
[2] Luke 4:29.
[3] I use the conventional English spelling of this word, more properly known by its Semitic name of Capharnaum – or Kefar (village) of Nahum. It has not been possible to identify the Nahum after whom the original village was named.
[4] John 2:12.
[5] John 7:5.

physically, under the impression that he was dangerously mad.[1] This was presumably because, when he performed his exorcisms, Jesus himself appeared to be possessed, as is the case with many exorcists.

Nevertheless, there is a mystery here which the New Testament does nothing to explain. At the beginning of his public life, Jesus appears to have been in a state of conflict with his family. His recorded utterances about the family as an institution are all hostile to it. Though he insisted on the necessity of monogamy, he praised those who left their mothers, fathers, brothers, sisters, and wives in order to be his followers. All this suggests that relations with his own family (and with his wife, if he had one) were, to say the least, tempestuous. Nevertheless, at the end of the story, the family of Jesus becomes extremely important. When his followers and friends had deserted him, it was his mother who stood at the foot of the Cross. And the early Church was presided over by the figure of James, the brother of Jesus, who receives almost no mention in the Gospel narratives.

There must be reasons for this. We are told by the Gospels that Jesus's family feared for his sanity, and there is every reason to suppose that they disliked his choice of companions which included not merely insalubrious types, such as swindlers, drunkards and whores, but also the much more dangerous company of those who sought to overthrow the power of Rome by armed insurrection. These are all strands which, as far as the Gospels go, remain loose ends, but we can probably gather them together without straying too far into the realms of fantasy.

Having thrown in his lot with his cousin John the Baptist, Jesus, as we saw in the last chapter, grossly disappointed John by failing to live up to any of his Messianic promises. The Gospels, in their present form, are far removed from the original family of Jesus. They are written in Greek for Gentile audiences. Even if, in origin, they contain traditions which are extremely old, they have been edited and altered to fit the teaching requirements of a Gentile church, who would have known nothing of Jesus's immediate circumstances.

The Synoptic Gospels therefore present Jesus's quarrel with his family very much as a division between earthbound, uncomprehending people and the divine saviour whom they fail to recognise

[1] Mark 3:21.

in their midst. The tone of Luke's Gospel – which scholarship would incline to say was the furthest from Jesus in time and place – suggests that the family's attitude was rather one of 'Who does he think he is? – healing the sick, preaching, – he is only a common man like the rest of us'. The tone of the Fourth Gospel is interestingly different. And it may be that here is one of the areas in which the Fourth Gospel retains a much older and more authentic tradition than the Synoptics. Jesus's quarrel with his mother at the wedding feast of Cana concerns, not his divine calling, but his timing. In that story, the mother of Jesus is asking him to perform a 'sign' – the transformation of water into wine. In other words, she is asking him to inaugurate a new era in Israel's spiritual history, when the old water is replaced by a vintage trodden in the winepresses of God. And he replies, 'Mine hour is not yet come'.[1] After the death of Jesus, as we shall see, it was his family who kept alive his message – a message completely at variance with that of the Gentile Church of Paul. From John the Fore-runner to James the brother of the Lord, it is a story of joint family concern, interrupted and misinterpreted by followers of Jesus who were not privy to the family secret. If they did not actually believe Jesus to be the Messiah, the family of Jesus believed that he had a unique role to play in the spiritual destiny of his nation, and the evidence rather suggests that Jesus was not willing to play the role which they had set up for him. If this interpretation of things is anything like correct, then we must change our picture of the quarrel. It is not the story of a simple carpenter getting ideas above his station, and being upbraided by his family for making claims for himself. It is, rather, a divinely chosen being stepping anarchically out of line. Instead of an austere call to repentance along the Baptist's pattern, it is the announcement that Jesus had good news to preach to the poor. No wonder they were baffled or disappointed. It was as if the Dalai Lama, instead of living the life of monkish austerity expected of so important a spiritual leader, should have chosen to sit in taverns and spin tales and drink with the common people. By a tragic paradox, in fact, it was only after the death of Jesus that his family were able to carry on the story as they had wished it to be fulfilled.

This is, of course, only a speculation, but it fits with some of the puzzles of the surviving New Testament evidence. If Jesus had, from

---

[1] John 2:4.

an early age, been trained up as a religious leader, and served for a time as an austere follower of John the Baptist in the Judaean desert, it would explain why there is indication in his teaching of remoteness from the actual workaday existence of the people whom he found so attractive – the common people among whom he chose to move and preach. One of Jesus's most famous stories, for example, is the parable of the sower, sowing his seed. Some of the seed falls on the footpath and the birds of the air peck it up. Some falls among the thistles, which grow up and choke it. Only a little falls in good soil, where it grows and yields a harvest.[1] As long ago as 1926, the German scholar Dalman in the *Palästina Jahrbuch* claimed to have discovered Palestinian farmers who employed this bizarre method of agriculture. No one else has ever seen farmers randomly scattering seed on unploughed land and expecting it to grow, and the simplest conclusion is that Dalman was mistaken. He visited Palestine in May and was told about the sowing-techniques which took place there in the autumn. In the Mishnah, the vast compilation of Jewish lore and wisdom of the rabbis, there is a list of work forbidden on the Sabbath. It includes, in this order, 'sowing, ploughing, reaping, binding sheaves, etc'. The commentary on this in the Talmud expresses puzzlement that the ancient writer should have forbidden 'ploughing, then sowing'. If a farmer behaved like the farmer in Jesus's story, or the equally bookish Mishnah, he would yield no harvest at all. In an excellent commentary on the parable, John Drury has written, 'We are either being presented with a farming method so inefficient that no one in his senses would use it for long, as Rashi and the Babylonian Talmud noticed, or the sower is a parable which resorts to the bizarre nonsense of riddle in order to jolt the hearer into perception, not of agriculture but of the mystery of the Gospel.'[2] What Drury does not go on to say, but it would seem a fair inference, is that the man who first told the parable of the sower had absolutely no experience of farming, though he might have been very well versed in the law-books of the rabbis. It would lend plausibility to Professor Vermes's suggestion that Jesus was a *tekton*, meaning, not a workman or a carpenter, but a scholar.

In one of his better-known carpentry analogies, Jesus again shows a fantastical imagination, and a sharp wit, but no practical knowledge

[1] Mark 4:3–9.
[2] John Drury: *The Parables in the Gospels* (1985), 58.

of what it was like to work in a carpenter's shop. 'Why beholdest thou the mote that is in thy brother's eye, but considerest not the beam that is in thine own eye?'[1] It has become a proverb to express the archetypal human tendency to be observant of other people's faults and blind to one's own. Like much that Jesus said, it is hyperbolic to the point of farce. It is actually extremely funny. But no carpenter in real life came anywhere near having a plank sticking out of his eye. Similarly, in the area of boating and fishing – if we except the incident of the Miraculous Draught of Fish in the Fourth Gospel which took place after Jesus rose from the dead – there is no evidence in the Gospels that Jesus had any practical skills whatsoever. When he accompanied the disciples on a fishing expedition on the Lake, and a storm blew up, his friends found that he had fallen asleep in the stern of the boat. 'We are sinking! Don't you care?' is their response.[2]

Jesus, then, does not appear to have been a practical man, nor one well-versed in a trade – unlike Paul who was a tentmaker, or Peter, Andrew, James and John the sons of Zebedee who earned their living as fishermen. Nor was he an experienced or observant agriculturalist. If he had been, he would not have told his hearers that the mustard plant was the tallest tree, so large that birds could settle in its branches:[3] another typical piece of hyperbole, which he probably derived from reading; the Talmud informs us that the mustard shrub was as tall as a fig-tree, which it is not.[4] Jesus told his followers to 'consider the lilies of the field', but he did not do so with a botanist's eye. As André Gide observes, there is not a single mention of colour in any of the Gospels.[5] None of this suggests the carpenter, carried away by his religious fervour into starting a movement. We should probably be closer to the truth if we imagined a boy who had been brought up to study the law books. Perhaps Luke's story of the boy Jesus, arguing with the doctors of the Law in the Temple at Jerusalem, contains a grain of truth. When he came to manhood, and began to preach his Gospel, and to work as a charismatic healer and popular leader, his family did not like it, and he decamped to Capernaum.

Nazareth was probably a very small place in Jesus's day. By

[1] Matthew 7:3.
[2] Mark 4:38.
[3] Mark 4:32.
[4] *Pal Talmud Peah*, vii 20f.
[5] André Gide: *La Symphonie Pastorale*.

contrast, the shores of the sea of Galilee were highly populated. It is hard to imagine today, as one drives along the shore of the lake, finding almost all the countryside between Tiberias (now a popular resort with five-star hotels, yachting marinas and Club Med-style cafes) and the Golan Heights almost devoid of population. Magdala, for example, which one passes on the way north to Capernaum, is a tiny Arab village, but in Jesus's time it was a thriving town with a population of 30 or 40,000. Capernaum, which was probably rather smaller, is now merely an archaeological site, a heap of ruins. It was a town of strategic importance to the Romans since it marked the point in the upper Jordan where the tetrarchy of Herod Antipas ended and the Golan territory, assigned to Philip, began. Its commercial links, to judge from coins and vessels unearthed there in recent times, were more with the north than with the south: Upper Galilee, Golan, Syria, Phoenicia, Asia Minor and Cyprus. The inhabitants seem to have had little commercial contact with Palestine to the south.

This part of the country was rich and fertile. Josephus, who was Governor of Galilee thirty years after Jesus died, tells us that 'the whole area is excellent for crops and cattle and rich in forests of all kinds, so that by its adaptability it invites even those least inclined to work on the land. Consequently every inch has been cultivated by the inhabitants and not a corner goes to waste. It is thickly studded with towns, and thanks to the natural abundance the innumerable villages are so densely populated that the smallest has more than 15,000 inhabitants.'[1]

In choosing to settle in Capernaum, Jesus was following those other disciples of John the Baptist, Simon Peter and Andrew, who ran a prosperous fishing business on the Lake. It is only since 1969 that excavations in Capernaum have proceeded in earnest. The remains of the beautiful synagogue are of a fourth-century CE structure, but the archaeologists have now shown the extreme likelihood that this magnificent edifice was constructed on the remains of another synagogue, built in the first century. If less magnificent than the fourth-century structure, this was clearly no mean building. Luke's Gospel tells us that the synagogue was built for the towns-people by an enlightened centurion.[2] If this seems fairly improbable,

---

[1] Josephus: *Jewish War*. It has to be said that Josephus is notoriously inaccurate with statistics.
[2] Luke 7:5.

then we can certainly believe that the synagogue at Capernaum was built by a cosmopolitan Jew, perhaps by one who had gone abroad, 'made good', and returned to his native town, determined to make a splash by erecting a good imitation of the sort of buildings he had seen in Greece, Asia Minor or Italy.

The Synoptic Gospels tell us that Jesus preached in this synagogue. On one occasion, he was interrupted by a man possessed by a devil, who shrieked at the top of his voice. Jesus confronted the demon and drove it out. [1]

It would seem that Jesus was much in demand as an exorcist, and that it was his skill in this area which first won him the widespread reputation which he apparently enjoyed in the area. He was not unique in his ability to 'drive out devils' or to heal the sick. In all primitive societies, there have been shamans, holy men, exorcists or witchdoctors who were able, by means of autosuggestion, to heal those who came to them in distress. [2] A very high proportion of the Gospel stories relate to Jesus's healing miracles. Modern scepticism will probably be more prepared to accept the stories of Jesus as a healer than those stories which relate his ability to walk on the waters of Galilee, or control the weather. As I have already said, there were other Galilean holy man of whom similar claims were made.

After Jesus had healed the demoniac in the synagogue, the narrative of Luke tells us that he went back to Simon's house: the house that is of Simon Peter. Mark too tells the story, placing it at the very beginning of his Gospel. He depicts the townspeople bringing the sick and the possessed to the door of this house – where Jesus also healed Simon Peter's mother-in-law, who was sick of a fever.

From Byzantine times, piety had marked the spot in Capernaum where this house stood, quite near to the synagogue. It was traditionally supposed to be the very house of Simon Peter. The archaeological excavations since 1969 have shown that beneath the octagonal

---

[1] Luke 4:31–37.

[2] Morton Smith's *Jesus the Magician* (New York 1978) compares Jesus with pagan magicians such as Apollonius of Tyana, and the occult practices described in the Greek Magical Papyri. There are many striking points of comparison – in particular, the Magical Papyri speak of the initiates becoming divine. 'Open to me, heaven! Let me see the bark of Phre descending and ascending . . . for I am Geb, heir to the gods . . .' This is likened by Smith to the Baptism of Jesus. If Jesus had not been a magician, Smith asks, why did the Pharisees and others accuse him of casting out demons by demonic means? That Jesus was in some sense of the word a 'magician' would seem beyond question, but by making comparisons with pagan literature, Smith begs many questions about Jesus and the world of contemporary Galilean Judaism.

Byzantine church erected on this site in the mid-fifth century CE there was a *domus ecclesia*, a house church, used for religious gatherings from the late first century CE, and that this house-church had been adapted from a house built in the late Hellenistic period. In other words, it is perfectly possible that this house was the very place where Simon Peter lived with his wife and mother-in-law, with Andrew his brother, and, for a period, with Jesus himself. The archaeologists have found physical evidence to support the testimony of the fourth-century Etheria, who wrote, 'The house of the prince of the Apostles in Capernaum was changed into a church; the walls of that house, however, are still standing as they were in the past.'[1] The house was built on the pattern of a Roman villa, with a central courtyard or atrium, and dwellings off it, not unlike the divisions of a cloister. It would appear to have been rather a comfortable and substantial house, and to give the lie to the popular cliché that Peter and the early followers of Jesus were all paupers.

Nevertheless, it was to the poor, to the 'lost sheep of the House of Israel', that Jesus addressed himself, and he did not detach his capacity to heal the sick from his spiritual remedy for the ills of Israel. We are told that there was a man in Capernaum who was sick of the palsy. By now, Jesus's reputation as a healer had grown, and when it was rumoured that he was in residence at Simon Peter's house, an immense crowd collected. He was presumably in one of the rooms off the courtyard, and the crowds were so dense that the family of the sick man, carrying him on a stretcher, were unable to get near him. They enterprisingly climbed on to the roof of the house, removed the roof and lowered the stretcher into the room where Jesus sat. Moved by their display of faith, Jesus pronounced that the sick man's sins were forgiven. We are told that there were 'scribes' sitting with Jesus; that is, those learned in the Jewish Law – a detail which suggests the company he normally kept when he was at home, unmolested by the mob. Perhaps these 'scribes' were his brothers. They protest that no one has the power to forgive sin except God. Jesus replied that the man's sickness, and his inner disease of sin, were one and the same thing, and that it was by assuring the man of his reconciliation with God that he was able to heal him. The paralysed man took up his stretcher and walked home.[2]

---

[1] Stanislao Loffreda: *Recovering Capharnaum* (Jerusalem 1985), 63.
[2] Mark 2:1–12.

From what we know of the various Jewish sects of the period, they all appear to have been exclusive. The Essenes and the Sadducees felt that the salvation of Judaism, and of the people of Israel, was to be found in narrowness. Opinions differ about whether the Pharisees, the *haberim*, were similarly exclusive, but certainly they are represented as exclusive by the New Testament, and this impression is not altogether contradicted by the Rabbinic literature. [1] It was a discipline too hard for ordinary people to follow, with their messy ways, their vague beliefs, their irregular marital arrangements. Religious extremists might well have believed that the presence of Roman soldiers in Jerusalem posed a threat to Judaism itself. The sects could not avoid being influenced by the Roman presence. Whether their attitude was that of the Qumran community, who sought to purify Israel by withdrawal, or whether like the Zealot movement they sought to purify it by armed struggle, by driving the Romans out by the use of force, the presence of the Roman legionaries posed for the Jews a constant religious offence. Pompey had profaned their Temple. Common sense told the Jews that they could not hope to withstand the Romans, and that they must compromise. But a measure of judicious compromise in these areas easily spilled over into the position of open collaboration; and that is why the Jews so particularly hated the 'publicans' – the tax-collectors, Jews who were prepared to work with the Roman authorities and collect levies for the empire.

If Jesus had chosen to be a member of some monkish and exclusive sect such as the community at Qumran, he could have opted out of this painful and muddled scene and refused to face up to the problems besetting his fellow Jews at the time. By a similar token, if he had not been a person of religious genius, addicted, suicidally addicted, to paradox, he might have chosen to ally himself to one of the existent causes, sects or groups available to him in his day. For the last hundred years, there has been no shortage of books attempting to show that, in spite of all the existent testimony, this is what Jesus did do. We have read of Jesus the revolutionary, Jesus the Zealot, Jesus the Essene, Jesus the supporter of the Pharisees. All these ideas have the vice of simplicity. They 'make sense' of Jesus, and the only evidence which we possess in the Gospels would suggest that his

[1] 'It is a mistake to think that the Pharisees were upset because he ministered to the ordinarily pious common people and the impoverished.' E. P. Sanders: *Jesus and Judaism*, 179. The whole book has many valuable insights into Jesus's relationship with contemporary Judaism.

contemporaries found it impossible to make sense of him; which is why they accused him of being mad, or possessed by the Devil.

The Synoptic tradition, and the Fourth Gospel, and Paul all suggest that Jesus chose to himself twelve followers to establish a new 'kingdom' of Israel. The numbering was significant. It corresponded to the number of the old tribes of Israel. The modern reader, remote from the world of Jesus and his contemporaries, can read the names of the Twelve without recognising how very distinctive and odd it is. They were Simon whom he renamed Peter; Simon's brother Andrew, who in the Fourth Gospel was the first of Jesus's disciples; the sons of the Galilean fisherman Zebedee – James and John; these he nicknamed Boanerges, the Sons of Thunder; Philip and Bartholomew, and Matthew and Thomas the twin; and James the son of Alphaeus; Thaddaeus, Simon the Zealot and Judas Iscariot. Who was Simon the Zealot, and what was he doing in the chosen band of Jesus's friends? We read much of the Zealots in the pages of Josephus. They it was who were most active, throughout the century, in armed struggle against the Romans. Even after the terrible sacking of Jerusalem in 70 CE by Titus, in which the population was first starved into submission, and then put to the sword, the Zealots retreated into the mountain-fortress of Masada near the Dead Sea and continued to keep up an heroic guerrilla campaign against the Romans for a further three years. When the Roman army finally surrounded them, the Zealots would not surrender, and having put their own families to the sword, they committed a mass suicide. They were above all things men of violence, albeit violence in a patriotic and noble cause. It is surely of supreme interest that Jesus chose a Zealot to be one of his close personal followers.

Another patriotic group mentioned by Josephus (and castigated by him as bandits) were the *sicarii*. 'Their favourite trick was to mingle with festival crowds [in Jerusalem] concealing under their garments small daggers with which they stabbed their opponents. When their victims fell the assassins melted into the indignant crowd, and through their plausibility entirely defied detection. First to have his throat cut by them was Jonathan the high priest, and after him many were murdered every day.'[1]

It would seem possible that Judas 'Iscariot' derived his name from membership of this violent band of *sicarii*. The presence of a Zealot

[1] Josephus: *Jewish War*, 135.

and one of the *sicarii* would seem to suggest that Jesus was indeed involved in some fairly straightforward piece of Jewish patriotism, and that the Twelve were little more than a group of armed rebels. ('Galileans,' says Josephus, 'are fighters from the cradle.')[1] But then we find among them the name of Matthew, who by tradition had been a tax-collector until he met Jesus, a figure whom Judas and Simon would not have been very likely to view as their natural ally. In 66 CE, King Agrippa II made an impassioned speech to the Jewish patriots who thought that they could fight a successful war against the Romans. He told them that their passion for liberty came too late: 'For the experience of slavery is a painful one, and to escape it altogether any effort is justified; but the man who has once submitted and then revolts is a refractory slave, not a lover of liberty. Thus the time when we ought to have done everything possible to keep the Romans out was when the country was invaded by Pompey. But our ancestors and their kings with material, physical and mental resources far superior to yours, faced a mere fraction of the Roman army and put up no resistance; will you, who have learnt submission from your fathers, and are so ill provided, compared with those who first submitted, stand up to the whole Roman Empire?'[2]

Perhaps Jesus, thirty years earlier, would have thought along similar lines. But he wanted his new kingdom to be a kingdom that was representative of all Israel. It was not an exclusive sect. It contained representatives of political activists and political quislings, because that was the condition of Israel at the time. It also contained men who, when they were not following Jesus, were engaged in busy trading on the Lake, and, we may assume, making a substantial profit out of it.

This group, the Twelve, became for Jesus a substitute for his family. Once, when his mother and brothers came to visit him at Capernaum, somebody pressed through the crowded room to tell Jesus that they were outside, waiting for him. 'Who is my mother? Who are my brothers?' he asked. And then, looking at the crowds of his admirers and followers, he said that it was they, rather than the family from Nazareth, who constituted his true family. Now it is possible that this story survives in the Synoptic Gospels not because Jesus actually said it, but because the Twelve-inspired

[1] Op. cit., 376.
[2] Op. cit., 145.

Churches of the Mediterranean did not like the family-dominated Church of Jerusalem, and wanted to make it clear to the new Church members that Jesus rejected his own flesh and blood. But it is equally possible that the incident took place. The Gospels contain occasions when Jesus was to take leave, not only of his family, but also of his followers. Having been rejected by Nazareth, he was in time to reject Capernaum.

The pattern of his 'Galilean ministry', as it is sometimes called, would seem to have been itinerant. He did not limit himself to Capernaum. He moved about the neighbouring towns and villages on foot, and he also crossed the lake on occasion to speak to the population there. Sometimes, he even preached from a boat, while the people listened to him from the shore. This would suggest that he had a commanding voice, which carried well across the water.

Boat traffic was common on the Lake, and in the wars against the Romans in the late 60s CE there were even some naval engagements. After Vespasian built a flotilla of rafts to confront the Jewish boats in 67 CE there was a terrible battle in which nearly 7,000 died, and after which the shores of the lake were strewn with wrecks. In happier times, we know from the remains of many harbours round the Lake and from literary evidence that boats were common in the first century.

Following a remarkable archaeological discovery by the shore of Galilee in 1986, we now have a better idea of the kind of boat in which Jesus might have sailed. Following a severe drought, the water level of the Lake went down. It was in late January 1986 that Moshe and Yuval Lufan, members of the lakeside Kibbutz Ginosar (*anglice* Gennesaret), found the wreck of a complete vessel in the mud. It was quickly dubbed the 'Jesus boat' by the press. There is nothing to link the boat with Jesus but it would seem that it could conceivably have been a craft which was in use during Jesus's lifetime. Experts have said that it is typical of boats of the period, even though no boat from an inland water has survived in so intact a condition. It is very like the boat in the so-called Migdal mosaic, which may be seen by the visitor to Capernaum. It is 8.27 metres long. It would have carried a minimum crew of five men, four rowers and a helmsman. The Gospels tell us that the boats used by Peter, James and John could have anything up to a seven-man crew,[1] though evidently

---

[1] John 21:2–3.

the sons of Zebedee had paid employees to act as crew for them. [1]
The boat found at Kibbutz Ginosar had cooking pots aboard, and it
was almost certainly of the sort which stored its seine net in the
stern. These seine nets, which could measure up to 400 metres in
length could also serve the double function of providing bedding for
any boatmen who wanted to spend the whole night on the water.
The discovery of this old boat, and the excavations at Capernaum,
have unearthed nothing about Jesus himself, but they bring vividly
to life the sort of world to which he belonged. Like the piece of
cooked fish in the Fourth Gospel they alert us to the fact that Jesus
did belong to a real world, a world which can be reconstructed by
a combination of archaeology and historical imagination. When I
read J. Richard Steffy's account of the boat's construction, having
seen the craft for myself, I felt supremely tempted to revise my view
that Jesus was not a carpenter. 'At first glance,' Steffy wrote, 'the
boat was a disappointment. It appeared to be a shoddily-built craft,
a far cry from the structural finesse found on Mediterranean hulls of
the Classical period, and one which had been frequently repaired by
an amateur. But that was a momentary observation, one to be
quickly reversed by more careful scrutiny. True, the wood used on
this vessel left much to be desired, but the workmanship was different in quality. There was a discipline here, a well-founded one that
was capable of producing a strong and practical boat in spite of the
lack of good compass timber. What at first appeared to be a series
of clumsy repairs was in fact the efforts of that master craftsman to
produce something substantial from something inferior.' [2] Could
there be a better description of what Jesus was trying to do when he
set out to call the 'lost sheep of the House of Israel'?

Jesus's reported fondness for life afloat was typical of his restless-
ness. It would seem as if he had not been all that long in Capernaum
before his impatience with the place erupted. Having paced around
the neighbouring Galilean town of Chorazin, and having performed
many works of exorcism and healing at Capernaum, Jesus is reported
to have been dismayed that they did not understand the significance
of these miracles. 'And thou, Capernaum, shalt thou be exalted unto
heaven? thou shalt go down unto Hades: for if the mighty works
had been done in Sodom which were done in thee, it would have

[1] Mark 1:20.
[2] 'The Boat: A Preliminary Study of its Construction' in *Atiqot*, Volume XIX, (Jerusalem
1990); 'The Excavations of an Ancient Boat in the Sea of Galilee', ed. Shelley Wachsmann.

remained until this day. Howbeit I say unto you, that it shall be more tolerable for the land of Sodom in the day of judgment, than for thee.'[1]

But what were the people of Capernaum supposed to have understood? It would seem from the Gospel accounts that the more healings and exorcisms he did, the greater Jesus's following became. Whether Jesus and his followers were actually fighting in the same campaign is a matter which the Gospels give us leave to doubt; but there are indications, even in the wholly Christianised view of things which the Gospels present, which suggest some of the ways that Jesus allowed his followers to get out of control.

An example of this occurs in the second chapter of Mark. 'One Sabbath day Jesus was "bypassing" through the cornfields. His disciples began to strip the ears as they made a path along. The Pharisees began to say to Him, "Look! Why are you doing what is not allowed on the Sabbath?" "Have you never read," He said, "what David did when he and his company were in need and hungry? How he went into the house of God, in the presence of High Priest Abiathar, and ate the shewbread – which none is allowed to eat except the priests – and gave it to his companions as well?" "The Sabbath," He said to them, "was made for the sake of man and not man for the sake of the Sabbath, wherefore the Son of Man is lord of (or 'on') the Sabbath."'[2]

Many things are going on in this short narrative. Some of them are going on in the text of Mark itself, in the preaching Mark wishes to convey. Some are going on in the events themselves, and we can say that because the other Synoptic writers so plainly misunderstand the story, and depict the Pharisees becoming angry with Jesus for a trivial little thing (as a Gentile would see it) like plucking a few ears of corn on the Sabbath.

First of all, the disciples are marching through a field of sown corn – they are causing a major inconvenience to a local farmer. Why are they doing this? Because they wish to 'bypass'. By bypassing a town you could avoid its Sabbath limits and reach an intended destination without being cramped by that limit. So, they behave as if

---

[1] Matthew 11:23. 24. It is of interest that Jesus's curse of Capernaum seems to have been effective, since it is now a derelict ruin. Sodom (or Sedom as it is named in the new Israel) is a flourishing 'health resort' where Scandinavian tourists and others, undeterred by the infernally sulphurous smells, go for saline cures, mud baths and immersion in the waters of the Dead Sea.
[2] Mark 2:23–28 The translation occurs in *The Making of Mark* by J. D. M. Derrett (1985).

they were observing the Sabbath. Or are they? Why does Mark make Jesus draw an analogy with King David, entering the Temple and eating the shewbread? In his narrative, there is a reason for this, though it is hard to see how much of this reason was apparent either to Jesus himself or to his disciples, if or when the incident actually occurred. The disciples strip the ears as they make a path. They strip the ears because they are hungry, and the hunger of the people becomes a metaphor in all the Gospels for what Jesus is trying to satisfy by his teaching. Mark makes Jesus the new King David by introducing the reference to David's indiscretion in the Temple. Even at the most urgent harvest time, however, there was no excuse for breaking the Sabbath, so it is not surprising that the Pharisees objected to the disciples picking corn to eat on the Sabbath day. But what about making the path? And what has King David got to do with it? And did Jesus really think that Abiathar was the High Priest – which he wasn't – or was this a mistake of Mark's? In the original story, David took the shewbread on the Sabbath and over-rode the ritual laws because he was the king. Similarly, since the time of the Maccabees, the Sabbath law did not apply to soldiers on the march, to men at war. So, Mark saw Jesus and his followers as men on the march, with Jesus as their king. What kind of kingdom were they proclaiming? A kingdom of abundance in which the hungry would be fed. Abiathar means 'Father of Superfluity'. [1]

Jesus was inaugurating a new 'kingdom', and the crowds were preparing to make him into their king. But what was the manifesto of this kingdom? If the modern reader, particularly the sympathetic agnostic reader, is chiefly interested in Jesus because of his teaching, the contemporaries of Jesus were chiefly interested in him because he was a healer and a wonder-worker. Yet, when we read of Jesus's impatience with his followers for their failure to understand his teaching, and when we consider the extensive passages in the Gospels which are devoted to examples of that teaching, we need to focus our minds on what that teaching was, always, of course, being aware that complete certainty about what Jesus taught is going to be impossible.

Sir Walter Scott, in the course of pursuing his passion for Ballads of the Scottish Border, had a brush with the mother of James Hogg, the Ettrick Shepherd. Margaret Hogg had a vast knowledge of these

---

[1] In all these insights I am endebted to J. D. M. Derrett: op. cit. 73—77.

old songs, but of Scott's *Minstrelsy of the Scottish Border*, she took a low view. 'There were never ane o' my songs prentit till ye prentit them yoursel', an' ye hae spoilt them awthegither. They were made for singin' an' no for readin'; but ye hae broke the charm noo, an' they'll never be sung mair.'[1]

It is a perfect example of the absolute difference in approach between an essentially oral tradition and the literary desire to freeze the words of those who have gone before us. Had Jesus lived to read one of the 'Gospels', and in particular their accounts of his teaching, he might well have reacted to them as Margaret Hogg reacted to Scott's *Minstrelsy*. 'They were made for singin' and no' for readin'.'

The sayings of Jewish teachers, like those of other oriental peoples, were not uncommonly collected up by their followers, not as written documents, but as orally repeated saws, stories, apothegms. They would often be encapsulated in some rhythmical or poetic form, and in many cases, like ballads and folk-songs, they would be sung. It is not impossible that some such process occurred in the record of Jesus's sayings. His most famous set of teachings are still sung today as a hymn in the churches of the East (Greek and Russian Orthodox) and they are readily memorable:

> Blessed are the poor in spirit: for theirs is the kingdom of Heaven.
> Blessed are they that mourn: for they shall be comforted.
> Blessed are the meek: for they shall inherit the earth.
> Blessed are they that hunger and thirst after righteousness: for they shall be filled.
> Blessed are the merciful: for they shall obtain mercy.
> Blessed are the pure in heart: for they shall see God.
> Blessed are the peacemakers: for they shall be called the sons of God.
> Blessed are they that have been persecuted for righteousness' sake: for theirs is the kingdom of Heaven.
> Blessed are ye when men shall reproach you, and persecute you, and say all manner of evil against you falsely, for my sake.
> Rejoice and be exceeding glad: for great is your reward in heaven: for so persecuted they the prophets which were before you.[2]

[1] James Hogg: *The Domestic Manners of Sir Walter Scott* (1909), 51–52.
[2] Matthew 5:3–12.

Jesus never wrote a book. He took the risk, therefore, of his say-ings being misremembered or misrepresented. Pedants are right to remind us that no phrase in the New Testament could be proven to be the *ipsissima verba* of the Master. That is not a reason for leaving out of account a discussion of Jesus's reported words. The words attributed to Jesus by the Gospels are so remarkable that they deserve to be studied and memorised, whoever said them. Nor is complete scepticism about their 'authenticity' entirely well-placed. Taken as a whole, the teachings of Jesus, both in the Synoptic Gospels and even, on occasion, in the Fourth Gospel, have a distinctive manner which it is difficult to believe was concocted by the four evangelists – each of whom wrote for different audiences, and in different times and places. When we read the Gospels, there emerges a peculiar mode of questioning, an ironic dialectic, which is sometimes totally at vari-ance with the fixed literary form in which they are recorded. The dialectic, with its disturbing conversational energy, bursts from the printed page like new wine bursting from old wine-skins. This is no proof that Jesus said all the words to which the Gospels attribute him, nor even that he employed such a method of dialectic. But if he did not do so, then we have to recognise that some other great religious genius taught the four evangelists to adopt this mode for themselves.

There is, of course, no fixed body of 'teaching', no blueprint for a new religion, in the Gospels. Jesus did not dictate a Koran, or a Book of Mormon. Behind all his utterances, there are the Hebrew Scriptures in which he implicitly believed, and which he neither wished to supersede nor to alter. 'Think not that I came to destroy the law and the prophets: I came not to destroy but to fulfil.'[1] All the wit, and disturbingness, and dynamism of Jesus's sayings are read against this firm foundation. What interested him was how to be a good Jew. He asked himself, and his people, this question at a time when Judaism was threatened: with violence and persecution from the Romans who were one day destined to destroy the very Temple of Jerusalem itself; and on the other hand from the Gentile world, with its imaginative inability to hold on to the monotheistic idea. What was the implication, for the Jews, of believing in their Scriptures, believing in their God, Who had been revealed to them in the Torah, and in the Prophets and in the Writings or Wisdom

[1] Matthew 5:17.

Literature such as the Psalms and the Proverbs? In making this exploration, Jesus was to say and ask things of universal significance, which stretch far beyond the confines of Judaism, and which were to have a universal appeal. That has always been the paradox of Judaism, and it would have been so even if Jesus had never lived: Judaism is both an exclusive religion meant only for those who have been born or (in rarer cases) received into it; it is also a religion which is universalist in that it worships the Maker of Heaven and Earth, and the dispenser of a universal moral law. The Jews are a 'God-bearing people' and it has been their destiny to be the conscience of the human race. We shall look in vain, however, among the words of Jesus for an ethical or theological *summa*, a considered blueprint of 'how to live'. We can discern in his reported sayings, however, a particular attitude to Judaism which was disruptive, perhaps even revolutionary; certainly it is dialectic not lapidary, organic not static. For Jesus, a Jew was not a man or woman who had merely received a set of truths on the tablets of stone delivered to Moses on Mount Sinai. The Jew must always, in Jesus's view, examine the implications of those laws in his or her heart, and in contemporary society. The Beatitudes provide a suggestion for how the kingdom of Israel can be reconstituted in spite of the Roman occupation and persecutions of the Jewish race. There is a positive blessedness, Jesus taught, in accepting the persecution, and in making peace, and in meekness, and in seeking first the kingdom of God and His righteousness. Then might dawn the promised Messianic Age in which God's kingdom can truly come.

We see how he digs down to the disturbing heart of things, and makes the Jews examine the implications of the Torah, in his teachings about marriage.

'Ye have heard that it was said, Thou shalt not commit adultery: but I say unto you, that every one that looketh on a woman to lust after her hath committed adultery with her already in his heart. . . It was said also, Whosoever shall put away his wife, let him give her a writing of divorcement: but I say unto you, that every one that putteth away his wife, saving for the cause of fornication, maketh her an adulteress: and whosoever shall marry her when she is put away committeth adultery.'[1] Matthew places these words in the 'literary' context of a 'sermon', delivered from the top of a moun-

---

[1] Matthew 5:27, 28, 31, 32.

tainside. In doing this, he is making a deliberate allusion to Moses who gave the Old Law to the Jews from Mount Sinai during their journey through the wilderness. The New Moses can thus be seen to give the New Torah. The Twelve, like leaders of the Twelve Tribes, sit at his feet and receive his doctrine. It is their task to mediate the teaching of Jesus to the crowds who sit, out of earshot, below. This is to be, in Matthew's 'Church' and in subsequent generations of Christendom, a justification for the successors of the Twelve – the apostolic bishops – to dictate to the faithful about such matters as whether they should be allowed to obtain a divorce.

But in its original setting, the teaching of Jesus must have seemed very different. True, he was an ardent defender of monogamy, just like John the Baptist, his cousin. Like the Qumran community, he felt that the Mosaic law of marriage was too lax; they too felt that it was unacceptable to divorce and remarry. But Jesus was not, as Matthew tries to make him do, laying down a new law. He was asking his Jewish hearers to make a connection between their religious and ritual observances on the one hand, and on the other, the deepest stirrings of conscience, when God speaks directly to the individual. They were no longer to think that they could please God by a minimalist observance of the Torah. Why had God told Moses that adultery was sinful? That is the disturbing question that Jesus posed. In sexual ethics, as in other areas, Jesus detects the source of trouble as the human heart, its capacity for self-deception and fantasy. For a Gentile reader of the Gospels, it is sometimes necessary to be reminded of the admissibility of private judgment within the community of Judaic faith. He did not very often answer ethical questions, because he wanted his hearers to go back and answer these questions for themselves. Professor Vermes reminds us of a legendary doctrinal argument which took place towards the close of the first century CE between Rabbi Eliezer ben Hyrcanus and his colleagues. 'Having exhausted his arsenal of reasoning and still not convinced them, he performed a miracle, only to be told that there was no room for miracles in debate. In exasperation, he then exclaimed, "If my teaching is correct, may it be proved by Heaven!"; whereupon a celestial voice declared, "What have you against Rabbi Eliezer, for his teaching is correct?" But this intervention was ruled out of order because in the Bible it is written that decisions are to be reached by majority vote.'

Jesus wanted the Jews of his own time to look into their own hearts and to reject collective answers, whether political, religiously sectarian, or military. Like Rabbi Eliezer, he could not convince people, even though he performed miracles, or heard voices from Heaven, because they did not have the confidence to step outside their own fatally bigoted and narrow party confines. His conflicts with 'the scribes and Pharisees' in the Synoptics, and with the Judaioi in the Fourth Gospel, are conflicts which are parallel to Eliezer's conflict with his rabbinical *confrères*. Asserting not merely the legitimacy, but the essential need for private judgment in the religious life, Jesus confronted his hearers with a series of questions of great penetration and profundity. Is there any virtue in having merely abstained from adultery if you have not recognised the sexual chaos within you? Do you think you have obeyed the Torah, and made your peace with God, if you have a heart that is full of anger and malice and revenge? Jesus is always saying, 'You think that you can serve God merely by following a regulation. But there is more to it than that.' And it is in this 'more' that the believer is led to an encounter with God Himself, an encounter which reveals not an unyielding lawgiver, but a Father, full of love.

The same quarrel with religious legalism is to be found in the notorious exchange between Jesus and the authorities about whether or not his disciples have observed the correct cleansing and washing rituals. 'Hear me all of you, and understand: there is nothing from without the man, that going into him can defile him: but the things which proceed out of the man are those that defile the man.' Jesus made this rather rumbustious exchange an analogy or parable of the spiritual life. Food is not dirty. Excrement is. By the same token, it is what comes of the heart which defiles. 'For from within, out of the heart of men, evil thoughts proceed, fornications, thefts, murders, adulteries, covetings, wickednesses, deceit, lasciviousness, an evil eye, railing, pride, foolishness: all these evil things proceed from within.'[1]

Mark, in relating these sayings about the dietary laws, adds the little note for the benefit of the Gentile readers: 'He said this making all foods clean'. A very different message from that of Jesus, who is merely telling the Jews to keep a sense of proportion about their dietary laws, and to search their own hearts; for unless they have repented and purified themselves, they will not 'see God'. Mark, of

[1] Mark 7:14, 15, 21–23.

course, is writing for Gentiles, who do not observe the Jewish dietary laws. He invents stories about Jesus talking with non-Jews. He exonerates Pontius Pilate from any responsibility for the purely Roman manner of Jesus's execution by claiming that this happened because Jesus had somehow or another been tried, on the eve of Passover, by the Jewish Sanhedrin. He even tells us that a Roman centurion, standing by the Cross of Jesus, asserts, 'Truly this man was the son of God'. [1] But then, like all the evangelists, Mark puts in a part of the remembered tradition which entirely contradicts his 'Christian' picture of Jesus. He tells us that a Syro-Phoenician woman approached Jesus for a miracle-cure for her daughter. He replied brusquely, 'It is not meet to take the children's bread and cast it to the dogs'. [2] This saying, when taken with the other sayings of Jesus which the evangelists have forgotten to cut out – that he did not wish to overthrow the Torah, that not one jot nor one tittle of the Law could be discarded, that his mission was entirely directed to the Jewish race and to 'the lost sheep of the House of Israel' – makes us realise that the Gospels do, in spite of themselves, contain words which are almost certainly authentic memories of his teaching.

But then again, we have to be careful. Take something as apparently simple as Jesus's injunction not to get involved in unnecessary litigation. The saying is to be found in Matthew[3] and in Luke. [4] Matthew has, 'Agree with thine adversary quickly, whiles thou art with him in the way; lest haply the adversary deliver thee to the judge, and the judge deliver thee to the officer, and thou be cast into prison. Verily, I say unto thee, Thou shalt by no means come out thence till thou have paid the last farthing.' The sense (and common sense) of the injunction seem pretty clear. Where possible, settle disputes out of court. We know from Paul's First Letter to the Corinthians[5] that the early Christians tried, whenever possible, to avoid coming before pagan judges. It may be that this saying of Jesus, however authentic, has been coloured by the experience of the Gentile Church. Luke, however, in his Gospel, interprets the saying in a completely different manner and you have to read the previous

[1] Mark 15:39.
[2] Mark 7:28.
[3] Matthew 5:25, 26.
[4] Luke 12:58, 59.
[5] I Cor. 6:5–7.

few verses to get its flavour. In Luke's version, Jesus has just been saying that the people know how to interpret clouds in the sky as signs of a coming storm, but they do not know how to read the signs of the coming Day of Judgment. Then it is that Jesus says, 'As thou art going with thine adversary before the magistrate, on the way give diligence to be quit of him: lest haply he hale thee unto a judge, and the judge shall deliver thee to the officer, and the officer shall cast thee into prison'.

It will be noticed, even from a translation, that the wording of the two passages is completely different. It seems as though Luke is translating a saying direct from Aramaic (the language in which Jesus himself spoke) whereas Matthew appears to have known the saying in Greek. Of Matthew's forty-four Greek words, and Luke's fifty, only twelve are the same. Same story; different origin; very different sense attached to it by two Gospel writers. In Luke, it has almost become a parable about the coming day of Judgment. 'You would agree with a dangerous opponent in the law courts before coming before the judge. Well, then – beware the coming of the judge!' A whole Protestant Midrash has grown up around this saying. The great Bultmann believes that it was originally a parable with an eschatalogical meaning. God is the judge. We should agree with our adversaries before we die, or God will condemn us.

Most scholars, particularly German scholars in the last hundred years, have realised that in preaching about his kingdom, Jesus was looking to the end of time when this glorious kingdom would be fulfilled. [1] Jesus is reported to have taught his disciples and followers a prayer. Although many New Testament scholars have questioned

[1] Joannes Weiss, in *Die Predigt Jesu vom Reiche Gottes* (Göttingen 1892), argued that Jesus imagined that the kingdom would come at the *eschalon*, the last time. Eschatology, the seeing of history in terms of the last days, overshadows most German New Testament scholarship for the next seventy years after Weiss. Most famously of all, Albert Schweitzer in *The Quest for the Historical Jesus* believed that Jesus had died a disappointed man, railing against God for his failure to bring the kingdom to pass in his own lifetime. The Messianic kingdom had not dawned, and Jesus, his life and his teaching, were to be seen as a pathetic failure. The English scholar C. H. Dodd in such books as *Parables of the Kingdom* (1935) tried to redress the balance by suggesting that Jesus preached a 'realised eschatology'. The kingdom was 'at hand': that is, it was real in the here and now. We did not need to await it as a future event when the Son of Man came on the clouds. While Dodd was right to suggest that Jesus was not simply preaching about the end of the ages, the fact remains inescapable that this element is strongly present in the recorded utterances of Jesus and the overwhelming likelihood is that he did, in common with many of his contemporary Jews, expect the redemption of Israel and the arrival of a Messianic Age as a physical event in history, and possibly within his lifetime. Whether he retained this belief to the end of his days is a matter of debate.

whether Jesus ever said these words, they are words which will always be associated with his name. The prayer, which is called the Lord's Prayer because of its association with Jesus, is a pure distillation of monotheist piety:

> Our father which art in heaven, Hallowed be thy name. Thy kingdom come. Thy will be done, as in heaven, so on earth. Give us this day our daily bread. And forgive us our debts, as we also have forgiven our debtors. And bring us not into temptation, but deliver us from the evil one. [1]

At the beginning of this prayer, after the acknowledgement of the fatherhood and the holiness of the Almighty, Jesus prays, 'Thy kingdom come!' The scholars are probably right to tell us that Jesus believed that, very shortly, God would establish a special kingdom on earth. The phrase the 'kingdom of God' is a very familiar one in the Old Testament and in the Rabbinic writings. [2] The kingdom is a metaphor which means many things. It can mean the covenant between God and Moses on Sinai. It can mean the individual Jew's covenant to live as a loyal child of God. Rabbi Joshua ben Karha said: 'Why does the section *Hear O Israel* (Deut. 6:4–9) precede [the section] *And it shall come to pass if ye shall hearken [diligently to my commandments]*? – so that a man may first take upon himself the yoke of the kingdom of heaven and afterward take upon him the yoke of the commandments.' (Berakoth 2:2). [3] Jesus doubtless did teach his followers that the kingdom would come as an actual event, as prophesied in Daniel. But he also plainly felt that the kingdom was very near in the sense that his followers could live in it. [4] As in the Prayer, so in his other sayings, there is the suggestion that the Jews should have an absolute and simple trust in the Creator. He 'clothed' the fowls of the air and the flowers of the field. He will likewise feed and clothe them. The Jews are specially set apart by God, like lamps to lighten a dark world, like salt to give savour to the whole earth, like leaven without which the bread will not rise. These sayings in Matthew make no real sense if they are applied to 'Christians', a type of person whom Jesus never of course envisaged as existing. They

---

[1] Matthew 6:9–13.
[2] For a very sensible overall survey, see N. Perrin's books *The Kingdom of God in the Teaching of Jesus* (1963) and *Rediscovering the Teaching of Jesus* (1967).
[3] E. P. Sanders: *Jesus and Judaism* (1985), 141.
[4] Mark 1:15.

are expressions of the Jewish vocation. 'Ye are the light of the world.'[1] The Fourth Gospel, which makes Jesus embody the true Israel, the true humanity's response to God, within himself, makes him say, 'I am the light of the world'.[2] But Jesus believed that the Jews were the light of the world, and it was his mission to teach them how to make that light shine brightly.

Where Jesus differed from many of his contemporaries was in his admission into the kingdom of 'tax-collectors and sinners': that is, of the traitors – those who have flagrantly disobeyed the Law of God.

The reason that Jesus had for admitting these people into the kingdom can be discerned from reading his many parables, which present a radical view of God. A man had two sons. One asked for his inheritance, and went away into a foreign country, where he wasted his substance on women and riotous living. Eventually, when he is reduced to hunger, and a job as a swine-herd (the impurest possible occupation for a Jew, where he is so hungry that he even shares the eating trough with these forbidden beasts – so much for the dietary laws!), this young man turns for home. He decides to beg his father's forgiveness, and ask if he can be received as one of his father's hired servants. But when he gets within sight of home, he sees that his father is awaiting for him a long way off. The old man receives him with open arms. He kills the fatted calf, and holds high festival. The other son, understandably enough, is furious. How could the father be rewarding the brother, who is a whoremonger, when he has never rewarded the virtuous brother?

Or again, Jesus told the story of a man going out to hire labour. He agrees with one group of men to work for a penny a day. Still, there are not enough labourers for the vineyard, so that he goes out at intervals throughout the day to hire labour. The terms are always the same. By the end of the day, the men whom he hired first are given a penny, for sweating their way through the hottest and most arduous hours of work. The wastrels and lazy men who came last and only worked for one hour are given the same wages: a penny.

Or again, there were two men. One was a rich man, who lived finely and ate well. Another was a poor man who lived in misery and poverty, covered in sores, which the rich man's dogs deigned to lick. Then the two men died, the rich man went to hell and the

[1] Matthew 5:14.
[2] John 8:12.

poor man went to heaven. There was nothing in the story to indicate that the poor man was virtuous nor that the rich man was wicked. The rich man in hell begs the poor man to come and relieve his sufferings, if only by offering him a drop of water. Abraham, however, in whose bosom the poor man reposes, will not allow it, saying that there is an unbridgeable gulf set between the poor man and the rich man.

Or again, a dishonest steward is dismissed from his lord's service. He calls to him one of the lord's debtors, and asks how much he owes. 'A hundred measures of oil.' The steward writes the man out a bill for fifty. The next debtor comes in owing a hundred measures of wheat and is only charged for eighty. When the lord finds out that his unjust steward has swindled him, he commends his ingenuity 'for the sons of this world are wiser than the sons of the light'.

The kingdom is a world where morality, on a simple level, does not seem to be as important as something else. Why, in Jesus's story about the tax-collector and the Pharisee praying in the Temple, does God favour the tax-collector and fail to listen to the Pharisee? Because the tax-collector allows God to be God. He takes no moral initiative himself. He is merely a passive instrument into which the forgiveness of God can be poured.

Throughout the Old Testament, there had been this strand of Jewish thinking about God:

> As far as the west is from the east,
> So far hath he removed our transgressions from us.
> Like as a father pitieth his children,
> So the Lord pitieth them that fear him.
> For he knoweth our frame;
> He remembereth that we are dust. [1]

It survives in modern Judaism as in the story told by one of he rabbis about the sinner who died and was confronted by God. 'Have you kept the Torah?' God asked him. 'No,' said the man. 'Have you remembered to say your prayers?' No. 'Have you at least been faithful to your wife?' No. 'Come into the kingdom,' says God. Why? asked the man – when I admitted that I was an adulterer, that I did not say my prayers, nor observe the Torah? 'Because you told the truth,' said God.

[1] Psalm 103: 12–15.

There is an element of this in Jesus's teaching, but he adds something to it which is highly distinctive: and that is the urgent, yearning
activity of God in relation not to the righteous but to the sinners.
A shepherd searches the hillside for one lost sheep, though he has
ninety-nine other sheep in his fold. The woman who has lost a single
coin scours through the house and even, absurdly, holds a party for
her neighbours when she has at length discovered this piece of small
change.

This is the measure of God's love and forgiveness. It extends
towards those who have not yet repented. John the Baptist, in
common with most other religious teachers of his day, taught that
sinners should repent and turn to God. The Pharisees also taught this,
and were not nearly so exclusive as, say, the Qumran community. So
long as a Jew was a righteous Jew, he could wait for the coming of
the Lord in hope, according to the Pharisees' faith. But Jesus upsets
all that. The active partner in the relationship between God and the
human race is God. His rewards are handed out arbitrarily, whether
or not you have been virtuous or powerful in worldly eyes. New
Testament scholarship has placed a false and sentimental emphasis
on the poverty of Jesus's followers. It was not their poverty or their
lack of education which scandalised his contemporaries. It was the
fact that Jesus appeared to admit them to his 'kingdom' *before* they
had repented. This was certainly not a practice which endeared him
to the Pharisees. Nor was it something which the 'Christians' made
the slightest attempt to follow, as we can tell from reading the Acts
of the Apostles, or the Epistles of Paul, in which 'sinners' are put
out of the 'Church', punished and even on occasion struck dead for
their misdemeanours. We can assume, since the admission of sinners
was not the custom of the early Church, and yet remains so distinctive
a part of the Gospels, that it was an authentic part of Jesus's message.

It is something which goes much deeper and further than a dispute
between an easy-going Galilean and a strict Jerusalem priest over the
question of ritual washing, or diet. The 'scribes and Pharisees' were
not only obsessed by ritual trivia, nor was Jesus entirely dismissive
of Jewish ritual practices. The difference is a deep imaginative and
theological gulf which is as great as the gulf decreed by Abraham to
divide the rich man and the poor man in Jesus's parable. On the
one hand you have an understanding of religion which places the
initiative on man's shoulders. The Jew can choose how obedient he
is to be to God's holy laws, and he can follow them, or not, as his

virtue or wisdom extends. In so far as he follows the Torah, he will please his Creator, and ultimately find serenity and joy. But for Jesus, this is not enough. Such a system of observance – by extension, any such system – could exist without God being alive, or indeed existent. Few religious thinkers have ever been less interested in Kant's categorical imperative than Jesus. It is not so much that he overthrew morality as that he asked how far it got you. His answer would seem to have been: not very far, if the end of your hopes is the building of the kingdom on earth. The kingdom was not complete for Jesus unless it contained the whole of Israel: and that meant the untouchables, the impure, the outcasts and the sinners. It was to such as these that God held out his hands in yearning love. Such a message was bound, in the initial stages, to be of tremendous popular appeal, particularly to this ragamuffin class themselves. Combined with his gifts as an exorcist and a healer, it is not surprising that Jesus should have been pursued all over the region of Galilee by eager crowds. Nor should we be surprised that when he spoke, his teachings should have been regarded as so revolutionary, 'for he taught them as having authority, and not as the scribes'. [1]

[1] Mark 1:22.

# VII

SHALOM: THE LOAVES

AT THE BEGINNING of Pasternak's *Doctor Zhivago* there is a remarkable conversation about the significance of Jesus Christ in history. One of the characters says that it is possible to be uncertain about the very existence of the Deity, 'and yet to believe that man does not live in a state of nature, but in history, and that history as we know it now began with Christ, it was founded by Him on the Gospels. . . What is it? Firstly, the love of one's neighbour – the supreme form of living energy. And secondly, the two concepts which are the main part of the make-up of modern man . . . the ideas of free personality and of life as sacrifice. . . .'[1]

Those from a non-Christian tradition who read these words might be surprised that the Russian Orthodox believed that Jesus alone can be held responsible for the existence of kindness and unselfishness in the world. Nevertheless, the Gospels present us with a whole range of different human types, whom Jesus is enabling to become themselves. A senior rabbi comes to him secretly by night – Nicodemus. True, this is the Fourth Gospel's metaphor for the old order of Judaism coming to Jesus in a state of unenlightenment, but that does not mean that some such encounter did not take place. Jesus told Nicodemus that he must be reborn; he must shake up all his old values, and begin to see the world afresh, like a newborn baby. Understandably, Nicodemus was baffled;[2] but he was a real person. We can read about him in Josephus. It is in the encounters with these real people that we can begin to form some impression of what Jesus was like.

The Gospels are full of people. In many cases, the evangelists have chosen to make of these people emblems to suit their theological

---

[1] Boris Pasternak: *Doctor Zhivago* (ET 1958), 19.
[2] John 3:1–10.

purposes. The servant's high priest becomes Malko, the king. It is no accident, in the Gospel of Mark, for whom the lives of the patriarchs were as a grid by which to measure the life of Jesus, that Jesus was handed over to the men of violence by Juda(s), just as it was Judah, the brother of Joseph in Genesis, who betrayed the dreamer into slavery.

Behind these interpretations of who they were, however, there lies the fact that these people probably existed. It is largely through his dealings with people that we can begin to glimpse what sort of a man Jesus was. Their response to him is revealing. He is accorded the authority of the exorcist and healer. In the fifth chapter of Mark alone, we encounter some very different people who confront Jesus with their needs.

First there is the wild lunatic who lives among the mountain tombs in the country of the Gadarenes on the eastern shore of the Sea of Galilee. He is an alarming figure. People had tried to bind him with chains, but such was the strength of his frenzy that he always broke loose. He wandered about in this rough mountain-place, shrieking and cutting himself with stones. Jesus met this man, and the 'devils' inside the lunatic shouted out that Jesus was tormenting them. Jesus asked the man's name. 'My name is legion,' he replied, 'for we are many.'[1]

It is an exchange which has all the ring of truth, and which could have taken place at any time, and in any place between a mad divided self, and a sane man. Jesus the exorcist and healer commanded the devils to come out of the man; and he 'sent' them into a neighbouring herd of pigs. Presumably, the wretched man's shrieks were enough to frighten the pigs, who ran violently down the slopes, and fell to their destruction in the Lake. The local farmers, understandably enough, came to ask Jesus if he would move on. It was one thing for visiting Jews to abstain from eating pigs; but another thing altogether when they invaded the farms of Gentiles and destroyed their livelihood.

Like all the stories in Mark, it has been adapted so that a preacher can use it to tell the early Church some truth, as they understood it, about Jesus. In his lifetime on earth, Jesus had a great power of healing. Jesus will, Mark teaches us, be able to heal our inward conflicts and divisions if we come to him. That is the sermonising

---

[1] Mark 5:9.

point of the story. But the wild man in the cave seems very real. More real, strangely enough, than Jesus.

Then we meet Jairus: a very different man. He was the ruler of the synagogue in Capernaum, probably the very synagogue whose foundations have been dug up within the last twenty years. He is a man in despair about his daughter, who is lying at the point of death. Jesus made his way to the house and on his way, he met another unhappy person: a woman who for twelve years had been suffering from haemorrhages – 'an issue of blood'. She believed that if she could only touch the hem of Jesus's clothing, she will be healed. She came up behind him in the crowd, and Jesus rounded on her. 'Who touched me?' The disciples were astonished, since he had been touched and jostled by so many people. Yet at that moment, we are told, he was aware of the healing power within him being used up. Goodness went out of him. Full of anxiety and fear, the woman came forward and admitted that she had touched him. And she is healed. After this healing, Jesus made his way to the house of Jairus, and found the full paraphernalia of a funeral in progress, with hired mourners wailing and the family in a state of shock. When Jesus said that the girl was not dead, he was laughed to scorn. Undeterred, he cleared the house of people and went to the young girl's bedside. '*Talitha cumi!* Damsel arise!' When the little girl opened her eyes, Jesus realised that she would be hungry. He told the family that they should keep the healing a secret and that they should give the girl something to eat.[1]

The words of Jesus to the daughter of Jairus were taken up as a rallying-cry among nineteenth-century feminists. 'Damsel arise!' were words which emblazoned colleges and schools which, for the first time in history, had been founded with the specific purpose of educating women. This was not completely fanciful. By contrast with St Paul and the early Christians, Jesus neither feared women, nor treated them as a sub-species. It would appear that he was prepared to defy convention in this regard and to befriend women in a time and place when the sexes were not supposed to mix on socially equal terms. Some of his closest associates were women.

Near to Capernaum was the town of Magdala, now a small village, but in Jesus's day numbering 30 or 40,000 people. The woman known to history as Mary Magdalen came from this town. Luke's

[1] Mark 5:35–43.

Gospel tells us that he cast 'seven devils' out of this woman. Presumably, this means that she was subject to epileptic fits. She became one of his followers, and she was to be with him in Jerusalem at the time of his death.

Unfairly to this woman's memory, she was identified in the early church with the prostitute who, in the seventh chapter of Luke, anointed the feet of Jesus in the house of Simon the Pharisee.[1] She was further identified with another Mary, who came from the village of Bethany, near Jerusalem.[2] There is no evidence in the New Testament that Mary Magdalen was a prostitute or a sinner. Still less is there any evidence that she and Jesus were lovers, or that they got married, as has been claimed in various absurd quarters. Nor is there any evidence for the ninth-century legend that she emigrated to France and is buried in Aix-en-Provence. But her presence in the Gospels, and her importance as a supposed witness of Jesus's Resurrection, are testimony to her closeness to him. The fact that he had so many women in his entourage of followers is one indication that Jesus was not planning to found a paramilitary movement to overthrow the Romans. Had he done so, he would have chosen male followers exclusively.

If Mary was not a 'sinner', the Gospels tell us that Jesus did not scorn the company of those who were. There is the story, to which I have already alluded, of the woman in the house of Simon the Pharisee. It is a story entirely in accordance with Jesus's parables, and there is no wonder that it should have made so profound an appeal to every Christian generation since the Gospel of Luke was written. Jesus entered the house of a Pharisee. 'And behold, a woman which was in the city, a sinner; and when she knew that he was sitting at meat in the Pharisee's house, she brought an alabaster cruse of ointment, and standing behind at his feet, weeping, she began to wet his feet with her tears, and wiped them with the hair of her head, and kissed his feet, and anointed them with the ointment.' The Pharisee protests, and says that if Jesus were truly a prophet, he would have known what sort of woman she was. Jesus replies, 'Simon, I have somewhat to say unto thee. And he saith, Master, say on. . . . Jesus said, Seest thou this woman? I entered into thine house, thou gavest me no water for my feet; but she hath wetted my feet with her tears, and wiped them with her hair. Thou gavest me

[1] Luke 7:37.
[2] See next chapter.

no kiss, but she, since the time I came in, hath not ceased to kiss my feet. . . . Wherefore, I say unto thee, that her sins, which are many, are forgiven; for she loved much.'[1]

A comparable fragment has been preserved in some of the manuscripts of the Fourth Gospel, though everyone realises that it is not part of the original text. (It bears all the hallmarks of belonging to the tradition of Luke.) That is John 7:53 to John 8:11, the story of the woman, taken in adultery, and brought to Jesus by the Pharisees for judgment. They remind him that in the law of Moses, it is stated that an adulteress should be stoned. 'But Jesus stooped down and wrote with his finger on the ground. But when they continued asking him, he lifted up himself, and said unto them, He that is without sin among you, let him cast the first stone at her. And again he stooped down, and with his finger wrote on the ground.' It is one of the most remarkably naturalistic details in the entire Gospels, this silent, brooding man, staring at the dust, and writing with his finger in the dust. The Pharisees are shamed into walking away, one by one, leaving Jesus, at length, alone with the woman. He asks the woman, 'Did no man condemn thee? And she said, No man. And Jesus said, Neither do I condemn thee: go thy way, from henceforth sin no more.'[2] If this story is so unlike the rest of the Fourth Gospel in style and vocabulary that scholars can discern at once that it is an interpolation, it is not wholly at variance with the ideas or theology of the Fourth Gospel. In the fourth chapter of that book, we read of the really astonishing encounter that Jesus had with the Samaritan woman at Jacob's well in Sychar (modern Nablus, from Neapolis or New Town, known in Hebrew as Shechem).

The manner in which this story has been told is typical of the way in which the Fourth Gospel extracts mystic meaning from the simplest everyday experiences. Jesus is thirsty. It is midday. The disciples had gone shopping and left Jesus on his own. A woman approaches. Jesus asks her to give him water. She expresses surprise that a Jew should speak to a Samaritan woman, since the Jews and the Samaritans refused to mix with one another. Jesus says that if she knew 'who he was', she would ask of him, and he would give her water which would be a well of eternal life springing up within her, and that she would never thirst again. She asks for this water.

[1] Luke 7:37–38, 44, 45, 47.
[2] John 8:10, 11.

'Go home and bring your husband, then,' replies Jesus. 'I don't have
a husband.' 'Too right, you don't have a husband – you've had five
husbands.' And then there follows the sublime discussion between
the woman and Jesus about the rival religious claims of the Samaritans and the Jews – whether God is most properly worshipped from
the Temple Mount in Jerusalem or the Samaritan Temple mountain
of Gerizim. The manner in which the scene is built up is typical of
the supreme literary and theological genius of the Fourth Gospel.
Behind the story are the Synagogue Lections, which explain the
perhaps surprising conjunctions: the talk about water and its religious
significance; the talk about worship and mountains; and the apparently gossipy details about the woman's *mouvementé* emotional life.
We are directed later in the chapter to the time of year – it is four
months before harvest. The Synagogue Lections by this grid will be
the story of Rebekah drawing water for Abraham's servant (Genesis
24) and the story of Moses, escaping from Pharaoh and receiving
succour from the seven daughters of Midian as he sat wearily on a
well. The reading of Ezekiel 16 gives us the woman with many
lovers. Moreover, if we assume that the story of the woman at the
well is meant to correspond to the readings of the second Sabbath in
Shebat, then, in the third year of such a triennial cycle the Lection
would be of Deuteronomy 27: the instructions by God to Moses of
how he is to be worshipped when the Hebrews enter Canaan. 'And
Moses charged the people the same day, saying, These shall stand
upon mount Gerizim to bless the people, when ye are passed over
Jordan' . . . and he names the tribes.[1] It is Mount Gerizim which
towers over Jesus and the woman as they meet by Jacob's Well. In
other words, the Fourth Gospel, with extraordinary allusiveness and
intricacy, has packed this 'ordinary' incident with Scriptural echoes,
as well as with foreshadowings of its own internal drama. It is the
sixth hour, and Jesus says that he thirsts. There will come a time
again, at a sixth hour, when Jesus thirsts.

Central to the whole dialogue which is placed on the lips of the
woman and Jesus by the Fourth Gospel is the idea that Jewish ritual
observance – indeed, by implication, any ritual observance, or fixed
religious organisation – is in future to be superseded by true and
spiritual worship. The woman says, 'Our fathers worshipped in this
mountain; and ye say that in Jerusalem is the place where men ought

[1] Deut. 27:11.

to worship. Jesus saith unto her, Woman believe me, the hour cometh when neither in this mountain nor in Jerusalem, shall ye worship the father . . . the true worshippers shall worship the father in spirit and in truth . . . God is a Spirit and they that worship him must worship him in spirit and in truth. . .'[1]

John 4 is one of the supreme examples of how the Fourth Gospel manages to present all its Gospel at once. A man asks a woman for a drink on a hot day; and out of this short narrative, we have deliberate (and for the Samaritans or Jews who first read this Gospel immediately recognisable) echoes of the Synagogue Lection; we have a foreshadowing of the sixth hour in which Jesus would thirst in his Sacred Passion. We have the Fourth Gospel classic anti-institutional, anti-ritualistic view of true worship, and we have the glorious symbolism of the well, the fountain springing up within us eternally, so that we never thirst again. Yet at the heart of it, there remains this story of Jesus and a woman. Obviously, having said so much about the artifice of its narrative technique, it will seem paradoxical of me to claim this as a realistic story; but that is how it reads. That is John's great paradox. The more he piles artifice upon artifice, trope upon trope, the more real his pictures become, to the point where it becomes almost impossible not to believe that some such conversation, with a Samaritan woman, must have taken place. Without forcing the historicity of this, or any other, event in the Gospels, however, we can notice one thing: the Gospels represent Jesus as being the friend of sinners. In his parables, and it would seem in his life, he preached the forgiveness of sinners. It would seem from his teachings that Jesus admitted sinners to the kingdom. And we can be fairly confident that this is the authentic teaching of Jesus, since it was not the teaching of the early Church.

When Paul hears that a Corinthian has married his step-mother, he declares that the whole Christian community should go into mourning. The man must be rooted out of their company and treated like a pariah. [2] Admittedly, Paul relented towards this unfortunate, but it is impossible to imagine the Jesus of the Gospels reacting in such a way to a man of whose marital status he disapproved. Likewise, the Acts of the Apostles make it abundantly clear that sinners were not welcome in church. Ananias and Saphira had reason to

[1] John 4:20, 23, 24.
[2] I Cor. 5:1–5.

regret their decision to be baptized, since they were struck dead by St Peter for the sin of giving a mere half of all their worldly goods to the Church. He had wanted all. [1]

There can be few more extraordinary moments in the Gospels than the Transfiguration, the occasion when three of Jesus's friends saw him shine with light, and realised that he was one of the Enlightened like Moses and Elijah. In the Synoptic Gospels, it is one of the two key moments in Jesus's story, the other being the miracle of the loaves. These moments are so important because they help to define Jesus in the eyes of other people. We can begin to imagine, not merely how these stories fit into the Gospels, but how they explain the formation of those Gospels – and before that, how they determine the course of Jesus's life.

It is interesting to note that the Transfiguration does not occur in the Fourth Gospel, for the simple reason that it was not necessary, by the theology of that book, for such a moment to be included in the story. To the fourth evangelist, the glory of Jesus, and the glory of God in the signs of Jesus, are revealed repeatedly. In that book, there is no need for a moment of enlightenment on the mountainside.

Matthew, Mark and Luke, however, tell the story that Jesus took three of his disciples up a mountainside. They are Peter, James and John. In their sight, he was transfigured. 'And his face did shine as the sun, and his garments became as white as light.' [2] In their vision, the three men saw Jesus in company with Moses and Elijah, that is with the Giver of the Law and with the greatest of the Prophets. The visionary experience faded. When the three men open their eyes, they 'saw no one any more, save Jesus only with themselves'. [3]

It is a moment of extraordinary intensity, which the Gospels themselves would seem to find impossible quite to describe. A comparable moment occurred in the life of the Buddha, when he met a mendicant on the road, who said to him, 'The senses of others are restless like horses, but yours have been tamed. Other beings are passionate, but your passions have ceased. Your form shines like the moon in the night-sky, and you appear to be refreshed by the sweet savour of a

[1] Acts 5:1–12.
[2] Matthew 17:2.
[3] Mark 9:8.

wisdom newly-tasted. Your features shine with intellectual power, you have become master over your senses, and you have the eyes of a mighty bull.'[1] Of all the personal encounters which Jesus had with friends and acquaintances, the Transfiguration is the most remarkable. Commentators have wished to persuade us that the incident is misplaced in the Synoptic tradition, and this vision of Jesus must actually have occurred after his death, when the disciples were fired with the faith of the Resurrection. One of the reasons for this argument is that if Peter, James and John had experienced their vision of Jesus during his lifetime, they would surely not have been able to forsake him at the end. But that is one of the humanly plausible things about the Gospels. Even those who had 'beheld the glory', in the Fourth Gospel phrase, were capable of the utmost disloyalty.

I have no difficulty in believing that the story of the Transfiguration refers to something which actually happened within the earthly life-time of Jesus. It would be crass to try to explain it. Certainly, the experience did not lead to anyone present on that occasion proclaiming that Jesus was divine, or a god, or the Second Person of the Trinity. The point is that they had seen the Revelation through him, not that he is himself a divinity. If this event had taken place in another culture or at another time, it would have been described in different ways. Had Jesus been an Indian, his followers might well have seen in him an avatar or incarnation of the divine. It seemed natural in the Hellenized world, as the Christian converts learnt to come to grips with the mystery of monotheism and to discard the polytheist legends which had sustained the old religions, to make Jesus into an incarnation also. It seems very unlikely that any such symbolic language was available within the imaginative framework of pure monotheism. It nevertheless makes sense to suppose that Jesus filled those whom he met with a sense of extraordinary closeness to the Heavenly Father. The healings and the teachings go hand in hand here. People flocked to him, not merely because his healing was effective, but because they believed that within the experience of healing, they had come to understand the love of their Creator. That is why Jesus, in common with other healers, proclaimed the forgiveness of the sick person's sin. The Pharisees objected to this on more than one occasion, and those who cling to the belief that Jesus was the Second Person of the Trinity, or the gruesome idea that human sin could only be forgiven by the death of Jesus on

---

[1] Buddhist Scriptures, in a new translation by Edward Conze (Harmondsworth 1959), 53.

the Cross must miss the point of such Gospel stories. Their Heavenly Father *had forgiven them*. That was of the essence of Jesus's teaching and this was what caused scandal to those, like the Pharisees or the Essenes, who believed that forgiveness could only be offered to the pure. At the same time, he would seem to have achieved a high level of purity and enlightenment himself. The Christian doctrine of Jesus's sinlessness is, like the idea of his being an incarnate divinity, one which threatens to deprive the central figure in the Gospels of his moral seriousness. A young man once ran up to Jesus and asked him what he should do to inherit eternal life. 'Good sir,' he said, 'what should I do?' Jesus corrected him. 'No one should be called good, save one.'[1] Even in the Gospels, we read of Jesus losing his temper, quarrelling with his family, making mistakes and climbing down again afterwards. He is depicted as a fully human being. But it was in the richness of that humanity that those who knew him felt close to heaven.

We have reached the climax of Jesus's work in Galilee: that episode which the Gospel of Mark calls the Loaves (not the miracle of the Loaves, just the Loaves). The Fourth Gospel distinguishes the incident from the signs of Jesus. 'Ye seek me,' says John's Jesus, 'not because ye saw signs, but because ye ate of the loaves.'[2]

The Gospels record Jesus's dismay that even his closest followers did not understand the Loaves. Is it possible that we can understand them – distanced as we are from the incident, not merely by time, but by generations of Christian Midrash on the story? Nothing can be certain, it is true, but a book about Jesus which shrinks from interpreting the Loaves is in obvious danger of misinterpreting him, since he is recorded as having placed a supreme and symbolic value on the event. Let us refresh our memory of the incident.[3] Since the Christian symbolism is so much more obvious to a modern eye in the Fourth Gospel version, I shall quote that in full.

[1] Mark 10:18.
[2] John 6:26.
[3] Mark has two such incidents, one in which Jesus feeds a crowd of 5,000 (Mark 6:30–44) and another in which he feeds a crowd of 4,000 (Mark 8:1–10). Some commentators have assumed that there was only one feeding, but that two stories survive about it. Others have pointed out the symbolic meaning of the feedings and seen the first (with its twelve baskets of leftovers, corresponding to the twelve tribes of Israel) as Jesus's mission to the Jews, and the second (with its seven baskets of leftovers) corresponding to the non-Jews, since this feeding happens in the Decapolis, the 'Ten Towns'. In limiting my discussion to the one feeding which occurs in both Mark and the Fourth Gospel, I am not suggesting that there was only one such demonstration on the part of Jesus. I am merely trying to concentrate on its meaning.

After these things Jesus went away to the other side of the sea of Galilee, which is the sea of Tiberias. And a great multitude followed him, because they beheld the signs which he did on them that were sick. And Jesus went up into the mountain, and there he sat with his disciples. Now the Passover, the feast of the Jews, was at hand. Jesus, therefore, lifting up his eyes, and seeing a great multitude coming unto him, saith unto Philip, Whence are we to buy bread, that these may eat? And this he said to prove him: for he himself knew what he would do. Philip answered him, Two hundred pennyworth of bread is not sufficient for them, that every one may take a little. One of his disciples, Andrew, Simon Peter's brother, saith unto him, There is a lad here, which hath five barley loaves and two small fishes; but what are these among so many? Jesus said, Make the men sit down. Now there was much grass in that place. So the men sat down, in number about five thousand. Jesus therefore took the loaves; and having given thanks, he distributed to them that were set down; likewise also of the fishes as much as they would. And when they were filled, he saith unto his disciples, Gather up the broken pieces which remain over, that nothing be lost. So they gathered them up, and filled twelve baskets with broken pieces from the five barley loaves, which remained over unto them that had eaten.

Mark's account is more spare, but it is essentially the same. In Mark, the crowd are simply given bread. In John, they are given barley loaves, because John wants his readers to remember the prophet Elisha who miraculously fed a hundred hungry prophets with barley loaves in the Second Book of Kings.[1] Mark does not name the disciples who discussed the feeding with Jesus. John tells us that it was Philip who doubted, and Andrew who showed the way. (In this Gospel, Philip and Andrew are from the first chapter, the ones who lead the others to follow Jesus.) Then again, John adds the very 'symbolic' detail that this feeding happened close in time to Passover. This would date it very specifically to some time in April (Passover is celebrated from 15 to 22 Nisan in the Jewish calendar) in the year 29 CE. And there is the little detail of the fish, the fact that the Fourth Gospel uses that 'trade word', *opsarion*.[2]

[1] 2 Kings 4:42–44.
[2] *Vide supra*, chapter three.

I would regard it as pointless to 'demythologise' this incident, but it is surely legitimate for the exegete to ask why, in both the accounts of Mark and John, Jesus is dismayed by the disciples' and the crowd's failure to understand the significance of the Loaves.

The miracle or sign concentrates on the feeding, and not on the multiplication of bread. Indeed, it is noticeable that in Mark's account, no one expresses the slightest astonishment at this incident. When Jesus cleanses a leper, or heals a blind man, the event is usually enough to 'astound' or 'amaze' everyone who hears about it. There is no amazement at all in Mark. In John we read that when the people 'saw the sign' they proclaimed that Jesus was 'the prophet that was coming into the world'. Also, highly revealingly, the Fourth Gospel says that thereafter they tried to make Jesus into a king, and that he was compelled to run away into hiding. Presumably, if we read the story naturalistically, the absence of amazement on the part of the crowds is to be explained by the fact that none of them knew that the multiplication had taken place. They simply assumed that they were being fed in a non-miraculous way. John and the Synoptic writers both want us to think of the followers of Jesus as a New Israel; so, his followers, like the followers of Moses in the wilderness, will be fed by God, just as the old Israelites were fed by manna, the mysterious wafer-like bread which descended from the sky. So, for the evangelists, it was natural to make this 'feeding' into a supernatural event, and to assume that Jesus himself had multiplied the loaves and fishes. Modern commentators, trying to unpick 'what really happened' from this story, have imagined that the crowd was fed because they learnt from Jesus how to share. He took the lad's five loaves and two fishes and shared them with someone else. In turn, the men, sitting down in the grass, looked in their knapsacks or bags and found that they had some food which they could share with their neighbour. Hence the 'multiplication'.

This 'explanation' for the miracle of the Loaves, or the incident of the Loaves, only moves a small way to understanding its significance. The Fourth Gospel adds an enormous commentary on the story, in which Jesus expounds the mystery of himself as the bread or manna sent down from heaven. There is even a passage which Christian scholars interpret as a reference to the Christian Eucharist, in which

Jesus is made to say, 'He that eateth my flesh and drinketh my blood abideth in me and I in him'. [1]

That this should have formed part of the Fourth Gospel in its earliest state seems highly unlikely, since that Gospel does not mention the institution of the Eucharist, and indeed, clearly did not believe that Jesus did institute the Eucharist. Quite possibly, the first version of John had not even come across the practice, invented by Paul, of eating and drinking the flesh and blood of Christ. A later reviser, embarrassed by this lacuna, added the paragraphs about eating and drinking Jesus himself. Even as they stand, it is hard to follow their symbolism very exactly. If the Fourth Gospel wished the Feeding of the Five Thousand to be a prefiguring of the Eucharist, would it not be necessary for the Christian Eucharist to consist of bread and fish instead of bread and wine?

The clue to the incident's meaning is in the original story, just quoted, and not in the elaborate commentary which a later reviser has added. 'Make the people sit down'. A truer translation is 'Make the men sit down'.

Make the men sit down! Make the Essenes sit down! Make the Pharisees sit down! Make Iscariot sit down, with his dagger, and make Simon the Zealot sit down, with his patriotic band of terrorist guerrillas! Sit down, O men of Israel!

Jesus had done much to make the women stand up, and in this he was eccentric, not to say revolutionary ('Damsel, arise!' 'Men, sit down!'). As has often been observed, warfare and physical strife are peculiarly male things. When we think of the battles of world history, they are fields full of *men* killing one another. You could not imagine Waterloo or the Somme filled with women. Somehow or another, the women, if serving in those armies, would simply not have continued with the killing. Jesus said, Make the men sit down!

We could if we chose read this, and quite legitimately read this, as a profound spiritual and psychological teaching. Suppress if you can the yang and exalt the yin! Keep down the urge to dominate, to score, to triumph, to fight, and exalt the urge to conciliate, to understand, to value. 'I shall not hurt or destroy in all my holy mountain.'

Much of this can be drawn from the story. It is there. In terms of Jesus and his contemporaries, however, it is a principle with an

[1] John 6:54.

absolutely obvious practical application. The fighting men of Israel must sit down. The differing sects, the sparring partners, the sectarians must sit down. It is not incredible that Jesus was quite consciously modelling himself on the great Hebrew Prophets of the Scriptures. Luke tells us that Jesus first preached from the 61st chapter of Isaiah. This could simply be the evangelist expressing to us how Jesus seemed like an embodiment of that prophecy. But it could equally be the case that Jesus himself took that text, and the many similar passages of the Scriptures, as a sign of how Israel should be living at that time. 'The Spirit of the Lord is upon me, Because he hath anointed me to preach good tidings to the poor: He hath sent me to proclaim release to the captives, And recovering of sight to the blind, To set at liberty them that are bruised. . .'

I believe that this was Jesus's self-conscious mission to his people. Like the Pharisees, and the Essenes, and so many others, Jesus believed that Israel should return to the Lord, in a spirit of penitence, and joy. Unlike many of these sectarians, Jesus believed that any Jew could turn back to the Lord, and that it did not require in him any great intellectual skill or spiritual energy. It required a simple trust in God. Love of God, and love of one's neighbour. These, Jesus taught, were the fulfilling of all the Torah. By its failure or success in being able to keep these laws, and be guided by them, Jesus felt that his people's history would depend.

That is the simple purpose of the Loaves. Jesus gathered together a huge crowd of people in a desert spot, and made them sit down together. Many of them were probably Zealots, or other patriots, expecting that this should be the moment when yet another military uprising against the Romans should be announced or planned. He made them sink their differences. He made them break bread together and eat a simple meal. It does not matter whether we believe that there were actually five thousand men or whether this is just a symbolic number, suggestive of the whole assembly of Israel.

The profound significance of the scene was only to unfold in the last year of Jesus's life. If the Fourth Gospel is right, and if this desert rally took place at Passover, then Jesus had just a year to live. The factors which were destined to destroy him were all present in that meeting. There is the volatile crowd, eager for leadership, eager for food, and eager for the spiritual food – his words and his healing – which Jesus had to give. They are not a united crowd. They are not an intelligent crowd. There are those among them – the *sicarii*, represented by Judas Iscariot, the Zealots, represented by Simon – who would be very happy if the crowd's enthusiasm for Jesus led to a popular upsurge against the Romans. These are fighting men, these five thousands. They are ruinously addicted to sectarianism and to violence. Jesus knows this, and will try to pacify them, and to warn them of the terrible dangers facing the Jewish religion and race if this sectarianism and this violence continue.

Yet he does not turn away from them until their implacability is made clear to him. Then he sees that 'they were about to come and take him by force, to make him king'. [1] While he preaches to them a kingdom not of this world, his hearers, struck by his charismatic powers of utterance and healing, look to him as their natural leader, their military leader, against the Romans. Some of the hotheads almost certainly believe that he is, or might be, the promised Messiah, and that the Feeding is a foretaste of the Messianic banquet. Jesus is destined to offend the men of violence by insisting that his is a kingdom of love, and that in using the word 'kingdom' he is speaking of that indestructible inner kingdom to which all followers of the Torah belong. He preaches the union of Israel, its mystic and indissoluble communion, and he urges the sectarians to put their differences aside. This is destined to anger some of those sectarians, and, much more serious, to excite a reasonable suspicion in the minds of the Roman authorities that a Jewish populist uprising is centred upon the purpose of this man.

Not for the last time in the history of the Jews, the hostility of their enemies, and their divisions among themselves, threatened their destruction. The Feeding is Jesus's greatest sign. Make the men sit down! Jesus was not the Messiah, and he did not teach that he was the Messiah. He taught that the promised age of blessedness could not dawn until Israel saw its true destiny, which was to behave as if the coming of the kingdom was imminent. That meant to live together in peace, and to accept their unity as the sons and daughters of the Creator.

If indeed the Feeding in the desert took place at Passover time, then the mind of Jesus would naturally have been with those who went up to Jerusalem for the festival, singing, as they approached the holy city, the Psalms of Ascent:

[1] John 6:15.

Pray for the peace of Jerusalem:
They shall prosper that love thee.
Peace be within thy walls,
And prosperity within thy palaces.
For my brethren and companions' sakes,
I will now say, Peace within thee.
For the sake of the house of the Lord our God
I will seek thy good. [1]

It was in Galilee that Jesus grew up, and made his impact. It was in Jerusalem that his idealistic vision was tested, with consequences of enormous portent for Jesus himself, for the Jewish people, and ultimately, for the history of the human race.

[1] Psalm 122:6–9.

# VIII

## THE MAN ON A DONKEY

JESUS, THE GREAT apocalyptic prophet, the visionary teacher, the widely popular healer and exorcist, was destined to die a humiliating death in Jerusalem at the hands of the Romans. This fact, more than any other, hangs over the Gospels, and explains their shape. They are not balanced biographies, in which an equal amount of space is given to Jesus's upbringing, the influences on his early thought, his circle of friends, his ambitions, his relations with his family, his unfolding public life. They are all really Passion narratives, and the accounts of Jesus's life and teaching could be said to be so much prelude to accounts of the last week of his life, his trial, his death, and his Resurrection.

The evangelists' manner of arranging and rewriting the material makes it extremely difficult to know how much they can be of use to the historian. As we have repeatedly seen in this book, the Gospels were written for those who were, for want of a better word, Christians – though they would probably not have been able to subscribe to the creeds of the later Church, such as the Nicene Creed of 325 CE. They probably all believed that Jesus was about to return to earth on the clouds, to gather his followers to join him in the sky, though the Gospel of Luke, with its companion-volume of Acts, seems to be coming to terms with the fact that this expected event has been for some reason delayed. They were written with the conviction that Jesus had risen from the dead, and left behind an empty tomb in Jerusalem to prove it; and that he had appeared in various mysterious ways to some of his followers.

The historian is bound to attempt some explanation of how the early Christians came to arrive at these beliefs. But at the same time, he is hindered from doing so by the intractable nature of the Gospel evidence. For the evangelists, all the historical evidence that Jesus was the prophet foretold in the Scriptures, or that he was the Messiah, is denied by their story. They know that – whatever will happen in the

future, when Jesus has come again – the actual story of his earthly
life was disastrously sad. He did not achieve any of the things which
he apparently set out to achieve. In so far as he had conflicts within
the body of Judaism it is now almost impossible to reconstruct what
those conflicts may have been about, and it would seem as though
neither side won. The Romans killed him, just as, forty years later,
they were to eliminate the great ritual embodiment of Judaism, the
Temple itself.

The fact that Jesus was a total failure in life, and that his mission,
whatever its original purpose may have been, ended on the Cross,
leads the evangelists in two contrary directions. On the one hand,
with a vividness which makes their Passion narratives unrivalled for
their poignancy, they depict Jesus as a figure of vulnerability who is
purely the victim of the situation. He is betrayed by one of his best
friends, forsaken by the others. He begs the Almighty to deliver him
from his fate and, at the end, even his Heavenly Father forsakes him.
Only the family remain to take down his corpse from the Cross.
Nor is it ever explained, in realistic terms, why all this had to happen
to Jesus. The lands of Israel and Judaea swarmed with men who had
very strong ideas about the religious destiny of the Jewish people.
There were many false Messiahs, as we read in the New Testament;
they were not necessarily killed, still less were they crucified, which
was a death reserved for those who had offended the Romans. This
is a fact which is extremely embarrassing to the evangelists, who are
writing for Gentiles, and writing for a world where the Jews were
beginning to be persecuted by the Romans, in retaliation for their
recalcitrant behaviour as the colonised. Those evangelists therefore
who wrote with an eye to readership in the wider Roman Empire
(and in their final stages of redaction, this includes all four Gospels,
whatever their origins) were as anxious as possible to suggest that
Jesus died at the hands of the Jews – the famous trouble-makers. The
fact that he manifestly was killed by the Romans, and must have
been seen at the time as a threat to the Romans, is an uncomfortable
one for the evangelists to swallow.

Uncomfortable, that is, politically. From the doctrinal point of
view, if they believed that Jesus was the great prophet chosen by
God to proclaim a new religion to the world, it is embarrassing for
them to suppose that his death, which cut him short in the prime of
life, should have been in any way a set-back. So, they all feel obliged
to tell us repeatedly that Jesus foresaw his death, and foretold his

own Resurrection after three days. If he had really done so, of course, his terror at the time of his arrest, and the drops of sweat which he shed in Gethsemane, would have been so much theatre. Why should a divine being, who is quite confident that he is going to come back to life again after three days, show the slightest terror of death?

So, the historian is faced with a double problem: the problem of seeing what, if anything, can be extracted from the Gospel writings which can be regarded as historical, and the problem of accounting for the faith which produced those writings in the first place. I am not here subscribing to the well-worn 'Pentecost' argument, which asks how a group of poor, frightened individuals whose master has been crucified could have been transformed into a group of highly articulate men and women, prepared to die in order to communicate their faith in the Gospel (sometimes called in such arguments 'the Resurrection experience') to the world. The poorness of this argument is that it presupposes that we know what 'the disciples' were in fact like before they had 'the Resurrection experience'. History is full of people who have been prepared to encounter persecution for the sake of their beliefs. The Resurrection is important not because of the change it effected in his disciples, but in the change it seems to have effected in Jesus himself, if we are to follow the early Church as the model of what the risen Christ taught.

At the risk of spoiling the suspense of my narrative, I had better confess in advance what I *think* might have happened in the last week of Jesus's life, always emphasising that it is no more than what I think, and that I might be wrong, as many others have been before me. I should also like to emphasise in advance that whatever one writes about this subject, there will always remain at its heart a very great area of mystery.

We know that Jesus quarrelled with his family, and we know, very strangely, that they were present at the end. They had consistently opposed him, and he them. 'Woman, what have I to do with thee?'[1] His family say, 'He is beside himself . . .'[2] 'And he answereth them, and saith, Who is my mother and my brethren?'[3] It is they, however who are the leaders of the movement associated with Jesus's name. It is they who, we must assume, are responsible for the burial of his body. Jesus, I submit, fell foul of his family because he would not

[1] John 2:4.
[2] Mark 3:20.
[3] Mark 3:33.

conform to their idea of what a great prophet should have been like. It
might even be that they hoped he would be the Messiah. If so, he bitterly disappointed them, above all by his doctrine that sinners could
be admitted to the kingdom, and his preparedness to mix with them.
On the one hand, this had led to scenes which seemed shocking to
propriety – a prostitute bathing the feet of Jesus with tears, drunkards
blubbering out their penitence over the dinner table, rather than
making acts of ritual self-abnegation before the priests, devils flying
from the mouths of lunatics into untouchable pigs, tax-collectors, the
most hated category in Jewish society, being admitted to his innermost
circle. As if this apparent moral anarchy were not enough, Jesus also
seemed to be taking the most absurd political risks, and to be either
too naive or too heedless of his own safety to be able to see what he was
doing. It was a country in which bandits, political terrorists, religious
fanatics, rebels, insurrectionaries, milled about, fighting one another
and plotting the overthrow of authority.

Such activities risked the severest repercussions, which would
affect not merely the rebels themselves, but the lives of their families.
Jesus, up to and including the miracle of the Loaves, had seemed to
be quite prepared to allow his popularity with the crowds to encour-
age the excitement of the Zealots and the *sicarii*, of whom Judas was
one. After that miracle, when, as the Fourth Gospel tells us, the
crowds planned to make Jesus into a king, he realised that he had
opened a Pandora's box. The kingdom which he wished to establish
was not of this world; but the very word 'kingdom', *basileia*, means,
simply, empire. If you were the commandant of a Roman fortress or
the procurator of a Roman province, and you heard that a charismatic
leader, with a following of thousands, had decided to set up a new
empire, you would not be reassured, particularly if it was happening
in the land of the Jews, not famous for their submissive attitude to
the Romans. Jesus, meanwhile, had various lessons which, as a
prophet, he wished to teach the Jews. Whether they all happened in
the last week of his life, as the Synoptic Gospels suggest, or whether
they happened over a longish period, and during several visits to
Jerusalem, does not really matter. But it surely does not strain credulity to imagine that Jesus did, in fact, overturn the money-changers'
tables in the outer court of the Temple at Jerusalem; that he did weep
over the city, and imagine that, if the Jews did not change their
ways, the Romans would destroy them, and the Temple. It is hard
to believe the evangelists when they say that Jesus foretold his own

arrest and death. It is easy, however, to believe that after that arrest, his followers forsook him. He was condemned by the Romans and crucified. He was buried in a tomb. Three days later, this tomb was found to be empty. In some versions, young men or angels inform the distressed female friends of Jesus that he has gone to Galilee. In other versions at least one of the women stays behind for long enough to see a man whom she thinks first of all to be the gardener, and then, Jesus himself. There follow a number of occasions in which the disciples see a stranger, whom they do not at first recognise, but whom they decide to 'be' Jesus. Their excitement and exaltation is tremendous, equalling that of Herod who, upon seeing Jesus, supposed that John the Baptist had risen from the dead. My guess would be that the followers of Jesus – Mary in the garden, the two disciples on the road to Emmaus, the fishermen by the lakeside in Galilee – had actually seen James, or another of the brothers of the Lord. The angels or young men who told the women that he had 'gone before them into Galilee' were members of Jesus's family, who had come in the garden tomb in order to take the body for burial nearer his home in Nazareth. James and the other brothers of Jesus took over as the leader of the group, teaching them a more austere 'Gospel', but one which was more in line with mainstream Jewry. The little group, far from wishing to break away from Judaism, or admit Gentiles, 'were continually in the Temple, blessing God'.[1] We do not know precisely what they were blessing God for, but clearly, in James, they recovered their sense of a leader, who could give them the confidence to await the coming of the kingdom which, in spite of the terrible disillusionment of the Crucifixion, they still expected. Thus, after a moment in which it looked as though the anarchic ideas of Jesus might gain some popularity, his followers settled back into a routine of austerity which would have made perfect sense to the Essenes, the Pharisees and the other groups which they in some ways resembled. Fourteen years later, very much to their alarm and surprise, they discovered that there was a new 'religion' taking root in the synagogues of the Diaspora. A Jew called Paul, whom none of them had ever met, had been preaching a doctrine which was esoteric, mystical, and wholly at variance with the Church of James – the doctrine of Christ's Atoning Death, of Justification by Faith Only, and, worst of all, the doctrine that in this new Church, which

[1] Luke 24:53.

had been founded in collaboration between St Paul and the Risen Jesus, there was to be no distinction between Jews and Gentiles. All the dietary laws had been scrapped. Circumcision was no longer to be practised. It was not even clear whether the divine Scriptures themselves were to be read and mastered by Paul's semi-literate pagan followers. Anxious that this regrettable development should be thought to have anything to do with them, the friends and relations of Jesus summoned Paul to a meeting in Jerusalem.

That is what I believe to have happened. I could not prove it, but I think that I could show that it was more likely than the New Testament account of things. Having admitted that, I shall continue with the narrative.


Jerusalem is a hill-town in Judaea, some seventy miles south of Nazareth. In the time of Jesus, it was the capital of a separate province, Judaea. As well as being the cultic centre of the Jewish faith, it was also a Roman garrison, and a Galilean, coming there for the first time, would have been struck by the sophistication of some of the architecture, and by the heavy presence of Roman soldiers. A modern visitor to the city, trying to recapture what it was like in those times, must realise that it occupied roughly speaking the site now covered by the Old City – though the present-day walls trace a different perimeter, and are of mediaeval origin. By far the most imposing building today is the Dome of the Rock, built after the Moslem conquest of the city in 638 CE to commemorate the holy place where Abraham supposedly offered his son Isaac as a sacrifice to God, and where the Holy Prophet Mahomet ascended into heaven. Six hundred years before the coming into the world of the Holy Prophet, however, the great monument in Jerusalem was the Temple. We have a strong sense of what that was like because of the extensive descriptions of it by Josephus, who was in Palestine at the time of its destruction, and was obsessed by it. The size and extravagance of the Temple of Herod were a source of astonishment to all who saw it for the first time. Roman conquerors, and Jews from the Diaspora, who had seen the architectural wonders of the world, were alike astounded by this building. The Inner Sanctum, which contained the Holy of Holies, was all that remained of the old Temple of Solomon, built in 986 BCE. Around this, Herod had built up a vast complex of grandiose courts. In the lower Temple courts, the stones were sixty feet long. There were double colonnades of which the pillars were nearly forty feet in height. This outer area covered a circuit of three-quarters of a mile. The visitor then passed through to a second court, through a stone balustrade measuring four and a half feet in height. At intervals, there were slabs, in Greek and Latin, reminding visitors of the laws of ritual purification if they wished to proceed further. This was the Sacred Precinct, and no Gentile was admitted. An inscription survives which reads, 'No foreigner may enter inside the barrier and embankment. Whoever is caught doing so will have himself to blame for his ensuing death.' So much for the fanciful idea, implausibly put into the mouth of Jesus by Mark, that the Temple should be a house of prayer for all nations.[1] So strictly did the Jews feel that the presence of a Gentile would defile their holy places that even the workers on the construction of the Temple had to be specially consecrated as priests.[2] The building of the main Temple was completed by Herod's workmen within eighteen months in 20–19 BCE. The whole complex of courts and special buildings was not finished until 64 CE, that is, six years before it was all utterly destroyed. In Jesus's time, therefore, we can imagine that there would still be scaffolding, stone-carvers and masons at work as visitors to the Temple made their exits and entrances through the various courts. Nine gates altogether had to be passed from the outer court to the Holy of Holies itself. Within the outer court was the Court of the Women; this was as close as they were ever allowed to come to the Sanctuary. Beyond that was the court of the Altar of Burnt Offering, and from this court, a priest was appointed on a daily basis to slaughter and burn the offering, and to carry the holocaust through into the further sanctum, where the shewbread and the altar of incense were to be found. Immediately to the west of the Holy Place was to be found the holiest place of all, the Holy of Holies. This was separated from the altar of incense by a great curtain or veil, and only the High Priest himself could enter it, and then only once a year on the day of Atonement.

Needless to say, such a huge cultic centre required a large religious 'staff' to keep it running smoothly. Already in Jesus's day, there were Jews who were becoming disenchanted with the predominance

[1] Mark 11:17.
[2] Floyd V. Filson: *A New Testament History*, 41.

of sacrifice in Temple worship; this was not out of a sentimental regard for the numbers of birds and animals which had to be killed; they feared that the priests were corrupt, and that the manner in which the sacrifices were carried out was offensive to ritual purity. At times of festival, when each pilgrim would have wished to sacrifice a lamb or a pigeon, the number of killings each day must have run into thousands. The stench of blood and of roasting flesh can hardly have been drowned by the smoke of incense; nor can the cries of traders, or the uplifted voices of priests and pilgrims at prayer, have drowned the screeching of the beasts as they had their throats cut, and their blood scattered in the time-honoured manner. Of course, in order to get your pigeon, you had to buy it, and in order to avoid defiling the Temple by bringing in foreign currency, which might be emblazoned with the idolatrous head of Caesar, it was necessary to change your Roman coinage into the sacred half-shekels which made up the Temple currency. This was the system upon which Judaism depended, and if there had not been money-changers, it would not have been possible for the sacrificial routines to be operative.

It is to this Temple that Jesus, in common with all other practising Jews, must regularly have come throughout his life. In the legendary account of Luke, we read of Jesus being presented here when he was circumcised, aged eight days. Here his parents made the statutory offering of a pair of pigeons, and here the wise old Simeon, perhaps a Temple priest, is supposed to have made the prophecy that Jesus would be the cause of the 'falling and rising up of many in Israel'.[1] Here, Jesus as a boy is supposed to have debated earnestly with the doctors of the Law.[2] Here, if the Fourth Gospel is right, he made regular visits throughout his adult life to keep the Jewish festivals – Passover and Unleavened Bread, celebrated in the spring (April or March); commemorating the Exodus of the Hebrew people from Egypt in the time of Moses; the Feast of Weeks or Pentecost, fifty days later, which marked the ending of the grain harvest; then, much later in the year, there was a Harvest Festival for the Grape Harvest – the Feast of Booths or Tabernacles, when pilgrims slept out under makeshift tents or huts; and on the first day of this feast the Temple was lit up. The Fourth Gospel, which follows these festivals so

[1] Luke 2:34.
[2] Luke 2:41–52.

closely, has Jesus saying things which are appropriate to each of them. On the Day of Lights when the Temple was lit up, for example, that Gospel has him saying, 'I am the light of the world'.

The Fourth Gospel represents Jesus as coming and going between Galilee and Jerusalem; and his conflicts with the Jews and the Pharisees have already reached fever pitch, in this account, months before the final confrontation. Moreover, to emphasise the idea that Jesus comes to overthrow Judaism and replace it with a new dispensation, the Fourth Gospel places the incident where Jesus overthrew the money-changers' tables at the beginning of the story. The other Gospels place it towards the end. For them, there is only one journey to Jerusalem, the journey towards Calvary and the Cross. The conflicts which Jesus had with Jewish officialdom, about such matters as ritual purification, or the observance of the Sabbath, happened in Galilee; though even here we are told that the altercations reached such a fever pitch that the scribes and Pharisees devised means by which they might put Jesus to death. All the Gospels seem quite convinced, or wish us to be quite convinced, that Jesus was put to death by the religious authorities, though they offer no proof of this, and it seems in some ways unlikely to have been true. The point is that for the Synoptic Gospels, the journey to Jerusalem is emblematic. It is a journey in which Jesus himself is becoming the sacrifice and oblation. The writers therefore are not troubled to burden us with, for example, topographical information, nor with such biographical information as where Jesus normally stayed when he came to Jerusalem, who his friends were, how well he knew the city, and how well the Galilean followers in his entourage knew it. Nevertheless, we find a set of narratives which all represent Jesus and his followers going up to Jerusalem, probably towards the end of March in the year 30 CE for the Feast of the Passover.

Since each of the Gospels has a slightly different tale to tell about the events of that Passover, we shall be compelled to turn from one narrative to the next at several junctures; but for the sale of simplicity, I shall concentrate at first on the version of Mark. It is extremely direct and circumstantial (for example, it tells us the time of day when the various events took place) and it is detailed. Nowhere, however, is the famous 'Messianic secret' of Mark's Gospel more closely guarded than in its chapters 11–14, which read like a mystery story of a singular character: a mystery, that is, where the secret is known to some of the characters, not all, and where the explanations for many of the most important clues have been withheld from the author himself: a paradoxical point, but one which must have struck every attentive reader of Mark. Inevitably, this has given rise to some interesting theories.

We can never hope to reconstruct Jesus's motives for behaving as he did in the last week of his life, but we can make some intelligent guesses about what was going on, always bearing in mind that they are only guesses and that they might be wrong.

In Mark's version, it seems fairly clear that Jesus knew something which his followers did not. Mark presents Jesus as a Galilean stranger to the Jewish capital, and yet, on two occasions – the triumphal entry into the city and the Last Supper – we find that Jesus has already prearranged matters.

He and his disciples arrived from Galilee on the Sunday of the week preceding Passover 30 CE. Jesus stayed at the village of Bethany, which is about three miles from the city itself. Jesus instructed his followers that if they went to the far end of this village, they would find an ass's colt. They were to fetch this animal for him. If anyone tried to stop them, they should say, 'The Lord hath need of him'. The disciples follow these instructions, and the donkey is released to them by its owner or guardians. It is the only occasion in the Gospels when we read of Jesus riding rather than walking, and for the evangelists, the episode is pregnant with meaning. So full of meaning is it for Matthew that he even doubles the number of animals involved. Jesus was fulfilling the prophecy of Zechariah: Tell the daughter of Zion, Behold thy king cometh to thee, meek and riding upon an ass, and upon a colt the foal of an ass.[1] The original words of the prophet employ typical Hebrew parallelism – 'riding upon an ass, the foal of an ass'. Matthew, who is intent that Jesus should fulfil the prophecies to the letter, imagines that there are two donkeys; then, having introduced the second beast into his story, he has to provide it with a function. Jesus rides on the ass, and they put their garments on the foal.

The point which can not be missed is that the King was coming to Zion. He was not coming to establish a kingdom of power, as would have been the case if he had come riding on a charger, but a kingdom of meekness and of peace. As Mark tells the story, there is a puzzle. The disciples have clearly been kept in the dark about this

[1] Zechariah 19: 8–9; quoted Matthew 21: 4, 5.

demonstration. Clearly, in Mark's version, Jesus had made previous arrangements with the owners of the donkey, arrangements to which the disciples were not privy. It would seem then that something was in the offing of which the disciples, sent to fetch the donkey, were unaware. The link with the passage from Zechariah would suggest that the Messianic kingship of Jesus was about to be revealed to the people. This does suggest to me that there was something in the nature of a plot afoot. There have been a number of extremely ingenious suggestions as to what this plot was, but the truth is that we do not possess enough evidence for more than intelligent guesswork. We do not, after all, know with any certainty how many of the details in the Gospel narratives bear any relation to historical reality. By their own confession, these accounts were written from sources based on the hearsay evidence of Jesus's friends, who deserted him at the time of his arrest, and could not possibly have been witnesses to any of the crucial events of his trial. None of this evidence makes a great deal of sense. But at least one explanation for that failure of it all to make sense could be that, at this critical stage of his career, *Jesus himself failed to make sense.* The prophecy or message which he had to give to Israel had begun to be a matter of high public interest since the Feeding of the Five Thousand in the desert. At that event, he had symbolically urged all the people of Israel to forget their differences, to abandon the way of political terrorism, and to submit themselves to God: Make the men sit down. It was after this, the Fourth Gospel says, that the crowds tried to make him into a king. Clearly, they went on thinking that he was going to be their king until the last week of his life.

What exactly the role of the Twelve was in all this is not clear. Some of them, presumably, were more 'in the know' then others. At the Last Supper, Jesus makes signals to Judas Iscariot which are not understood by any of those present. They are afterwards interpreted to mean that Jesus knew of his approaching arrest. The Fourth Gospel has Jesus saying to Judas, 'That thou doest, do quickly. Now no man at the table knew for what intent he spake this unto him . . .'[1] Matthew tells a story, in many respects highly improbable, of Judas going to the 'chief priests' and offering to betray Jesus to them for a sum of money.[2] What all these confusing stories retain

[1] John 13:27, 28.
[2] Matthew 26:14–16.

– 177 –

is the tradition that few of Jesus's immediate followers knew what was going on during the last week of his life, and few of them afterwards were able to make sense of his actions. Apart from the theological interpretations which they were able to place upon his last actions, his suffering, and his death, the followers of Jesus must have been puzzled about the exact circumstances of his arrest and trial. We can say this with some confidence because there is no other reason why these puzzling details should have been retained in the theological works which the Passion narratives became. There is a striking consensus between the Fourth Gospel and the Synoptics about this: Jesus was in touch with people other than the Twelve in Jerusalem; he was planning something which they did not fully understand; he was involved in a series of actions in which his death was seen as inevitable.

Beyond this, the historian cannot go. A blend of intelligent historical guesswork, with a cautious comparative reading of other Semitic texts, can make us sketch a picture which is probably not far from the truth. One method of reconstructing the possible authenticity of Jesus's sayings is to see how they translate from the Greek in which they are written into the Aramaic in which they must have been spoken. In Luke 17:24, for example, we read of Jesus saying, 'as the lightning, when it lighteneth out of the one part under heaven, shineth unto the other part under heaven; so shall the Son of Man be in his day'. This is not a sentence which can be rendered into feasible Aramaic, and it can therefore be rejected quite certainly as something which Jesus did not say. At least three of the sayings, however, in which Jesus prophesied his own death[1] can be rendered into Aramaic; they are sayings in which Jesus predicts that the Son of Man will die for his people as a ransom, and rise again. Similar tests of authenticity of Jesus's sayings make it seem quite possible that he made such predictions about himself. He used metaphors such as drinking of a bitter cup, preparing himself for a baptism, and completing a great work, when he spoke of this final consummation. There would also seem to be no reason to doubt that Jesus told his disciples, as Luke records, that 'it cannot be that a prophet perish out of Jerusalem'.[2]

It would not be impossible, then, to suppose that Jesus foresaw

[1] Mark 14:21; 8:31; 10:45.
[2] Luke 13:33.

his death, and in a way wished for it. He had by now come to see himself as a 'king', a man who could unify Israel and inaugurate the new 'kingdom of the saints'. Opinions could differ about whether this would mean that Jesus believed himself to be the Messiah. The point is that by his prophetic witness, begun in Galilee and completed in Jerusalem, he thought that he would inaugurate the new age. When he had died, he would rise again; by implication, not only would he rise again, but so would the rest of the redeemed Israel. The rule of the saints would begin. Jesus, riding into the city on a donkey, believed that some such process was about to start. We know that among his friends there were Zealots who believed that this rule of the saints could not start until they had led another rebellion against the Romans; we know that the *sicarii*, to which Judas probably belonged, thought that the rule of the saints would be advanced by a few random stabbings in the crowd at festival time.

Jesus had evidently been the focus of enough public attention to attract that of the authorities, religious and civil. It is conceivable that they feared some uprising at the time of the Passover, and that there was reason for such a fear. Even if Jesus himself was not involved in a paramilitary plot, we know enough about him to know that he numbered among his friends those who were. If Jesus believed, which is more probable than not, that he was about to inaugurate a new age on 15 Nisan of the year 30, and if the chief priests got to hear of this, there is no doubt that they would have panicked. Such a thing would certainly have caused civil unrest, and possibly a major riot in the city, when tens of thousands of pilgrims were squeezed into the narrow streets. The Romans would certainly exact reprisals. It was necessary to isolate Jesus, and to put a stop to the trouble-making before it went any further. The haste with which, in the Gospels, the authorities wish to try Jesus, and the need to get rid of him before the Feast, suggest that they knew of some plot which was timed to take place at the time of the Feast.

The stage is set, then, for an extremely confusing drama. Whether or not Jesus knew what was going on, we shall never know, but if our cautious guesswork is anywhere near correct, it is possible that Jesus knew of the 'tip-off' to the authorities, and had decided to make of his arrest, and possibly of his death, a demonstration of the power of the Most High to inaugurate the Messianic Age. Here is the scene: there were the Zealots, or similar political and military groups, planning an insurrection, and providing Jesus with the 'props' for his proclamation. For them, he was the best leader they could find of a revitalised Jewry, which drew on all classes and all sects to unite against the Romans. There were also the Sadducees, the upper-class priestly sect based on the Temple, who would have been quite determined to stamp out yet another cranky sectarian development within Jewry, particularly since it was heretical (Jesus admitted the sinners to the kingdom) and, which came to the same thing, Galilean. There were also the Romans, perpetually frightened that the Jews would prove ungovernable – as indeed turned out to be the case – and need subduing by the most terrible display of force – as happened forty years later. There were also the small circle of initiates, close to Jesus, who presumably thought they knew what was going on. And there were the Twelve, some of whom, like Judas, knew what was happening, and others of whom seemed to have been in complete ignorance, as the king mounted his ass on that Sunday afternoon, and rode into Jerusalem.

In the second century BCE – the incident is recorded in the Book of Maccabees – a great Hasmonean reformer called Simon Maccabeus had entered Jerusalem 'and purged the citadel of its pollutions. And he entered into it . . . with praise and palm branches, and with harps and with cymbals and with viols and with hymns and with songs.'[1] Perhaps Jesus was consciously imitating Simon when he climbed on to the donkey. If Mark's account of Jesus's entry into the city bears any relation to the truth, we must assume that the crowds had been prepared for his entry. True, at festival time, the pious were sup-posed to make their journey into the holy city on foot, so that by riding, Jesus made himself stand out; but without prior warning of the demonstration, it is hard to see why crowds should have run after him crying out, 'Blessed is the kingdom that cometh, the kingdom of our father David'.[2] On this first day of the demonstration, in Mark's account, Jesus did no more than enter the city, go to the Temple, and look around. If we believe that this is what he did, then one motive for his behaviour would have been to show himself to the public. Though a popular figure in Galilee, Jesus was virtually unknown in Jerusalem. Few would have known what he looked like, and in those dense crowds a man with a veiled head would in any case have been hard to distinguish. After this 'triumphal entry' into

[1] I Macc. 13:50, 51.
[2] Mark 11:10.

the city, Jesus, at a late hour, returned to Bethany where he was staying with friends.

Since all the Gospels are agreed that Jesus spent the last week of his life staying at Bethany, it is all the more surprising that the Synoptic Gospels make no mention of his most spectacular miracle. They do not even speak of Jesus's friend Lazarus whom he raised from the dead. The Fourth Gospel tells us that news of the death of Lazarus reached Jesus and his disciples when they were still in the north, on their way down to Jerusalem. The disciples urge Jesus not to go back to Judaea where they fear that he will fall foul of 'the Jews'; but Jesus is unable to restrain himself. 'Our friend Lazarus is fallen asleep; but I go that I may awake him out of sleep.' There is no more dramatic story in the New Testament. When Jesus reached Bethany, he found that Lazarus had been lying in the tomb for four days. The burial is over, but the mourners are still keeping up their dirge, and Jesus was caught up in the emotion of the occasion. 'Jesus wept. The Jews therefore said, Behold how he loved him!' Jesus went to the mouth of the 'cave' where Lazarus was laid and asked them to roll away the stone which covered the doorway. Martha, one of Lazarus's sisters, protested that by this time the body would have begun to decompose and stink. Jesus authoritatively called out to Lazarus – 'Come forth!' And the dead man came forth, bound head and foot in his grave clothes.

The story forms the first great climax in John's Gospel. It is the culmination of Jesus's signs. The second half of the Gospel will be devoted to his discourses, and then the 'sign' of his own death and triumph over death, which the raising of Lazarus foreshadows. We will come again to a narrative in which there is a tomb, and a stone rolled across it as a door. For reasons which are not immediately penetrable, it is the raising of Lazarus which persuades the Pharisees that Jesus is trying to usurp their religious authority with the Romans. 'The Romans will come and take away both our place and our nation.' And it is on this occasion that Caiaphas the High Priest makes his prophetic announcement, 'that it is expedient for you that one man should die for the people, and that the whole nation perish not'. [1] The incident is swathed in Johannine theology and the literary ironies which we should expect from that source. The unbelieving Jewish High Priest speaks truer than he can know about the true

[1] John 11:50. The whole story of the raising of Lazarus is to be found in John 11.

High Priest, Jesus, whose death – like the serpent lifted up by Moses in the wilderness – will draw all true believers to himself, and give them the gift of eternal life.

What, if anything, lies behind this story, or is it just pious legend? As so often with questions relating to the Fourth Gospel, the answer must be ambivalent. It was not until 1958 that Professor Morton Smith of Columbia University, New York, deciphered an eighteenth-century letter, scrawled on the end paper of a seventeenth-century edition of the works of St Ignatius of Antioch. This letter was a transcription of a letter purporting to have been written by Clement of Alexandria in the second century CE and was addressed to a certain man called Theodore. It referred to a secret Gospel of Mark – evidently a Gnostic version – 'for those who were being perfected' or 'initiated into the greater mysteries'. Many conditionals must attach themselves to Morton Smith's theory, which lead, as we have already mentioned, to the conclusion that Jesus was a magician. *If* the eighteenth-century letter is truly a transcription of a letter written 1600 years earlier; *if* the 'Secret Gospel of Mark' is indeed an authentic Marcan tradition, rather than merely being a garbled, Gnostic version of the Fourth Gospel story. . . Those are two very big *if*s. And we need not necessarily conclude that narratives so eccentric and with such tenuous textual history necessarily take us closer to the historical Jesus. Having said that, Morton Smith's theories should not be dismissed lightly. We are told that Jesus baptized not with water but with the Spirit; we read of him in the Gospels having an overwhelming effect upon people as a charismatic exorcist. It is imaginable that such a figure should have taken part in the bizarre rituals which Morton Smith describes: rites of initiation, in which the newly-admitted catechumen would be dressed up in grave-clothes and then called to 'new life' in the Spirit. If this were the case, then the Fourth Gospel's account of the 'raising' of Lazarus begins to look different. Supposing that the Lost Gospel of Mark comes first, and the Fourth Gospel second. In that case, we have first the account of the ritual. Then, at one remove, we have a narrative in which the inner meaning of the ritual has been translated into an event, a 'sign'. The catechumen in his grave-clothes becomes an actual dead man in grave-clothes, coming forth to be initiated into the Baptism of Spirit, the Baptism of Eternal Life. Before the story is out, we shall meet another figure wearing grave-clothes – a strange young man who makes two appearances towards the close of Mark's gospel, once in the Garden of Gethsemane, and once at the tomb of Jesus himself.

Until the moment occurs in our narrative when it is appropriate to ask ourselves some questions about this young man, let us return to follow Jesus to Bethany. There is an incomprehensible little exchange at the end of the Fourth Gospel in which it is stated that Peter asked Jesus, after he had risen from the dead, 'What shall this man do?' referring to 'the disciple whom Jesus loved'. 'Jesus saith unto him, If I will that he tarry till I come, what is that to thee? follow thou me. This saying therefore went forth among the brethren, that this disciple should not die; yet Jesus said not unto him, that he should not die; but, if I will that he tarry till I come, what is that to thee? This is the disciple which beareth witness of these things, and wrote these things; and we know that his witness is true.'[1]

There could be many reasons why the brethren said that the Beloved Disciple should not die, but one of them could be that they believed him already to have risen from the dead. That is to say, he could have been Lazarus. Quite conceivably, the Synoptic Gospels drew on contrary traditions, which positively rejected the claim that Lazarus had literally risen from the dead. It is interesting that they tell us of Jesus's friendship with the Bethany family, while omitting any mention of Lazarus. Mark merely tells us that Jesus stayed at Bethany, and mentions that he visited a Pharisee named Simon. Luke tells us the story of Martha and Mary, and of Jesus rebuking Martha for being 'cumbered about much serving', rather than joining in the conversation like her lazier sister. Both the tradition of Mark and that of the Fourth Gospel made the scene of Jesus's anointing by the woman (in Mark a prostitute, in John, Mary the sister of Lazarus) a foreshadowing of his death and burial. This is implicit in the Johannine story, but in Mark, Jesus spells it out: 'She hath done what she could: she hath anointed my body aforehand for the burying'.[2] If Morton Smith is right, and if the symbolism of burial clothes and rising again to new life, could be enacted by the *living* in their rites of Baptism, we can probably detect here a place where confusion could arise between actual events and ritual performances. Mark writes from the point of view that Jesus broke free from death, and was raised up by God on the third day. He also believes that such a

[1] John 21:21–24.
[2] Mark 14:8.

rising-up is possible for all believers. But also, and this is where the confusion arises, he is, in his Secret Gospel, deliberately or inadvertently preserving a tradition where the living went in for ritual enactments of death and resurrection.

It is a ripe field in which fine religious symbolism and feeling can grow. It is rather more difficult to find, amid these profuse growths, anything which could be isolated as an historical fact. Everything which Jesus did or said, as it appears in the Gospels, is pregnant with celestial meaning; but this is doubly true for the evangelists' descriptions of what happens to him from now onwards. An example of what I mean is found in the scene which Mark places the day after Jesus's triumphal entry into the city: the scene in the Temple, when Jesus overthrows the money-changers' tables. For the Fourth Gospel, this is a purely symbolic act. That Gospel places the incident at the very beginning of the story, in chapter two. As always in that Gospel, a Galilee-sign is matched by a Jerusalem-sign, both making the same point. In Galilee, Jesus turned the water in those pots (after the Jews' manner of purifying) into intoxicating new wine; in Jerusalem, he drove out the money-changers from the Temple, and said, 'Destroy this Temple and in three days I will raise it up'.[1] In other words, Jesus is bringing to birth a new way of approaching God in which the ritual observances of the Jewish faith – the ritual purifying of the water-pots, the ritual sacrifices of the Temple – will be replaced by the free worship of the heart. As he told the much-married woman of Samaria at Jacob's Well, 'the hour is coming and now is, when true worshippers shall worship the Father in spirit and truth'.[2] So much for the symbolism of the Fourth Gospel which, however early some of the traditions upon which it draws, had probably gone through a final redaction after the destruction of the Jerusalem Temple, and after the separation of early Christianity from Judaism.

Mark describes several visits of Jesus to the Temple in the last week of his life. On one visit, he overthrows the money-changers' tables, and makes the specific point that the Temple has been made a house of prayer for all nations, 'but ye have made it a den of robbers'.[3] The chief priests are surprised by this saying, and decide that they must destroy Jesus on the strength of it. We are further told

[1] John 2:20.
[2] John 4:23.
[3] Mark 11:17.

that, walking in the Temple, Jesus had a quarrel with the religious authorities about John the Baptist. They ask Jesus by what authority he speaks and acts. Jesus replies that he will answer the question if they tell him whether or not John's Baptism was 'from heaven or from men'. Since they had not followed John in his lifetime, they fear to say that his Baptism was heavenly. But they fear the mob's reaction if they say that John was not divinely inspired. Another Temple-incident this week occurs when the disciples and Jesus are watching pilgrims throw money into the huge treasury. They see a poor widow come along and throw in two mites, the smallest possible item of currency. 'This poor widow,' said Jesus, 'cast in more than all they which are casting into the treasury: for they all did cast in of their superfluity; but she of her want did cast in all that she had, even all her living.'

Later, as they are coming out of the Temple, looking at the huge stones of Herod's architectural extravaganza, Jesus says, 'Seest thou these great buildings? there shall not be left here one stone upon another, which shall not be thrown down'.[1] The question then arises, whether we can determine, as historians, the attitude of the real Jesus to the actual historical Temple; whether it is likely that he predicted its overthrow; and whether this would in itself have been enough to make the religious authorities in Jerusalem seek for Jesus's destruction.

The Gospels in their final form are the product of Christian communities. They come to us from religious groups which have been separated from Judaism, with little or no actual memory of what the Temple was like. The symbolism of the Temple, both Solomon's Temple in the Jewish Scriptures, and the Second Temple which Jesus would have known, therefore becomes all-important for them. They wrote with the knowledge that the Temple had been destroyed; and they saw in this cataclysm the ultimate vindication of their own point of view: that is to say, Judaism in its visible form was finished, and the New Israel, founded by God in Christ, was the Church. It is from this *Sitz im Leben* that we can imagine Jesus saying that he would pull down the Temple, and rebuild it in three days. ('But he spake of the temple of his body.')[2]

If the 'cleansing of the Temple' actually happened, what was its

---

[1] Mark 13:2.
[2] John 2:21.

significance? Jesus must have meant it as a demonstration. As the Gospels present not merely the cleansing demonstration but all Jesus's sayings about religious formalism in general, it is tempting to interpret his angry gesture as suggesting the overthrow of Judaism. A difference between the versions in Mark and in the Fourth Gospel should put us on our guard against this interpretation. In the Fourth Gospel, Jesus says to the Jews, 'Destroy this Temple and in three days I will raise it up'. [1] In Mark, he says, 'Seest thou these great buildings? there shall not be left here one stone upon another'; this is distorted by the false witnesses at his trial as, 'We heard him say, I will destroy this temple that is made with hands, and in three days I will build another not made with hands'. [2] So, in no version is Jesus himself quoted as saying that he would destroy the Temple himself, either in a physical or spiritual sense. It may have been that in his anti-ritualistic remarks, he upset some of the religious leaders to the point where they threw up their hands and exclaimed – for example about his lax attitude to ritual purity – 'This is the last straw – he is destroying everything – next thing, he will be destroying the Temple!' But that is hardly the same thing as his saying that he would destroy it or that he would wish to destroy it. Nor is there any saying in the Gospels, which might plausibly be attributed to Jesus, which suggests that he wanted to start a new religion for Gentiles, still less make the Temple available for Gentiles to worship in. So, when he went into the Temple precinct and overthrew the tables of the money-changers, it is impossible to believe, as Mark does, that this was a demonstration against the exclusion of Gentiles from the Temple.

In the Fourth Gospel, he says, *Lusate ton naon touton*, destroy this sanctuary – I am the one who will build it up! It has been convincingly argued [3] that the significance of Jesus's prophetic action was not threatening, so much as admonitory. Jesus, according to Professor Sanders, is foreseeing the coming of the kingdom. In turning over the money-changers' tables, he was not expressing horror at the idea of animal-sacrifice (which was integral to the Jewish way of worship in which he himself participated); nor was he expressing a distrust of the Temple itself (his followers after the Resurrection were continually in the Temple, we read); he was foretelling a time

[1] John 2:19.
[2] Mark 13:1 and Mark 14:58.
[3] E. P. Sanders: *Jesus and Judaism*, 61–76.

when God would overturn the present order and raise up Jesus, together with his followers, in three days. I accept Professor Sanders's dismissal of those scholars who see the overturning of the money-changers tables as a protest – either against the corruption of the money-changers themselves, or against the religion of the Temple. Jewish prophets traditionally performed dramatic gestures to give flesh to their teachings. Riding the donkey into Jerusalem was such a demonstration. Overturning the money-changers' tables was another. But I find it less difficult than Professor Sanders to believe that Jesus might actually have foreseen, forty years before it happened, that the Jewish race would suffer the most terrible overthrow at the hands of the Romans. *Lusate ton naon touton!* You are bringing down destruction upon yourselves! That, I believe, is the message of Jesus. It is the same as the message at the desert Feeding: *Make the men sit down.* Jesus shared with all the religious enthusiasts of first-century Jewry, a sense that the kingdom would not come until Israel had reclothed itself in an attitude of loyal sonship to God. Where he differed from so many of his contemporaries was in seeing this as a unifying, not a sectarian ideal. He dreamed of a simple Judaism, stripped of its besetting sins of moralism and sectarianism. The ascetics of Qumran and the Pharisees thought that the kingdom would come because they were not as other men. Jesus taught that it would not come until they recognised that they were as other men. Not until they could be as responsive as children to God, and as indifferent as possible to the blasphemous presence of the Romans in their midst, could the Kingdom come.

The cleansing of the Temple in Mark is therefore all of a piece with the trick question which is put to him by the Pharisees and the Herodians: 'Master, we know thou art true, and carest not for any one: for thou regardest not the person of men, but of a truth teachest the way of God'. (And there is no reason to suppose that this was an ironical or sarcastic question; they believed it to be true; but if it was true, how did he reconcile such a view with the existence of the hated tax to the Romans, which his Zealot friends believed to be not merely an economic burden but a blasphemy?) 'Is it lawful to give tribute unto Caesar, or not?' Jesus asked for someone to give him a Roman coin, and held it up to them. It displayed the head of the divine Caesar. His lapidary reply is as destructively unworldly as his gesture of overturning the tables of the money-changers: 'Render unto Caesar the things that are Caesar's, and unto God the things that are God's'. [1] The Jews were of the belief that God would establish His kingdom on earth. Jesus probably believed this too, but he could see that any attempt to help the Kingdom on its way by armed rebellion, or even by civil disobedience, would have a calamitous result. He urged his people to detach themselves from the Maccabean dream. If this is true, then the significance of overturning the money-changers' tables becomes very specific in its symbolism. Unless they abandoned their recalcitrance towards the Romans, then their city, and the Temple itself, would be overturned. The reason why they should be prepared to swallow their pride was not cowardly. It was because by their divisions among themselves, and their obsession with expunging Rome, they were forgetting the reason why a Temple had been built in the first place. The prayer of Solomon, at the opening of the First Temple, had recognised that though monotheism was adorned by architecture, it did not require it: 'behold heaven and the heaven of heavens cannot contain thee: how much less this house that I have builded!' [2]

This is all of a piece with the Jesus of the Fourth Gospel, who tells the Samaritan woman that the father is to be worshipped neither on her holy mountain, nor in Jerusalem, but in spirit and in truth. It was for the recovery of this essential and simple thing that Jesus spoke out and for which, whether or not this was his intention, he was to die.

[1] Mark 12:13, 14, 17.
[2] I Kings 8:27.

# IX

## THE MAN WITH THE PITCHER AND THE NAKED BOY

THE FEAST OF Unleavened Bread was now near, and Jesus, with his disciples, and the hundred thousand pilgrims who crammed into the city, were preparing for Passover. The normal population of the city was between 25 and 30,000 thousand, so that the crowds were dense. The Paschal Lamb had to be eaten by the pilgrims within the confines of the holy city. Bethany, the village where Jesus was staying, fell outside the 'catchment area'. Any Jew who tried to eat the Paschal Lamb outside the sacred confines could be punished by the religious police with a beating of forty strokes.[1] The hundred thousand pilgrims therefore surged into the city for their meal. In spite of the extreme cold at that time of year,[2] many pilgrims had to eat their meal out of doors, at the door of their tents, or squeezed on to rooftops, or even within the Temple Court itself, near the very spot where the lambs were sacrificed. Mark tells us that already, by this stage, the religious authorities in Jerusalem were plotting the death of Jesus, but he offers absolutely no reason for such a plot. More is always going on behind the narrative of Mark than we, or perhaps he, can understand. Unexplained figures, like the men who had the donkey ready for the Triumphal Entry, slip in and out of the narrative without introduction or explanation. Another such figure is the man carrying the pitcher of water.

Mark tells us that it was on the first day of Unleavened Bread Jesus's disciples asked where they should eat their Passover meal. Since they had made no arrangements, they were perhaps expecting that they would have to eat their meal out of doors, like the poorer or more feckless pilgrims who had not made previous arrangements. Jesus told them to go into the city, where they would see a man carrying a pitcher of water. They were to follow him, and

[1] Mark 3:3. See Joachim Jeremias: *The Eucharistic Words of Jesus*, 16.
[2] Mark 13:24, 25.

when he turned into a house, they were to ask, 'The Master saith, where is my guest-chamber, where I shall eat the Passover with my disciples? And he will show you a large upper room furnished and ready.'[1]

We shall never know who the man with the pitcher of water was. Astrologers have seen him as Aquarius. Others, more prosaically, have noticed that it was the function of women to carry water, so that the man carrying the pitcher would have been very conspicuous. He would have needed to be if the Disciples were to find him in those dense crowds and those narrow streets. We are not told who provided the money for the large guest-chamber, though it is hinted that Judas looked after Jesus's money for him, and perhaps it was he who was behind the arrangements for the Upper Room.[2] It was to this room that the friends of Jesus made their way on that cold dark evening (of 14 Nisan or 7 April 30 CE?). It is easy to imagine the noise and the smell of Jerusalem, as, all around them, a sacred barbecue was being cooked for a hundred thousand people. Every meal was the same, as decreed by the Book of Exodus: 'Your lamb shall be without blemish, a male of the first year: ye shall take it from the sheep or from the goats: and ye shall keep it up until the fourteenth day of the same month: and the whole assembly of the congregation of Israel shall kill it at even. And they shall take of the blood, and put it on the two side posts and on the lintel, upon the houses wherein they shall eat it. And they shall eat the flesh in that night, roast with fire, and unleavened bread; with bitter herbs they shall eat it. Eat not of it raw, nor sodden at all with water, but roast with fire; its head with its legs and with the inwards thereof. And ye shall let nothing of it remain until the morning: but that which remainest of it until the morning, ye shall burn with fire. And thus shall ye eat it; with your loins girded, your shoes on your feet, and your staff in your hand: and ye shall eat it in haste: it is the Lord's Passover. For I will go through the land of Egypt in that night, and will smite all the firstborn in the land of Egypt, both man and beast: and against all the gods of Egypt I will execute judgments.'[3]

The significance of all this for some of the Jewish contemporaries of Jesus must have been obvious. For 'Egypt' read 'Rome'. Was the

[1] Mark 14:14. 15.
[2] John 12:6 and John 13:29.
[3] Exodus 12:5–12.

Almighty going to repeat, for His people, the miracle which had been performed at the first Passover, when a small band of faithful Jews had been delivered from slavery to a mighty empire?

Mark tells us that in this week, Jesus delivered to his Disciples a great apocalyptic address, drawing his imagery from the Book of Daniel, to describe the Coming of the Lord. 'Then let them that are in Judaea flee unto the mountains, and let him that is on the house-top not go down nor enter in . . . The sun shall be darkened, and the moon shall not give her light, and the stars shall be falling from heaven, and the powers that are in the heavens shall be shaken.'[1] It is surely conceivable that Jesus believed that the Day of the Lord was about to happen, at that very Passover. It is equally possible, in spite of his attempt to unite all the various factions of Judaism in his kingdom, that those who heard him put very different interpretations on his words. Some of his friends were Zealots and assassins, and Jerusalem at great festivals always attracted such desperadoes. Other friends of Jesus included the Pharisees. We are told that in the last week of his life he ate a meal at a Pharisee's house, and he numbered among his friends members of the Sanhedrin, such as Nicodemus and Joseph of Arimathea. As the story is told, it would seem as though Jesus invested this particular celebration of the Passover with great significance, as though the Messianic Age were indeed about to start, with signs and portents in the sky – of which it is not impossible that Aquarius, with his pitcher of water, was one. (The Qumran ascetics, in common with most of their contemporaries, were believers in astrology, and Jesus was probably no exception.)

It was in a state of unusual suspense that the Twelve gathered in that Upper Room. As a symbolic enactment of how he wished his followers to regard their fellow men, Jesus removed his outer garments and draped himself with a towel. Then he began, like a common slave, to wash the feet of his guests. Simon Peter protested at such an action. His mind had not begun to absorb Jesus's extraordinary reversal of hierarchies, his proclamation that in the new kingdom the first should be last, and the least in the kingdom the greatest. Peter was not ready for the kingdom that night; neither were his friends. Jesus seemed like a man completely alone; his companions failed to understand him. He had by now heard of the plan to arrest

[1] Mark 13:24, 25.

him, but when he announced to his friends that one of them would betray him, they were all astounded, and were unaware of what he meant.

The meal began, and Jesus would probably have read or recited to his Disciples the account of the Exodus: 'And it shall be when thy son asketh thee in time to come, saying, What is this? that thou shalt say unto him, By strength of hand, the Lord brought us out of Egypt, from the house of bondage'.[1]

The meal which took place in the Upper Room was a ritualised affair, but it was unusual in other respects. First we may notice the very striking fact that it was a male-only occasion. Jesus had excluded the women. He must have guessed that the evening was going to end in violence of some kind, and not wished his mother, with his other female followers, to be present. At the Passover meal, it was customary for the Jews to demonstrate their liberty as the sons of the Lord by reclining, not sitting, at the table. So, Jesus and his companions lolled. 'Whereas the slaves eat standing, at the Passover, people should recline when they eat, to signify that they have passed out of bondage into liberty,' as a Jewish writer of 300 CE was to explain.[2]

Another ritualised element of the meal was in the provision of wine. Although Jesus had a reputation as a toper,[3] he would have been very unlikely to drink wine habitually with every meal. According to the ritual requirements of the day, everyone at the Passover meal had to drink four cups of wine 'even if it is from the poor dish'. It was conventional for alms to be given at the time of Passover to enable the poorest of the poor to drink their ritual four cups. When, towards the end of the meal, Jesus sent Judas Iscariot out, the disciples assumed that he was going to make some such provision of alms for the poor.

In fact, Judas was going out to betray his master: as tradition has it, to the authorities. There have been any number of sentimental and fanciful explanations for why he should have wanted to do this. They range from the Gospel explanation – that Judas was bribed by the high priests – to notions of his being disillusioned with Jesus for political reasons. None of the explanations quite fit. If Judas was expecting Jesus to lead a great armed rebellion against the Romans,

[1] Exodus 13:14.
[2] Jeremias: op. cit., 36.
[3] Matthew 11:19.

and now realised that no such rebellion was planned, he would hardly have gained anything from handing Jesus over to the authorities. He could not know that Jesus, under torture, would not have given away the names of his fellow conspirators. If, as Jesus said at the time of his arrest, Jesus had become a notorious figure in Jerusalem during the previous week, it is strange that they needed Judas's help in identifying him – though it is true that the arrest happened in the dark, and Jesus would presumably have had his head covered. The only plausible sense in which Judas could have helped the authorities was in drawing their attention to Jesus's whereabouts in that crowded city, on that darkest of nights.

The whole story is swathed in mystery. The likeliest explanation for what was afoot was that the authorities had got wind of some planned uprising, just before the Feast of the Passover. Perhaps Judas had been found out by the authorities and, rather than betray the true secret of the uprising, he had decided to betray Jesus. Perhaps Jesus's talk about the kingdom, his apocalyptic prophecies, his triumphal entry, his overturning of the money-changers' tables, had made the authorities fear that he was going to be at the centre of such an uprising, and they had decided to scotch it at night, when most of the pilgrims were still eating their meal, rather than risking a public outcry by arresting Jesus in broad daylight when he was speaking to the crowds or walking about in the Temple courts. So, Judas left the supper table, and all his friends assumed that he was going to give alms to the poor. In fact, he was going to reveal to the authorities the whereabouts of Jesus's post-supper rendezvous. The Fourth Gospel tells us that Satan had entered Judas's heart, and as the wretched man goes out on his mission, that Gospel adds one of those pregnant short sentences which make it such a memorable book. *And it was night.* In Greek, it is no less monosyllabic and even shorter: *en de nux.* It is one of those moments where, in the powerfully economical prose of that evangelist, symbolism and realism join. Darkness indeed. And now the forces of darkness muster themselves against the Lord of Light.

Famously, it is at this point that the Fourth Gospel and the Synoptics differ about what took place after Judas had left the Upper Room. According to the Fourth Gospel, Jesus now delivered a long discourse to his Disciples, culminating in a very long prayer to the Father that he, and the Father, and the Church might all be one. These chapters (John 14–17) contain passages of high sublimity – 'I

am the way, the truth and the life',[1] 'In the world ye have tribulation: but be of good cheer; I have overcome the world'[2] – but they
are obviously a purely literary creation. They bear no resemblance
to the way that Jesus is supposed to have spoken in the Synoptic
Gospels; nor are they much like the way he speaks in the earlier part
of the Fourth Gospel itself. They are concerned with Church, and
with a collective view of the Christians which seems unlike the indi-
vidualist Jesus, who confronted Nicodemus and the Samaritan
woman in single encounters and promised that the way to the Father
was through individual rebirth, not by Church membership. ('I am
the vine, ye are the branches'.)[3] These chapters of the Fourth Gospel, which speak of the Christians being driven out of the synagogues
because of their view of Jesus, and their kinship with the Father
through their beliefs in Jesus, bear all the hallmarks of being inter-
polated into the Fourth Gospel itself. It is impossible to believe that
any such discourse fell from Jesus's lips at the Supper.

For the fourth evangelist, in any case, the Supper was not the
Passover meal, but a preparation meal. It may be that the evangelist
believed, as a matter of historical fact, that this was so; but the
symbolism of it is obvious, and it could be the supreme example of
his rearrangement of material in order to make a theological point.
His Jesus is the true Paschal Lamb, who dies a day earlier than the
Synoptic Jesus. He shows forth his true nature to believers by being
lifted up on the Cross at the very hour when the Paschal Lambs were
due to be sacrificed in the Temple. One explanation[4] for John's
silence on the subject of the Eucharist could be that he did not wish
the Eucharistic formula to fall into the wrong hands. He kept the
ritual secret in rather the manner that freemasons, today, might wish
to conceal from the rest of the world their rituals and the words
which accompany them. We know that from early times Christians
met together to break bread and to bless wine, and we know that
this was regarded as no ordinary meal. Only a quarter of a century
after Jesus's death, Paul was writing to his converts in Corinth, and
quoting something which was clearly remembered as a piece of
ritual, a mantra. 'For I received of the Lord that which also I delivered
unto you, how that the Lord Jesus in the night in which he was

[1] John 14:7.
[2] John 16:33.
[3] John 15:5.
[4] Jeremias: op. cit., 73.

betrayed took bread; and when he had given thanks, he brake it and said, This is my body which is for you; this do in remembrance of me. In like manner also the cup after supper, saying, This cup is the new covenant in my blood; this do as oft as ye drink of it, in remembrance of me. For as often as ye eat this bread, and drink this cup, ye proclaim the Lord's death till he come.'[1]

As in so many cases in the history of religion, it is impossible to say which came first – the cult, or the story which explains the origin of the cult. Undoubtedly the early Christians met together for the breaking of bread. It is generally assumed that they did so each week, and that there has been a continuous repetition of this mystic act, from the time of the Last Supper until the present day. Many purple passages of devotional prose, and many glorious hymns, most notably those of St Thomas Aquinas, have been written on this assumption. For Christians who believe that Christ lives in the holy bread which they even now consume, it is axiomatic that Jesus should have established a rite which was a token of his perpetual presence in the world. It is what they should expect of one who founded a new religion which was intended to spread far beyond the confines of Jewry to the entire Gentile world. Once it is recognised as inconceivably unlikely that Jesus founded a church, or felt himself to have any mission to neighbouring Gentiles in Palestine, let alone to Italians, Ancient Britons, or Hottentots, then the origins of the Eucharist seem more puzzling. Another explanation of why the Fourth Gospel does not attribute Jesus with having blessed bread and wine and told his Disciples to do this in memory of him is that he did not in fact do any such thing at the Last Supper. That he ate a meal with his friends, we may believe. That one of those friends – perhaps John, perhaps Lazarus – was especially dear to Jesus and laid his head on Jesus's breast during the Supper is a pious story which might well be true.[2] It is hard to envisage the circumstances which could have prompted Jesus to 'institute the Eucharist'.

All the New Testament writers presented Jesus, particularly in his last days, as the fulfilment of stories and prophecies in the Old Testament. He himself becomes the sin-offering, the Paschal Lamb. The breaking of bread and wine itself becomes a sacrifice, an offering of this Lamb. The imaginative and emotional power of the rite, and

[1] I Cor. 11:23–26.
[2] John 13:23.

the fact that it is the focus of the religious lives of so many people to this day, can blind us to the unlikelihood of Jesus ever having instituted the Eucharist. What would he have meant by doing so? It only makes sense if you believe that he founded a church for Gentiles, with its full complement of bishops, priests, deacons, sacraments and so forth. For the unlikelihood to become apparent, you only have to imagine the figure of Jesus returning to earth today and attending, let us say, High Mass at St Peter's in Rome. Imagine trying to explain to him what was going on. You would either say that the priest was turning the bread into the actual body of Jesus, or you would say that in some way which it was hard to convey in words, he was calling up the mystic presence of Jesus. There is no fundamental difference between the Catholic teachings of St Paul about the Eucharist, and the ritual customs and beliefs of modern Christians. But there seems an absolute gulf between the modern Christians and Jesus. If, as some Christians believe, the Last Supper was the First Mass, then how could his presence in the bread and wine have been more of a reality than his actual presence reclining at the table? If, like more orthodox Christians, you do not believe this, if you believe that the First Mass was Calvary, when Christ was offered to the Father, then the Last Supper was simply, as it were, a dry run for future celebrations of the Eucharist. You have to imagine that Jesus anticipated the Catholic theology of Saint Paul. It is something which is historically unimaginable. Jesus, after all, was in a state of high excitement. Something was about to happen which none of the Disciples knew about or understood. Jesus was either expecting that the Day of the Lord was about to dawn, or that he was about to be arrested. In either circumstance, it is hard to see why he should have gone to the trouble of teaching his followers a new rite. If he was correct in his prophecies, there would be no time for further rites. Perhaps this is the meaning of the strange saying in Matthew at this point: 'I will not drink henceforth of this fruit of the vine, until that day when I drink it new with you in my Father's kingdom'. [1]

So important for Christians is the cult of the Bread and the Cup that for them the entire significance of the Supper in the Upper Room is to be found in this action. Mark, Luke and Matthew all repeat the *mantra* known to (invented by?) St Paul. Actually, the

[1] Matthew 26:29.

institution of a new rite at this point is a narrative intrusion. The Fourth Gospel makes better sense at this stage: that Jesus spoke to his Disciples at the Supper, and that when he had finished speaking, he went forth over the brook Kidron to Gethsemane.[1]

The narrative of Mark notes that the Disciples sang a hymn before making their way towards the Mount of Olives. This would have been the Hallel, sung as a grace on these occasions, and taken from Psalms 114 to 118. These psalms speak of the deliverance of the Jews from the Egyptians and of a merciful Providence: 'I love the Lord because he hath heard my voice and my supplications. . . The cords of death compassed me and the pains of Sheol gat hold upon me. I found trouble and sorrow. Then I called upon the name of the Lord.'

The words which were traditionally sung on this occasion suggest to the evangelist the narrative which is to come. Jesus is indeed in danger of his life as he makes his way to the Mount of Olives, a place which Luke tells us (oddly, since the Lucan Jesus has hardly visited Jerusalem in adult life) was a favourite spot. It must in fact have been a place of rendezvous, a place known about by Judas. It is hard to know exactly what Jesus thought was going to happen when they reached Gethsemane. This is a place which may still be seen today, still planted with ancient olive trees, some of which might conceivably have been in the garden when Jesus was there. Until the modern Israeli government build an hotel on top of the Mount of Olives, the whole of that side of the city must have altered little from the time of Jesus. The other 'holy places' in Jerusalem were for the most part invented by the Empress Helena, who arrived in Jerusalem three hundred years after Jesus had died and decided, more or less arbitrarily, where the site of, for example, Calvary, or the Holy Sepulchre, can have been. Likewise, the exact footsteps of Jesus as he carried his Cross through the streets of Jerusalem have been invented for Christian pilgrims along the Via Dolorosa. Gethsemane is different from these places. It is an actual place which we know from the Gospels to have been associated with Jesus. He was here on the last night of his life. Places have memory; so do trees. Almost all visitors to Gethsemane are forcibly struck by its atmosphere, which is one of intense sadness and solemnity. Jesus was preparing himself for the end – but for the end of what? The Gospel writers all assume with hindsight that Jesus was looking forward to

[1] John 18:1.

his certain death, and that it was for this reason that he was filled with fear and sorrow in the garden. If this was the case, then Jesus must have committed some capital offence of which we know nothing, and which he was sure would lead to an instant carrying-out of the death penalty. Since no record of Jesus having committed such an offence exists, we cannot imagine what it might have been.

It would seem likely, or at least possible, that Jesus thought that the apocalypse was about to dawn in the Garden of Gethsemane. He had warned his Disciples that the Day of the Lord was going to come, and that it would be terrible. We find it hard, perhaps, to reconcile the violent imagery of the Book of Daniel, with which Jesus is said to have laced his apocalyptic prophecies, with the irony and humour and kindliness of some of his other apothegms. But Jesus was neither a theologian nor a philosopher. He had not worked out a system. He was a visionary, who saw into the life of things and did genuinely suppose that the last days were about to happen. He told his Disciples that even women, and infants at the breast, would not be spared when that terrible day came. This could be seen as an evangelist simply describing the siege and destruction of Jerusalem after the event. That is how the majority of liberal Protestant commentators on the New Testament have seen it. But there is no reason why Jesus should not have foretold the destruction of the city. On the other hand, it would be wrong to think that Jesus was making purely political forecasts or statements about military strategy when he foresaw the disasters which could lie ahead for the Jews. He saw these disasters as the visitation of their Almighty Judge. He undoubtedly believed in hell, and in future punishment, and it was perhaps of this that he thought in the garden. There is another possibility, and that is that some of Jesus's more belligerent followers had heard that the Day of Judgment was staged to take place that evening, and decided that they would help it along its way by having an armed uprising against Rome. Jesus could very well have known of some such plot and his attitude would most likely have been one of profound disapproval. The Disciples did not know, and still less do we, why Jesus sent Judas out of the Supper early. The betrayal theory of the Disciples has not been proved. Any number of things could have happened to Judas between the time he left the Upper Room, and his arrival at Gethsemane. He could have been sent by Jesus to the Zealots, or whoever were planning the uprising, asking them to come to Gethsemane and listen to reason one last time. Jesus could even have asked Judas to go to the religious authorities and take them into his confidence about the planned uprising. The information could have gone astray. The chief priests could have panicked and insisted that Judas take them, with their troops, to Gethsemane to identify Jesus and to 'bring him in for questioning'. Or, Jesus could have sent word to his other followers – the Zealots and the men of violence – that they *should* consider an uprising in the city that night. Judas could have been intercepted by spies, and forced to come to Gethsemane. For the historian, there can be nothing but frustrated and rather fruitless guesswork.

For the Christian believer and theologian, the Agony in the Garden is one of the most solemn moments in the Passion. It is the point where Christ in his human nature wishes that the cup of suffering could pass from him, but in his divine nature he knows that he, and he alone, can take upon himself the expiatory death which will deliver the world from sin. Such thoughts could not have passed though the mind of the historical Jesus, but an account of what actually went on in the Garden of Gethsemane would probably be unable to penetrate, as the Gospel accounts do, to the very heart of suffering, so that every listener to the story is caught up in the agony. Jesus is never more representative of humanity than when he prays to the Father to have the cup of suffering taken from him. He was by now accompanied by three of his Disciples, Peter, James and John, the same three who had seen a glimmer of the *shekhinah*, the ineffable glory, on the mountainside of Transfiguration. Now they are called to witness Jesus in his suffering and they cannot do it. They fall asleep. The sheer naked suffering of Jesus at this point – by implication, the sheer naked suffering of humanity itself – cannot be faced. Unused to drink, the Disciples have had their ritual four cups of wine at the Supper, and they are slightly drunk. So they fall asleep, and fail to witness the confrontation between Jesus and his Heavenly Father. By definition, since the Disciples are asleep, and Jesus would hardly have been able to write down an account of his evening in Gethsemane before being crucified the next day, his prayer in agony is a literary creation. It is one of the most superb of all literary creations, outstripping the *Iliad*, and Aeschylus and Shakespeare at their most august and terrible.

We are told that 'being in agony, he prayed the more earnestly, and his sweat became as it were great drops of blood falling upon the ground'. [1]

There is a whole school of 'forensic' readers of the New Testament, whose delight is to take the unlikeliest details in the Gospels and find modern parallels, usually from the medical schools of the United States, though not always. For those who like this sort of thing, it might be of interest to know that there is a condition known as haematidrosis, in which blood vessels rupture into the exocrine sweat gland, causing the patient literally to sweat blood. [2]

Jesus is now out of any sort of imaginable sphere. The hymn is literally true: 'we may not know, we cannot tell What pains he had to bear'. We can only watch from now onwards. The drops of bloody sweat which fall from him spring from an unimaginable agony. Perhaps they are caused more by frenzy than by fear. While the Disciples sleep, we know that there are other figures at large in Gethsemane. Another of Mark's extraneous figures drifts into the narrative quite soon; another of those figures whom the narrator does not quite know what to do with, like the man with the pitcher of water. He is the young man (*neaniskos*) wearing a shroud (*sindon*). We keep our eyes upon him because he is going to make an appearance once more before Mark's Gospel is over. It is hard to know what Mark makes of him. Professor Morton Smith, who considers that Jesus was a magician, thinks that the young man has assembled for a naked initiation rite in the garden.

Whether he had come for Baptism, or because he had heard that the End of Time was scheduled for that evening, we are never going to know. It is inevitable that scholars should seek and seek for explanations; in the last resort however, it is wrong to wish to explain everything and wrong to tie up too many loose ends. It is Gethsemane, and it is night. *En de nux*. We are in darkness. What happens in the next twelve hours will baffle us for as long as we continue to read the Gospels. We become even more puzzled if we speculate about what Jesus thought was going to happen. Few incidents in the history of mankind have been more dramatised, rehearsed, ritualised, meditated upon, and mythologised as the final twelve hours of Jesus's life, what believers call his Passion. This makes it impossible to understand on any level other than the cultic. But as the story is told

[1] Luke 22:44.
[2] See Ian Wilson: *Jesus the Evidence*, 120.

it remains the most extraordinarily vivid series of scenes. It is no surprise that so many pictures have been painted of Jesus in his agony, Jesus being arrested, Jesus before Pilate, and so forth. The Gospels give us the most vivid sense of it all, on an emotional level. It is a literary paradox, since their technique is the reverse of 'realistic', and it was largely built up by a system of Midrash, as we have seen, of commentary upon Old Testament stories. Thus, Jesus at this point in the story is understood by reference to Joseph, betrayed by his brothers, and sold into the hands of slavery Judas/Judah by his brother. We could very well wonder whether, if Joseph in Genesis had been sold into slavery by Reuben, whether the Gospels would not mysteriously have supplied Jesus with a treacherous friend called Reuben. We have already alluded to the fact that the whole of the Gethsemane episode is also a Midrash on the prophecies of Zechariah, right down to the detail, to which we must now return, of that servant of the High Priest, 'Malchus'.

Gethsemane found Jesus in an agony of anticipation. It was his hour of destiny. Piety and scholarship are silenced by this. His followers self-protectively have fallen asleep. At supper they had all professed their loyalty to him, but he had predicted that one of them would betray him. Peter had protested that though everyone else deserted Jesus, he would stand by his master. Jesus had replied that before the night was out and the cock had crowed twice, Peter would have denied him thrice. Now, in the garden, as Jesus awaits some great event, Peter was hardly able to keep awake. And then, through the olive trees, they see the lights of torches and they hear the clank of swords and armour. A posse of armed men was advancing upon them.

What happened next was a scuffle. The armed men were, according to the evangelists, sent by the chief priests to place Jesus under arrest. Judas was with them. The Synoptic Gospels tell us that Judas kissed Jesus in order to identify him to the soldiers. Luke adds the incomparable detail that Jesus said, 'Judas, betrayest thou the Son of Man with a kiss?'[1] The greatest archetype of human betrayal is encapsulated in those few words. Another of the great Gospel icons is born – the theme of countless paintings and works of art. For Dante, Judas, together with Brutus and Satan himself, becomes the very type of treachery, and confined thereby to the lowest place in

[1] Luke 22:48.

hell. As a matter of historical fact, it is hard to see how the Disciples knew that Judas had betrayed Jesus. That he was the instrument by whom Jesus was handed over to the authorities (and the word to betray in Greek means to hand over) seems likely; but he might have been the unwitting or unwilling instrument. For example, he himself might have been arrested during the time that Jesus and his other friends waited in the garden, and he might have been forced to identify Jesus. The fact that someone was needed to identify Jesus suggests that the charges on which he was being arrested were rather nebulous – as though a disturbance had been feared, and as though Jesus were suspected of being the ringleader of some outrage or seditious act. Certainly, if Jesus had been expecting that the heavens would open, and the Day of the Lord was about to dawn, he must have been hideously disappointed.

A small fight broke out. Although it was generally forbidden to bear arms at Passover time, it was (and still is) permitted to the Jews to act in self-defence during the festival. By tradition, Simon Peter drew his sword and struck at the ear of the servant of the high priest who had come to supervise Jesus's arrest. In Mark, the ear is cut off. In Luke, Jesus picks up the ear and miraculously appends it once more to the head of the High Priest's servant. Only in the Fourth Gospel is the servant given a name – Malchus, meaning the king. In an earlier part of this book, we discussed how the arrest of Jesus becomes a Midrash on the prophecy of Zechariah. It is from this prophecy also that the evangelists derived their idea that Judas had been paid thirty pieces of silver for betraying Jesus.[1] ('So they weighed for my hire, thirty pieces of silver. And the Lord said to me, cast them unto the potter,[2]' which in the Gospel becomes the story of Judas returning to the high priests, casting the thirty pieces of silver at their feet, with which they buy the piece of land known as the potter's field.)

But the High Priest's servant. Let us concentrate for a moment upon him. In my chapter on Paul, I remarked on the fact that Paul's obsession with the Cross and the Crucifixion of Jesus is nowhere explained. New Testament scholars repeat, as an axiom, that Paul and Jesus never met, without offering any suggestion as to how Paul developed this obsession. If, as I surmise, Paul, or Saul as he was

[1] Zechariah 11:4ff.
[2] Zechariah 11:12, 13.

then, had a minor but significant part in the drama of the Crucifixion itself, might not 'Malchus' be our man? In his letter to the Galatians, one of his most autobiographical letters, Paul revealed that he bore in his body 'the marks of the Lord Jesus'. [1] Some commentators have gone so far as to wonder whether Paul did not, like Francis of Assisi and many other Christian devotees, receive the mysterious marks of the stigmata, the actual wounds of crucifixion in his hands, feet and side. *Ego gar ta stigmata tou Iesou en to somati mou bastazo.*

At Paul's conversion, the mystical vision of Jesus told him, 'It is hard for thee to kick against the goad'. [2] In the vision, Jesus was both the man whom Paul was persecuting, and a man who is stabbing Paul with a sharp instrument. Nothing could be proved, but one way of reading Paul's admission to the Galatians was that he spoke the literal truth: he bore in his body wounds inflicted when he arrested Jesus. If I had the chance to return in time and meet Paul, I should take a close look at his ears.

You might say that if so important a figure as Paul was to become in Christian history had been present at Gethsemane, this would surely have been mentioned. This is not necessarily the case. To the original hearers of Mark (followers of the Pauline cult of the Cross) it could be that the phrase 'servant of the High Priest' was a phrase as readily identifiable as 'the Beloved Disciple' was to the Fourth Gospel community of believers. For subsequent generations, these phrases are impenetrably obscure. No one knows for certain who 'the Beloved Disciple' was, but it was clearly not a phrase used in the first instance to obfuscate or confuse the hearers of the Gospel. In the 1980s in Britain, the Prime Minister was so famous that she could be alluded to by kennings or phrases – 'the Iron Lady', or simply 'the Lady' or 'the Right Honourable Member for Finchley', referring to the fact that she represented the north London suburb of Finchley in Parliament. If after some disaster of war or earthquake London were destroyed, and all that survived of twentieth-century British history were a few newspaper articles, mistranscribed and then translated into another language, historians could be puzzled about their references to the Iron Lady. Some would claim that she had obviously been a mythological being, while others would suggest that some such person might conceivably have existed though

[1] Galatians 6:17.
[2] Acts 26:14.

they did not know her name. Then, one day, perhaps, archaeologists might unearth a railway-station sign-board emblazoned with the word FINCHLEY and one part of the puzzle would be solved. Finchley was, after all, a real place, even though most 'Iron Lady' scholars had persuaded themselves that it was purely imaginary.

My guess is no more than a guess; and some will say that it is a fantastical guess. But supposing that the first generation of Christians, those who were loyal to the Jewish inheritance of Jesus, perhaps, and who disliked what they heard of Paul's missionary activities, supposing that they called him 'the servant of the High Priest'; or supposing, even, that they called him 'the king', since his name, Saul, was the name of the first of the Jewish kings. 'The servant's name was the same as that of a king/*malcho*: that is, the servant's name was Saul.' If, as Acts 15 suggests, there was a fundamental rift between Peter and Paul and in their interpretation of Jesus and his message, it would make sense that his followers – those who began to compile the Synoptic tradition – should not have named Saul as having been instrumental in the downfall of Jesus. Rather, they preferred to vilify Peter as the man who was prepared to deny Jesus in his hour of greatest need.

Whatever happened during that scuffle in the dark, it ended. The soldiers knew their man. Peter, or whoever it was who attacked 'Malchus' with a sword, ran away into the darkness; so did all Jesus's other friends and followers. The soldiers grabbed hold of one other person. He was a young man, dressed like a catechumen expecting Baptism, in a shroud. The armed men grabbed this garment, but the young man shook himself free, vanishing, like everyone else in the scene, and like all the scholarly explanations for it, into the darkness. He was naked. Jesus was left alone with his captors.

X
=

# THE TRIAL

PONTIUS PILATE, THE Prefect of Judaea from 26 to 36 CE, was normally resident at the sea-port of Caesarea, where the Roman remains may be inspected to this day. At times of potential national emergency, such as festivals, it would seem that he moved, with a large number of soldiers, to Jerusalem. He probably stayed not in the Tower of Antonia at the northwest corner of the Temple area, but in the castle which had been built by Herod the Great on the western hill of Jerusalem. The knowledge that someone had been proclaimed king in Galilee at a huge gathering in the wilderness must have filled him with alarm, although Galilee was outside his immediate jurisdiction. Now he heard that Jesus the King of the Jews had reached Jerusalem. There had been a demonstration of his kingship when Jesus rode into the city at the beginning of the week on a donkey. There had been the disturbance when Jesus turned over the money-changers' tables in the Temple. Reports of what Jesus had been doing were probably confused. Some of Pilate's informers would have told him that Jesus had quarrelled with the scribes and Pharisees about questions of ritual observance. If so, such news would hardly have interested Pilate, since the Jews were always quarrelling among themselves about religious questions which, to an outsider, were wholly opaque. Others might have told Pilate that Jesus had attracted huge popularity as a miracle-worker, healer and exorcist. This was more disturbing, since no military ruler likes crowds. Where a crowd gathers, insurrectionaries flourish. Other witnesses will have told Pilate that among Jesus's followers were members of the Zealots and the *sicarii*. If so, it would not be in the least surprising if it had been Pilate himself who had arranged for the abduction of Judas. Pilate already had some Jewish patriots arrested and ready to die by crucifixion that day. There was a man who had the same name as the Galilean 'king' – Jesus Barabbas, and there were two others. To avoid any chance of rebellion or further disturbance, the Roman ruler would have had no hesitation in condemning Jesus to death.

The processes which led to Jesus's arrest, and what went on at his trial – whether in the strict sense he had a trial at all – are matters which will remain forever hidden from the historian. The followers of Jesus, from whose testimony, presumably, the early traditions arose which led in turn to the formation of the Gospels, were, by their own confession, in hiding from the moment of Jesus's arrest, though one or two of them followed him at a sheepish distance. None of Jesus's family or followers was present while he was being interrogated, and we are not told that any of them spoke to Jesus again until he was crucified. It follows that all the Gospels must have invented the trial scenes, and that there is very little in them which could be treated as historical. The only hard historical fact which we possess is that Jesus was crucified: that is to say, he was condemned by the Romans, and this is a fact which the early Christian Church, themselves fearful of persecution from the Romans, did their best to obscure. They therefore blamed the death of Jesus on the Jews, invented the idea that Jesus had been condemned by the Jews for blasphemy, or for plotting to destroy the Temple. By the Gospel accounts, Pontius Pilate is no more than a bureaucrat, almost genial, unwilling to condemn Jesus, but urged on to do so by the seething malice of the chief priests and other Sadducean leaders. Such a distortion of history would not have been so serious had it not been used as an excuse for two thousand years of Christian anti-Semitism. Even so benign a witness as Ernest Renan in his *La Vie de Jésus* can blame the Jews, not merely for the death of Jesus, but also for all the subsequent eighteen hundred years of religious persecutions exacted by the Christian Church. '*Le christianisme a été intolérant; mais l'intolérance n'est pas un fait essentiellement chrétien. C'est un fait juif.*'[1]

Having admitted that the Gospel-narratives must be treated with circumspection, however, it would be careless to dismiss them altogether. There appear to be three strands of Gospel tradition about the last hours of Jesus, those of the Fourth Gospel, of Luke and of Matthew and Mark. Of these only the Fourth Gospel makes any claim to material based on eye-witness accounts. Having isolated these different traditions, the historian must decide how they might

[1] E. Renan: *La Vie de Jésus*, 342.

legitimately be used. The criterion which I adopt is a simple one. How much could any of this evidence, plausibly, and by its own standards, be based on first- or even second-hand accounts? Episodes in the Passion-narratives which fail this rather generous test must be dismissed at the outset as unhistorical. I have therefore tabulated the accounts before making any comment upon them. In the appended table,[1] and in the discussion which follows, M. stands for the Mark/Matthew tradition; L. stands for Luke and J. for the Fourth Gospel.

What can we make of this evidence? From the moment when Peter denied Jesus in the courtyard of the High Priest to the moment when Jesus appeared, having been tortured by the Roman soldiers, arrayed like a parody of a king, wearing a purple robe and a crown of thorns, we know nothing. We can deduce certain probabilities from the meagre evidence which survives. Some of this evidence is negative. Peter, James and John were not arrested by the Romans. If they had been in any way implicated in a plot or an armed insurrection against the Romans, we can be perfectly certain that they would have been rounded up and executed. All the Gospels suggest that there were those present at the Supper who did not share Jesus's full range of acquaintanceship in Jerusalem. The sources on which the Gospels are based did not know, for example, who those men were who provided the donkey for the triumphal entry into Jerusalem. They did not know exactly how, in that overcrowded city, Jesus managed to secure a large upper room furnished for the Supper. Nor did they know on what charges Jesus was arraigned before Pilate, nor the reason why he was condemned to death. As we read the Gospels, it would seem that Jesus was crucified among strangers; but that is merely because the evangelists did not know, or did not choose to tell us, who the *lestai* were alongside whom Jesus was crucified. *Lestai* were bandits, political terrorists.

Having tabulated the Gospel accounts and compared them, what does the historian find that they can tell him?

All the Gospels agree that after his arrest, Jesus was taken to the house of the High Priest. They differ about who took him there. We can discount L.'s claim that the high priests themselves went to fetch Jesus from the Garden of Gethsemane on the grounds of sheer improbability. M. is vague and merely says that it was a number of

---

[1] See appendix One.

men who arrested Jesus. J. alone is specific about the identity of the guard itself: they were the *huperetai*, or constables of the court, backed up by a *speira* under the command of a *chiliarchos*. That is, they were Roman soldiers, a cohort under the command of a tribune, accompanied by Sanhedrin police. There is no need to suppose that the whole cohort came out to arrest Jesus. But the use of the word *speira* by J. at this point, particularly with the definite article ('the cohort', rather as Londoners might speak of 'the Guard', referring to that regiment of soldiers on duty to protect the Queen on a particular day), authenticates the detail. There was a garrisoning arrangement at the Tower of Antonia during festivals. 'The usual crowd had assembled at Jerusalem for the Feast of Unleavened Bread, and the Roman cohort [*he speira*] had taken up its position on the roof of the portico of the Temple; for a body of men invariably mounts guard at the feasts to prevent disorders from such a concourse of people.' So we read in Josephus.[1] In all three Gospel traditions, we read of Jesus's surprise at the guard. He asks them if they suppose he is one of the political terrorists, the *lestai*, that they should have arranged a full military arrest. Clearly, from a later moment in the narrative, when it is revealed that Jesus Barabbas had been guilty of a murder in 'the uprising'[2] (what uprising?), as had the other two *lestai* who were crucified alongside Jesus of Nazareth, we see that the Romans had not been slow to arrest Jews whom they suspected, at precisely this moment, of being involved in a plot. Jesus must have been implicated in this plot, as far as the Romans were concerned; but they cannot have reached this conclusion without the connivance or advice of the high priests.

In the passage relating to Jesus's interrogation at the house of the High Priest, it is once again J. who is specific while the other two witnesses are vague. J. provides us with a reason for this. 'The other disciple', one of the eye-witnesses who contributes to J.'s narrative, was known to the High Priest.[3] This is of the greatest significance, since neither of the other witnesses, M. nor L., can claim to have been near Jesus at this stage of the night. While the Jewish authorities are interrogating Jesus, we are allowed to overhear a scene which in its simple and poignant way is unique in the literature of the ancient

[1] *Jewish War*, 2:224, quoted Robinson, 241.
[2] Mark 15:7.
[3] John 18:15.

world: Peter's denial.[1] A crowd had collected in the courtyard, where fires were burning against the intense cold, and Peter stood among them to warm himself. In Mark, it is a servant-girl who recognises him. She said, 'Thou also was with the Nazarene, even Jesus. But he denied, saying, I neither know, nor understand what thou sayest: and he went out into the porch; and the cock crew. And the maid saw him, and began again to say to them that stood by, This is one of them. But again he denied it. And after a little while again, they that stood by said to Peter, Of a truth thou art one of them; for thou art a Galilean. But he began to curse, and to swear, I know not this man of whom ye speak. And straightway the cock crew. And Peter called to mind the word, how that Jesus said unto him, Before the cock crow twice, thou shalt deny me thrice. And when he thought thereon, he wept.'[2]

In J., it is perhaps significant that the person taunting Peter is not the maidservant but our old acquaintance, the 'servant of the High Priest', but that I merely note in passing. This is not the moment for riding hobby- horses. No one reading that story can fail to be moved by it. In a passage already quoted,[3] a great literary historian establishes the uniqueness of the incident on the grounds that it fits no existing genre: it is neither strictly tragic, nor comic, nor biographical as the ancients would have understood these categories. Nor is it theological. The most painstaking attempt to make every word of the Gospels into a Midrash on the Old Testament would have difficulty here, and since it adds nothing to what we might be expected, as convert readers of the Gospels, to believe about Jesus, we must assume that in broad outline, this part of the story is true. It has, moreover, the powerful narrative effect of distracting our attention from the matter in hand: what was passing between Jesus and the High Priest.

M., which does not even claim to be based on eye-witness accounts, provides an elaborate narrative of a 'trial' before the High

---

[1] See E. Auerbach: *Mimesis: The Representation of Reality in Western Literature* (ET 1953), 45. 'A scene like Peter's denial fits into no ancient genre. It is too serious for comedy, too contemporary and everyday for tragedy, politically too insignificant for history – and the form which was given it is one of such immediacy that its like does not exist in the literature of antiquity. This can be judged by a symptom which at first glance may seem insignificant: the use of direct discourse. . . I do not believe that there is a single passage in an antique historian where direct discourse is employed in this fashion in a brief direct dialogue' (quoted Robinson, 245).
[2] Mark 14:67–72.
[3] Auerbach, footnote 1.

Priest. It culminates (in Matthew) with the High Priest tearing his robes at the 'blasphemy' of Jesus. The blasphemy seems to have consisted in two pieces of evidence from 'false witnesses': first, the claim that Jesus had promised to destroy the Temple and rebuild it in three days, and, secondly, the identification of himself with the 'Son of Man' in Daniel's prophecies. These ideas – that Jesus in some spiritual sense has 'rebuilt the Temple' and that he is 'the Son of Man' whom we can expect to come on the clouds on the Day of the Lord – are of course Christian ones. They come from the world of belief which produced Matthew's and Mark's Gospels, and it may well be that in some synagogue where they were first aired, a rabbi denounced them as blasphemous. Actually, in the strict sense of the word, it is hard to see that they are blasphemous. As we have already observed, it was not blasphemous to believe that you were the Messiah, even if the religious authorities did not share your belief; and there are many cases of the Sanhedrin *not* condemning the deluded false Christs who, inevitably, surfaced from time to time in the turbulent world of first-century Judaism. So, even if the 'trial' before the High Priest and the Sanhedrin took place, it is less than probable that Jesus was arraigned for blasphemy. In fact, one cannot easily believe that such a 'trial' took place at all. It is inherently improbable that the whole Sanhedrin, or even a significant quota of Sanhedrin members, would have been summoned from their beds in the middle of the night for a sort 'show trial'. If Jesus was supposed to have committed a serious offence against religious law, there would have been a long and elaborate trial. It would have been much too important a matter to rush through in the middle of the night when everyone was tired. Neither M. nor L. know anything about Jewish legal procedures; and modern scholarly debates about the nature of the trial before the Sanhedrin ignore this very simple point. In J., by contrast, there is no 'trial' before the High Priest. Jesus is merely examined by the High Priest, slapped in the face for his impertinence to his interrogator, and handed over to Pilate.

This is something which we can well believe took place. It is clear from Josephus that the Jewish rulers, and in particular the chief priests, mediated between the Romans and the populace. They were held responsible by the Romans for outbreaks of civil disturbance.[1] If 'King Jesus' was in fact going to start a rebellion, or a riot, Pilate

---

[1] See Sanders: op. cit., 314–315 which gives several examples from Josephus of the Sanhedrin being held responsible by the Romans for rounding up those responsible for political insurrections.

would certainly have come to the chief priests and asked them why their police had not known about it; why they had not acted upon it, arrested the ring-leader and handed him over to the proper authorities. Josephus is full of examples of buck-passing. Florus was insulted by some member of the Jewish populace, and insisted that the chief priests and the powerful Jews (*dunatoi*) find the culprit and bring him to justice. [1] The leaders replied that it would be impossible to find the culprits. The Romans therefore took reprisals. They entered the market, massacred a large number of the populace, and dragged off some token culprits to be crucified. After this action, the chief priests implored the crowds not to do anything to provoke the anger of the Procurator.

It is in this terrifying context that one must read the 'trial' of Jesus. Christian tradition sees it as a grand theological event in which the Incarnate God is walking among the blasphemous Jews who do not know his identity and yet are also meant to be blamed throughout eternity for his death, even though this death brought salvation to the world. (Quite a number of contradictions there! Since the Jews plainly did not know that Jesus was the Messiah, why should they be blamed for their ignorance; and since his death was supposed, in Christian terms, to have removed the sins of the world, it seems perverse to blame the alleged, if unwitting, instruments of this deliverance.) To those involved in the interrogation of Jesus at the time, none of these questions would have been uppermost in the mind. What would have mattered would have been the question of whether Jesus constituted a threat to public safety and order.

It would not even have mattered whether he was involved in a plot to lead a rebellion or not. The point was a crowd had proclaimed him king; he had ridden through the streets of Jerusalem and attracted the crowds once again. There had been some sort of demonstration at the Temple – something to do with the money-changers. This was enough for wishing to arrest Jesus and if necessary give him to the Romans as a scapegoat.

There can be no doubt that the authorities regarded Jesus as guilty of a capital offence. Whether they had decided this before they arrested Jesus, or whether they decided the matter during the interrogation at the High Priest's house, we have no means of knowing. The Jews themselves had no power, under the Roman administration, to

[1] *Jewish War*, 11:305.

execute their prisoners. Even the Romans themselves could not easily carry out the death sentence under law. This was a power reserved to the supreme governors. [1] It was therefore necessary, if Jesus had committed, or was believed to have committed, a capital offence, that he should have been brought before Pontius Pilate.

It is at this point in the story that Matthew tells us of the death of Judas Iscariot. It is safe to dismiss every word of this story as legendary. None of the disciples, by their own account, knew why Judas had left the Supper, and none of them can possibly have been present at the time when Judas was supposedly accepting bribes from the High Priest, and then returning with the thirty pieces of silver and throwing them at the High Priest's feet. The story grows directly out of the prophecies of Zechariah who tells us of the breaking of the brotherhood between Judas and Israel. 'And the Lord said unto me, Cast it unto the potter, the goodly price that I was prised at of them. And I took the thirty pieces of silver, and cast them unto the potter in the house of the Lord.' [2] In Matthew, the chief priests use the thirty pieces of silver to buy the potter's field, which is known 'to this day' as the field of blood. The one small detail in the story which could, conceivably, be true is that of Judas's suicide; but perhaps he killed himself in order to avoid torture and crucifixion rather than out of remorse for a 'betrayal' of which he was very likely innocent.

We now come to the 'trial' of Jesus before Pilate, which all witnesses agree happened first thing in the morning. Once again, J. is rich in plausible historical details which the other two strands of witness lack. It has the detail that Jesus was led to the Praetorium, but that the priests would not follow him, for fear of being defiled. Pilate had to come out to them and hear their complaints. The priests told Pilate that if Jesus were not a criminal they would not be handing him over. As happens in several cases in Josephus, the Roman governor tries to pass the buck. It is a religious matter, why could not the Jews try to sort it out among themselves? In L., we have the possibly authentic detail that when Pilate discovered Jesus was a Galilean he tried to hand him over for trial to Herod, the Galilean tetrarch. We feel in these exchanges the supreme and electrifying fear of the situation. What, exactly, was happening – the exact details of

[1] A. N. Sherwin-White: 'The Trial of Christ' in D. E. Nineham *et al: Historicity and Chronology in the New Testament* (1965), 108.
[2] Zechariah 11:13, 14.

the feared uprising or plot – we shall never know. But the Jews fear a Roman reprisal, so they bring their scapegoat before Pilate. But the Roman Procurator in his turn feels fear. If they are asking him to punish a 'King of the Jews', does this mean that he is being asked to put down a popular leader? Will there be an uprising, with all its consequent bloodshed?

The Fourth Gospel at this point, outside the Praetorium, creates one of those grandly dramatic exchanges which is so powerful that we do not care whether or not it is historically plausible. The representative of the empire, in the person of the Procurator, confronts a ragamuffin victim of a chaotic situation. To Pilate, the internal squabbles of the Jews must have seemed incomprehensible. His only concern at this moment is to draw that delicate line between asserting his authority and, by overstepping the mark, exciting worse violence than he has quelled. And before him stand the querulous priests with their prisoner. The charge: that he has made himself into a king.

'Art thou the King of the Jews?' asked Pilate. To which Jesus replied, 'My kingdom is not of this world'. [1] If the historical Jesus said words such as these, he must have meant, at last in part, that his kingdom was not now, but to come; that his kingdom, the Messianic kingdom when all Israel would enjoy the rule of the saints, was nothing to do with the present *saeculum*. But of course this is one of those great moments in the Fourth Gospel where the central figure says something so grandly memorable that it is lifted entirely out of its historical context and becomes an archetype. The representatives of religious and secular power in this world – the priests and the Procurator – would appear to have this man exactly where they want him. But, in fact, he calmly announces that their power is all illusory, that for those who follow him in spirit and in truth, such manifestations of human authority will always seem fantastical, and even in their most terrifying manifestations, absurd. *My kingdom is not of this world.* It was with this text written in his heart that Tolstoy could undermine the imperial authority of the Tsars, just as Mahatma Gandhi, fed on such Tolstoyan books as *The Kingdom of God is within You*, could overthrow the might of the British Raj. In countless less dramatic ways the essential anarchy of Christ, as he is depicted in the Fourth Gospel, has woven through history a loose thread. Only a very few tugs can make the neat tapestries of Christendom come

[1] John 18:35.

unstuck. This icon, of the ragamuffin before the Roman governor, destroys them. The empires and churches and papacies which have been established in Christ's name are all revealed to be ridiculous by this text. Pilate probably crucified thousands of men, not just hundreds. The numbers of innocent who have stood before procurators, inquisitors, interrogation officers since must run into millions. Jesus establishes this strange icon: not that the powerful have no power. They have the power to torture and kill and destroy: but that there is another kingdom, of whose existence they are unaware and which is ultimately stronger.

It is at this stage of the story that we are told of the custom – mentioned by no Jewish historian or writer outside the New Testament – that at the Feast of the Passover the Romans were used to providing a minor amnesty by releasing to the populace a prisoner. In J., we are to imagine a negotiation about this matter taking place on the steps of the Praetorium. In M., absurdly, there is a huge crowd, all being asked their opinion of this delicate matter by Pilate himself. Since the Romans took every pain to quell civil disturbances, it is highly improbable that either the chief priests (as in M.) or Pilate himself would have allowed the mob to decide. It may very well be, however, that this story of the mob enshrines one particular truth, namely that the priests and Pilate both *feared* the mob. Barabbas was not a robber, as in our familiar Bible translation, but a political terrorist. As Mark tells us, he had committed a murder during 'the uprising' – an event to which this Gospel casually alludes, but which must have been of supreme importance at the time. If the crowds could be pacified by the release of Jesus Barabbas, they could perhaps be cowed into submission by a cruel public display of what happens to Jews who use words like 'kingdom', *basileia*, empire, to the Roman governor. Having made his decision to make an example of Jesus, Pilate and the Romans did it in cruelly sadistic style. Jesus was scourged, a common enough punishment, and then led off to be tortured by the Roman soldiers.

It is probably reasonable to assume that this was happening in Herod's palace, rather than in the Antonia. The archaeologists think that the palace was built with an esplanade, a *lithostrotos*, a word which Josephus uses for this pavement outside the residence, and which the Fourth Gospel tells us was called *gabbatha* in the Hebrew tongue. It was on to this pavement that Pilate caused to be set up a tableau of horrifying savagery. We are so conditioned by two thousand years of Christian art to think that the Jews would somehow have enjoyed this display, that we sometimes forget what it must actually have been like to be a Jew in 30 CE and to witness the charade which followed. The Romans had set up a stage outside the palace of Herod, more or less next door to the Temple. Pilate sat there, surrounded, presumably, by his guard in great numbers. Jesus was then produced for the crowd. 'And Pilate saith unto them, behold the Man!'[1] He had been tortured and beaten. The soldiers had plaited a crown of thorns and rammed it on to his head, and they had arrayed him in a purple robe of kingship. Pilate then asked the Jews whether they wished him to crucify their king. 'The chief priests answered we have no king but Caesar.'[2] This is often cited as an example of terrible cynicism. But, like so many of the exchanges in this chapter of the Fourth Gospel, there is an archetypical quality to it which echoes and reverberates in history. The timorous abbots and abbesses who did not risk martyrdom, and who were prepared to sign their allegiance to Henry VIII, would have understood the chief priests' dilemma; so would the mayors and petty officials and army officers in Lithuania, Latvia, Siberia if it was suggested to them that they should stand up for their own local interests rather than submit to Stalin. 'We have no king but Caesar.' Many in France and Belgium echoed the words during 1940–44. Better that a few should die horrible deaths at the hands of Caesar than that thousands should be exterminated in 'reprisals' for acts of national heroism.

The Gospels represent the priests and Jesus as being on opposite sides in this 'trial' tableau, but once Pilate has entered the scene this is not the case. It is a story of the Jews versus the Romans. In order to save their skin, the Jews found a scapegoat. It was expedient that one man should die for the people. Jesus was, in this sense, selected as a 'saviour' of his race. Pilate was not content to accept the scapegoat without having a little fun at the Jews' expense. 'Who did you say that your king was?' 'Caesar, Caesar!' And what is this person – this wreck – this figure with bleeding temples and a bedraggled purple robe? What is he? Look at him! Behold the man! The Jews have been looking at many such figures ever since. With tragic irony, we can see that Jesus was never more truly the representative of his race than

[1] John 19:5.
[2] John 19:15.

when he was being tortured and killed. This, quite as much as the burden of God-bearing conscience, has been the destiny of the Jews in history – to be tortured and killed for reasons which neither they nor their persecutors fully understand.

We do not know who else has been arrested during the night, nor why, exactly, the Romans have fixed on Jesus as the man whom they will make into their example. According to the Gospels, the Romans do not know themselves. It just seems like a good idea. Christian traditionalists say that none of Jesus's followers were arrested and that this proves beyond doubt that Jesus was not guilty of any political involvement. If the Twelve had actually been a political terrorist organisation, the Romans would have had no compunction about rounding them all up and crucifying them in a row. While this is indisputable, the truth is that we do not know, and nor do the Gospels appear to know, exactly who Jesus's friends were, nor exactly what he thought he was doing during the last Passover of his life. Mark and Matthew do not know who the providers of the donkey were. The man with the pitcher of water is as obscure as the naked boy. We know that they were on the scene, but the Gospels tell us nothing about them, probably because the Gospel tradition *knew* nothing about them.

As I have already said, the traditional explanation for the death of Judas is not necessarily the right one. He might have been implicated in a betrayal of Jesus; but it is just as likely that he hanged himself to avoid a worse fate at the hands of the Romans. The evangelists did not know everyone involved in this story. Or, if they had done, it would hardly have been in the Christian interest to point it out. The Christians were terrified of Roman persecution. If there were a body of oral tradition which suggested that Jesus mixed with terrorists, it would have been ironed out of the written accounts. We do not know for certain that the *lestai*, the political terrorists who were crucified alongside Jesus, were strangers. For all we know, they might have been as close to him as Peter, James and John. After the horrific parade on the Praetorium, of Jesus as a mock king, the Gospels tell us that Jesus was compelled to drag his own cross to the place of execution.

M. and L. say that Jesus was helped to carry his cross by Simon, the father of Rufus and Alexander (M.), evidently two persons known to the M. Church at least by reputation. Possibly the Rufus is the same member of the Roman Church to whom Paul alludes in his letter to that community.[1] J. alone is specific about the Hebrew name of the place – Golgotha, the place of the skull. (Actual Hebrew *Gulgoleth*, Aramaic *Gulgulta*.)

We do not know exactly where, in Jerusalem, this was. Eusebius, the fourth-century ecclesiastical historian, was present, as a boy, in the year 336 CE, when the Holy Sepulchre and the site of Golgotha were 'discovered' by Bishop Macarius of Jerusalem. They were beneath a Temple of Venus which had been erected by the Romans after the desecration of the city in 70 CE. Beneath this temple, there was a tomb, or sacred cave, and when the Empress Helena found out about it, she lost no time, with the assistance of her fellow Christians, in finding the True Cross, and the Crown of Thorns, and the spear with which the side of Christ was pierced. From 336 CE onwards, those who venerate the Crucified Christ have done so in the spot where Macarius found his Calvary; but Macarius was not an archaeologist, and there is absolutely no reason to associate the present site in the Church of the Holy Sepulchre with the place where Jesus died. We are told that Jesus was crucified outside the city walls. Kathleen Kenyon's excavations in the 1950s revealed that the present Church of the Holy Sepulchre, former Temple of Aphrodite, would in fact have been outside the city walls in the time of Jesus. This was not information known a hundred years ago. The Macarius Calvary is now visibly within the (mediaeval) city walls, which is what led nineteenth-century archaeologists and romantics to go in search of other Calvaries. By far the most impressive is that favoured by General Gordon, the hero of Khartoum. It lies just outside the Damascus Gate of the present-day Old City. If you stand just beneath the bus station there, you can see a hill which is called (or was this Arabs being wise after the event to impress the tourists?) the Place of the Skull. It is a rocky little hill, where the holes in the bare stone make a distinct skull-face – two cavities for the eyes, and so on. Moreover, hard by, there is a garden, in which archaeologists found a first-century tomb which, even if it is not the tomb in which the body of Jesus was lain after crucifixion, must resemble that tomb. The Gordon Calvary and tomb attract us because they look right; that is to say, they look like nineteenth-century watercolour illustrations to Bible stories.

In 1968, in the course of the Giv'at ha-Mivtar excavations, one of

[1] Romans 16:13.

the ossuaries was found to discover the skeleton of a man who had been crucified. He was a male in his mid–twenties, who had a cleft palate. His heel–bones were pierced and joined together by a single large nail, seventeen centimetres long. His name was Jehohanan. In order to append his body to the upper part of the cross without the weight of his body ripping his hands, or causing asphyxiation by pressure on the lungs, both wrists were nailed to either end of the cross–beam. It would appear that in order to stay alive on the cross (and some victims are known to have survived for as long as three days) the weight of the body had to be allowed to rest on the legs. Once the legs were broken, death followed almost automatically. Jehohanan had his legs brutally smashed. This would appear to have been a concession by the Romans to Jewish ritual custom, since it was contrary to their law for a body to be left dying on a cross after sundown.

The 1968 discovery gave further reason to suppose that J. does contain a considerable body of plausible historical material. There is nothing incompatible between J.'s description of the Crucifixion of Jesus and the archaeologists' speculations about the crucifixion of Jehohanan. Over the Cross of Jesus, Pilate caused the *causa poenae* to be affixed. This was a common part of Roman punishment, that a criminal would be compelled to have a charge sheet.[1] J. tells us that the chief priests complained to Pilate about the wording of this trilingual inscription. In three languages – Latin, Greek and Hebrew – Pilate had caused to be written over the Cross: JESUS OF NAZA-RETH KING OF THE JEWS. Trying to maintain their dignity in a situation which was obviously calculated, by Pilate, to humiliate them, they went to Pilate and said that he should have written, 'This man said that he was King of the Jews'. Pilate's briefly insulting reply – 'What I have written, I have written'[2] – is full of Johannine ironies. 'We' know that what Pilate has written is true, even though neither he nor the 'Jews' are aware of the secret. Jesus is indeed the King of the New Israel. In history, as opposed to theology, it would seem much likelier that this *causa poenae* must have seemed like a routine piece of insult to the Jews. 'Let this be a warning to any Jew who thinks that he can start a *basileia* not of this world, or a kingdom independent of the Roman Empire.' The crassness of the inscription

---

[1] Suetonius: *Caligula* xxxii:2; *Domitian* x:1; Dio Cassius: *Histories* 54:3–7, quoted in Harvey: *Jesus and the Constraints of History*, 13.
[2] John 19:22.

is something which even J., for all his sense of irony, does not truly
exploit.

All the Gospels mention that the Roman soldiers cast lots for
Jesus's clothes when he had been nailed to the Cross. This is a reference to Psalm 22 (verse 18), one of the most desolated poems in the
Bible, and one which all the evangelists draw upon to convey the
absolute degradation and horror of the scene. 'They part my garments among them, And upon my vesture do they cast lots.' J. goes
into more detail than M. or L. about this, and tells us [1] that Jesus
had worn a seamless robe, woven in one piece from neck to hem.
This extraneous piece of information suggests that Jesus had been
wearing clothes which were worth something. When put together
with the archaeological excavations at Capernaum of a villa of substance where Jesus lived, and the grandeur of the figure who emerged
after the death of Jesus to bury his body, this suggests that he
was very far from being a pauper, which adds considerable pathos
to the fact that he was compelled to die the death of a rebellious
slave.

Christian devotion to the vulnerable figure of Jesus on the Cross
did not begin until a thousand years after the Crucifixion. Anselm,
the Archbishop of Canterbury from 1093–1109, was one of the first
devotional writers to dwell on the pathos of the scene. Crucifixes,
that is to say, representations of a dying, vulnerable young man on
the Cross, are of mediaeval origin. The Byzantine way of conveying
the meaning of Calvary was to depict Christ in triumph, robed and
crowned on the Cross like a high priest.

The reality of the scene must have been one of unspeakable nasti-
ness, no less horrific for the fact that it was such a familiar sight in
the Roman Empire. It is customary for authors of lives of Jesus
to apostrophise him at this terrible moment. Even when they are
non-Christians, or ex-Christians, they have been so programmed to
sing hymns to the Crucifix that they cannot resist saying something
florid about this terrible spectacle, either by sensationalising its gorier
aspects, or by sentimentalising and softening the figure of Jesus in
his suffering. [2] It is refreshing to return to the reticent eloquence of
the Gospels which entirely lack this vulgarity.

L. names no witnesses, but he introduces us to the figure of the

---

[1] John 19:24.
[2] See Renan: 'Sa tête s'inclina sur sa poitrine, et il expira. Repose maintenant dans ta gloire, noble
initiateur. Ton oeuvre est achevée' etc. etc., 351.

Penitent Thief, crucified alongside Jesus. He is the last of the Lucan penitents, and his prayer – 'Lord, remember me when thou comest into thy kingdom'[1] – has understandably become one of the great prayers of Christendom, repeated endlessly in the liturgy of the Orthodox Church. M. names witnesses to the scene – Mary of Magdala, Mary the Mother of James and Joses and Salome. We notice that the family of Jesus has reappeared, after an absence which has endured throughout his 'ministry'. J., who insists that he is writing an eye-witness account of the scene, has two poignant exchanges between Jesus and those who stand at the foot of his Cross. One, a Midrash on Psalm 22:15, and a deliberate echo of the scene between Jesus at Jacob's Well with the woman of Samaria, has him saying, 'I thirst'.[2] Vinegar is put on a sponge and held to his lips on the end of a long pole. J. also has the scene in which Jesus speaks to his mother, and entrusts her to the protection of the 'Beloved Disciple'. How much these 'words from the Cross' represent historical memories and how far they are pious legends, we shall never know. They are not inherently improbable. It would seem as though Jesus, who had been estranged from his family at the beginning of the Gospels, was effecting a reconciliation with them at the end. This would be of small interest to those churches which produced the M. and L. traditions, which were probably far in time and place from any of Jesus's immediate family in the Jerusalem 'Church'. In J., Jesus dies after the vinegar has been thrust into his mouth. In L. he dies with a pious prayer on his lips from Psalm 31 – 'Into thy hands I commend my spirit'. It is in Matthew that the commentary on Psalm 22 continues to the end, with Jesus shrieking out the opening verse of the psalm – 'Eli, Eli, lama sabachtani', 'My God, my God, why hast thou forsaken me?' It is the most dramatic of the four accounts of Jesus's death, and for that reason it is the most haunting. Schweitzer said that Jesus was crucified for the sake of his parables. He meant that the Jewish religious authorities resented the liberality of Jesus's view of God, and the implied disrespect for the Torah which is shown in such stories as the Prodigal Son and the Publican and the Pharisee praying in the Temple. Schweitzer could not have literally believed that Jesus was crucified because of the parables. Another Midrash one could weave through

[1] Luke 23:42.
[2] John 19:28.

Matthew's use of the desolate psalm as the last words of Jesus would lead in a more devastating direction still. We could say that Jesus, in his passivity, defied not only Pilate, and the chief priests, but God himself. Jesus had come into the world and told the Jews that God was a Heavenly Father who loved his children as Jesus loved children. Jesus had blessed children in his arms. He had healed them from illness, and even appeared to have raised them from the dead – restoring the young man of Nain to his widowed mother and the damsel to her grieving father Jairus. Jesus had healed the blind and the lame and the deaf and the deranged. He had foretold the coming of a kingdom of love, which would be brought into being by an apocalyptic fanfare when God would show his true nature, which was love. Then, every tear would be wiped from the eye, and the lion would lie down with the lamb, and Israel would be restored in peace and unity. Until that time, it would be legitimate, we must logically conclude, to suppose that something was amiss with the world. Since Jesus did not know anything about St Paul's doctrine of Original Sin, he would not have found it very convincing that the only thing wrong was the wickedness of the human heart. He had specifically dismissed the idea that a man had been born blind because of his own sin, or that of his parents. There is only one who would be held responsible for the sheer cruelty and unhappiness of the universe and that would be, if such a being existed, its creator. The life and death of Jesus can be seen as the ultimate declaration of monotheistic faith, of faith that is to say not merely in a God who created the world but who sustains it and loves it. The rabbis in the concentration camps put God on trial, and found him guilty, for human wickedness itself was not enough to justify or explain the horror of the Holocaust. Jesus had put his trust in God and had assumed that the Day of the Lord would come, bringing justice to the poor, and healing to innocent suffering. He had put himself in the position of the poorest of the poor, making himself a slave to all, in that last ritual gesture at supper among his friends, the girding himself with the towel and washing his Disciples' feet. His reward had been arrest, torture and public humiliation. He had prayed for the Kingdom to come, and it had not come. If he did not utter the first verse of Psalm 22 as he hung on the cross, then he justifiably might have done. *My God, my God, why hast thou forsaken me?*

Jesus was alive on the Cross until the ninth hour, that is to say until three o'clock in the afternoon. M. and L. state that from the sixth hour until the ninth, darkness fell upon the land, and it has generally been assumed that Jesus only lasted three hours before dying. If so, there would be nothing very surprising in this. If the Gospel accounts give an even faintly accurate account of his last days, he must have been near to exhaustion and collapse even before his arrest. He had found himself being made into the figurehead of a great popular movement, and had done his best to escape the crowds in Galilee. In Jerusalem they had surged back, and he had undertaken his triumphal journey on the donkey. Perhaps he had not slept all week. In Gethsemane it is said that he was sweating blood; and after this experience he was taken away for a night's interrogation and torture. Although there are cases of crucifixion lasting for as long as three days, many of the victims must have died sooner. It would only have taken a torn ligament in the angle through which the big nail was hammered to ensure a collapse of the whole body, and death by asphyxiation. Some have speculated that the vinegar on the sponge contained some drug; and, perhaps needless to say, there have been suggestions that it contained, not a deadly narcotic, but some substance which merely put the body to sleep before its 'resurrection'. Such speculation is the stuff of which detective stories are made, but by far the likeliest explanation is that Jesus died on the Cross after a short time. J. contains the authentic detail (which is exactly what we should expect since the excavation of the skeleton of Jehohanan) that, as the day drew to a close, the soldiers came around among the crosses, thinking to break the legs of the crucified so that they could be buried before sundown in accordance with Jewish custom. We are told that when they came to Jesus, they found him dead already. Instead of breaking his legs, the soldier pierced his side with a spear, and there gushed out what seemed like a combination of blood and water.

After the death of Jesus, M. tells us that there were a series of paranormal happenings in Jerusalem. The veil of the Temple, separating the Inner Sanctum, the Holy of Holies, from the rest of the congregation of Israel, was torn, symbolising the destruction of Judaism, and the opening up of access between man and God by the atoning death of Jesus. In anticipation of his own forthcoming triumph over death, several tombs opened, and the dead walked the streets of Jerusalem, rather as the 'sheeted dead did squeak and gibber in the Roman streets' on the eve of Julius Caesar's assassination. It is interesting that these fascinating phenomena are not described by any other historian of the period and that L. and J. neglect to mention them.

It is desirable, in Jewish Law, for anyone who dies to be buried before sundown. Perhaps it was an added source of grief to Jesus's mother and brothers that he could not be buried in Galilee, but help was at hand, when they undertook the gruesome business of taking the dead body down from the Cross. J. tells us that this task was undertaken by the rich member of the Sanhedrin who had come to see Jesus by night 'for fear of the Jews' – Nicodemus – and his friend Joseph of Arimathea, whom tradition states to have been Jesus's cousin. L. and M. both have the tradition that Joseph of Arimathea buried Jesus. In M. Joseph approached Pilate, asking his permission to bury Jesus, and Pilate was astonished that his young prisoner should have died so soon.

It is clear, from his connection at the end with Joseph of Arimathea, Nicodemus, and such as these, that Jesus had acquaintance, if not close associates in Jerusalem who did not necessarily have much to do with his Galilean fishing-friends. Joseph, we are told, was a rich man, who had a tomb cut into a rock, where no body had yet been lain. J. tells us that this tomb was in a garden not far from the place where Jesus was crucified. It is a strange fact that, although popular Christianity should have depicted Jesus as having been hounded to his death by 'the Jews', and persecuted for his opposition to the religious hierarchy of his day, he should actually have been buried and anointed by two of the most senior members of the Jewish Sanhedrin – just such people as Jesus's brother James, and the early 'Christians' in Jerusalem, who were 'continually in the Temple' after Jesus's death. In J., they anoint the body for burying and place him in the tomb, cut in a rock. In M. and L., the women anoint the body with ointment and in M. alone, a stone is rolled across the entrance of the tomb.

To recapitulate very briefly: no real evidence can be found for Jesus's arrest and execution. It would seem impossible that he was tried for blasphemy, and it is almost certain that he was not tried by the Sanhedrin. The chief priests might well have been those responsible for handing Jesus over to Pilate as a potential trouble-maker. Pilate might (L.) or might not (M.J.) have wished to hand this Galilean over to Herod Antipas for examination (Galilee being within Herod's jurisdiction). Since Jesus once called Herod an old fox, we could perhaps surmise that if this stage of the 'trial' did take place, then Jesus's chances of acquittal were very much reduced. Jesus's family had by now returned to the scene. We have not met them since his early quarrels with them in Galilee. They witnessed his death, and perhaps the man who arranged for his burial, Joseph of Arimathea, had some family connection with Jesus. He was buried in accordance with Jewish ritual tradition. It was either on the evening, or the eve of the Passover.

Any reader who has followed the story thus far must realise how difficult it is to sift the evidence offered us by the Gospels concerning the life and death of Jesus. As we have repeatedly discovered, the evangelists were not attempting neutral *reportage* (if there is such a thing) and the death of Jesus was, for them, so full of religious significance that they inevitably chose to tell the story by reference to the Jewish Scriptures. They wrote in the certainty that the death of Jesus was no ordinary death. The experience of their shared faith in Jesus and his teachings made them feel that every event during those gruesome last twelve hours of Jesus's life was charged with theological meaning. For M. and L. there is a vivid sense of weakness and pathos and agony in the tortured picture which they paint. For J., the pathos is almost removed – in spite of the 'Woman behold thy son' and the 'I thirst'. It has been said that the story of the Crucifixion in the Fourth Gospel is no more a Passion-narrative than *Murder in the Cathedral* is a detective story, so certain is the author that the Crucifixion was a saving event; and that 'as Moses lifted up the serpent in the wilderness, even so must the Son of Man be lifted up: that whosoever believeth may in him have eternal life'. [1]

But in spite of the highly distinctive manner in which the evangelists chose to tell the story, we have to say that it is extraordinarily detailed and vivid. Of how many other figures in the ancient world, even of emperors, are we told so much in their last hours, as of Jesus? The paradox is that, while wishing us to believe in his name, and find salvation thereby, the evangelists have told us so little about Jesus himself. His death and Passion have a power to move and to change human lives because, from the very beginning, they seem to come before the hearer or reader as archetypes. The human race has looked to the Cross of Jesus for salvation. But the story partly appeals so strongly because we know so little about Jesus. If the Gospels had given us full documentary accounts of the exact nature of his

[1] John 3:14.

apocalyptic beliefs, or the exact quarrels which he had (if any) with the Jerusalem hierarchy, we should feel alienated. We should realise what must in fact have been the case, that Jesus was a man in his time, preoccupied by matters which for the most part would seem insignificant or incomprehensible to those of other times or other cultures. The figure of a helpless and apparently innocent man on trial for his life before the Roman governor is, however, an icon to which any member of the human race could respond. It is precisely because we know so little of the trivial things in the story that we can respond so powerfully to the large things – to his silences, to his apparent forgiveness of his captors, to his loneliness, and to his suffering. Paul, for whatever reason he was drawn to Jesus, saw the enormous imaginative appeal of this when he said that 'God chose the weak things of the world, that he might put to shame the things that are strong'. [1]

Paul and the evangelists find redemption through the death of Jesus, which they believed to be an atoning death. We cannot begin to extrapolate from any of their writings *why* they believed this. That the Cross of Jesus has been a focus of religious consolation and fascination for two thousand years is beyond question. What the New Testament so unsatisfyingly fails to reveal is the nature of Jesus the man. We can discern from his parables and recorded utterances that he was a person of intelligence and wit. There seems no reason to question that he was a man of self-giving virtue, gifted with healing powers, and an apocalyptic, perhaps a Messianic vision. The Gospels, however, are so intent to suggest that Jesus was a man through whom the power of God was at work, a man through whom the glory of God was revealed, that they do not offer us many instances of virtue on Jesus's part – virtue, that is to say, as it is universally or traditionally understood. Matthew tells us that Jesus told a story about the Day of Judgment. The righteous will be rewarded when the king, the Son of Man (by implication, Jesus himself), says to them that they are to inherit the kingdom. 'For I was an hungred, and ye gave me meat: I was thirsty, and ye gave me drink: I was a stranger and ye took me in; naked and ye clothed me: I was sick and ye visited me: I was in prison and ye came to me.' [2] The lesson is obvious: that in doing good to others, we serve

[1] I Cor. 1:27.
[2] Matthew 25:35, 36.

God. Formal religious observance is not enough. 'Many will say to me in that day, Lord, Lord, did we not prophesy by thy name, and by thy name cast out devils, and by thy name do many mighty works? And then will I profess unto them, I never knew you, depart from me, ye that work iniquity.'[1] Jesus worked and taught firmly within the tradition of the Jewish prophets that God could only be pleased by human kindness and goodness. Mysticism, exorcism, the power to heal or to cast out devils were no substitute for justice and virtue. When Christianity became a world religion, it took much of this spirit to itself, and in so far as it has ever been a force for good in the world, it is because of those among its numbers who have been inspired by this strand in the teaching of Jesus. It would be cynical to suppose that he had never exercised such virtue himself. We know that he mixed with sinners and proclaimed to them the forgiveness of God. We read that he saved an adulteress from stoning; that he restored swindlers and tax-collectors to a right sense of their own worth before God, just as he restored the sick. But there is so little anecdotal evidence of such acts of kindness, and such a complete absence of character-analysis in the Gospel pictures of Jesus that we can only be surprised that an historical figure of whom so little is known should have attracted to himself a reputation such as theology would wish to give him. Among the elements which inspired the New Testament writers to form their beliefs there must have been the memory of an extraordinary person; but in what that extraordinariness consisted, they are unwilling or unable to say. The feelings of the historian about Jesus must be analogous to his feelings about Shakespeare, who managed to achieve fame and wealth and notoriety in Elizabethan London, and who left behind him a body of literary work without parallel, but whose 'personality' remains almost invisible.

[1] Matthew 7:22, 23.

# APPENDIX

There are three strands of tradition concerning the last hours of Jesus: Mark/Matthew (hereafter M.); Luke (hereafter L.); and the Fourth Gospel (hereafter J.). Of these, only J. claims to use eye-witness material.

| INCIDENT | M | L | J |
| --- | --- | --- | --- |
| Identity of those who arrested Jesus. | A number of men sent by chief priests. | A number of men, including the chief priests themselves. | Roman soldiers. |
| The first place to which Jesus was taken after his arrest. | The High Priest's palace. | The High Priest's house. | The house of Annas, the father-in-law of the High Priest Caiaphas. |
| Peter's denial. | The story of Peter's denial is common to all three traditions. | | |
| Jesus on trial. The trial before the High Priest. | Full assembly of Sanhedrin before daybreak. The High Priest tears his clothes at Jesus's 'blasphemy' – applying Daniel 7:3 to himself. | Similar to M. A nocturnal trial before the Sanhedrin. | The 'other disciple' is known to the High Priest. No trial before High Priest. An 'examination', during which guards slap the face of Jesus. He is then sent on to trial before Pilate. |
| The trial before Pilate. | – | – | Priests refuse to enter the Praetorium. |
| Pilate asks 'Are you the King of the Jews?' | Jesus refuses to reply to the charges. | Jesus says, 'The words are yours'. | Jesus asks, 'Is that your own idea, or have others suggested it to you?' . . . 'My Kingdom is not of this world.' |

| INCIDENT | M | L | J |
|---|---|---|---|
| – | Pilate washes his hands, symbolising the innocence of the Gentiles. In Matthew, the High Priest says, 'This blood be on us and on our children', implying that the Jews alone are responsible for the death of Jesus. | Pilate attempts to pass the buck to Herod Antipas, since Jesus, a Galilean, does not fall within the jurisdiction of Judaea. Pilate releases a man imprisoned for riot and murder, having attempted to release Jesus. The Jews insist that Jesus should die. | There was a custom to release a prisoner at the Feast of Passover. The Jews choose not this man, but Barabbas. |
| The soldiers in the Praetorium crown Jesus with thorns. | The soldiers crown Jesus with thorns. | Roman violence towards the person of Jesus omitted. | Jesus is crowned 'King of the Jews'. The Jews respond, 'We have no king but Caesar'. |
| Carrying the Cross. | Simon of Cyrene, the father of Rufus and Alexander, helps to carry the Cross. | Simon of Cyrene helped to carry the Cross. | Jesus carries his own Cross alone to the Place of the Skull – Golgotha. |
| – | – | On his journey to the Place of the Skull, Jesus pauses to address the women of Jerusalem – 'Weep not for me, but for yourselves'. | – |

| INCIDENT | M | L | J |
|---|---|---|---|
| Crucifixion. | Jesus is crucified alongside two political terrorists. | Jesus is crucified alongside two criminals. | Jesus is crucified with two others. |
| – | An inscription over the Cross reads 'The King of the Jews'. | An inscription over the Cross reads, 'This is the King of the Jews'. | The inscription over the Cross reads, 'Jesus of Nazareth – King of the Jews'. The inscription is in Hebrew, Latin and Greek. |
| Jesus's sayings on the Cross. | *Eli, Eli, lama sabachtani'* (Psalm 22:1) 'My God, my God, why hast thou forsaken me?' | 'Father forgive them; they know not what they do'. He promises the Penitent Thief, 'This day thou shalt be with me in Paradise'. He dies with the words: 'Father, into thy hands I commend my spirit'. | He commends his mother to the care of the Beloved Disciple – 'Behold thy mother!' He says, 'I thirst'. He dies with the words *'Consummatum est'* – 'It is accomplished', i.e. the Redemption of the World is achieved, the task is done. |

| INCIDENT | M | L | J |
|---|---|---|---|
| Jesus's death. | When Jesus dies the sky becomes dark, the veil of the Temple is torn from top to bottom, the graves open and the dead rise up. The centurion asserts that Jesus is the Son of God. | Darkness descends. The veil of the Temple is torn. The Roman centurion asserts that Jesus was innocent. | The Roman soldiers come round breaking the legs of the crucified to hasten their deaths and allow them Jewish burial before the festival. Jesus is already dead when they come to break his legs. They stab his side with a lance and there flows forth blood and water. |
| Witnesses of the Crucifixion and death of Jesus. | At a distance, Mary Magdalen, Mary the mother of James and Joseph, and the mother of the sons of Zebedee. Mark says that Salome was present. | 'His friends and those who had accompanied him from Galilee.' | His mother, her sister, Mary wife of Clopas, Mary Magdalen, the Beloved Disciple and (if this is a separate person) the eye-witness who saw the piercing of Jesus's side. |

| INCIDENT | M | L | J |
|---|---|---|---|
| The burial of Jesus. | Pilate is surprised that Jesus is so soon dead. He gives permission to Joseph of Arimathaea, a rich man, to bury Jesus in an unused tomb, cut into the rock. He rolls a large stone against the entrance. Mary Magdalen and the other Mary keep watch by the stone. The Jews, fearful that the Christians will claim that Jesus has risen from the dead, ask Pilate for soldiers to guard the tomb. This guard is provided. | Joseph of Arimathaea, a member of the Sanhedrin, asks for permission to bury the body. Pilate grants this. The body is laid in a tomb which had never been used before. The stone at the door of the tomb is mentioned in his Resurrection stories, but he does not tell us that Jesus's tomb was sealed with a stone at the time of burial. Nor is there mention of a guard. | Joseph of Arimathaea buries Jesus in a new tomb in a garden near the site of the Crucifixion. The men anoint Jesus and wrap his body in strips of linen cloth according to Jewish burial customs. In Jesus's Resurrection stories a stone at the door of the tomb is mentioned. In the accounts of the burial, however, it is not stated that the tomb was sealed, nor that it was guarded. |

# XI

## JESUS CHRIST

EVEN AS YOU read these words, someone in the world is deciding that Jesus Christ is still alive. Although the membership of the Christian Churches would seem to be in irreversible decline, there remains no shortage of persons from all over the globe who would wish to attest to the living presence of Jesus in their lives.

Such testimonies can range from highly specific visions of Jesus, such as those of Marguerite-Marie Alacoque, to whom Jesus revealed his Sacred Heart in December 1673[1] to less visual, but no less certain awarenesses of the presence of the risen Jesus. Of such an experience, a good example would be that of Simone Weil, the brilliant young philosopher-mathematician who was gradually drawn to theism, through a combination of reading, personal suffering, and visiting two Christian shrines – Assisi and the monastery at Solesmes. It became her custom to recite George Herbert's poem *Love*, about the soul's encounter with Christ; and, as she confided in a Dominican priest, Father Perrin, it was during one such recitation that 'Christ himself came down and took possession of me. In my arguments about the insolubility of God I had never foreseen the possibility of that, of a real contact, person to person, here below, between a human being and God.'[2]

To non-Christian religious believers it must remain incomprehensible why such certainty of a presence should move to a certainty that the presence is Christ. To put it another way, it is not easy, when reading or hearing such testimonies, to understand the connection between the risen Christ, making his mystical presence felt, and the historical Jesus. Theology has concerned itself almost exclusively, from the beginning, with the risen Christ; so it is unsurprising that theologians are, and always have been, so uninterested in the

---

[1] *Vie et oeuvres de la bienheureuse Marguerite-Marie Alacoque*, ed. L. Gauthey, 3 vols, (Paris 1915).
[2] Simone Weil: *Attente de Dieu*, (ET) 1969, 35.

historical Jesus. Simone Weil, for example, identified the inspiration of Homer's *Iliad* with the spirit of Christ, and found intimations of Christ in Euripides and Pythagoras.[1] Paul in his letters said that the rock, from which water sprang to refresh the Israelites in the wilderness 1500 years before the birth of Jesus, 'was Christ'.[2] When Paul had his vision of Christ, risen from the dead, it was the most vivid possible example of what Simone Weil called 'a real contact'. In earlier pages of this book, I have offered very speculative explanations for Paul's preoccupation with Jesus, and with the followers of Jesus. These explanations were of course not explanations at all; there will never be an explanation of why Paul decided in defiance of, or independently of, Jesus's other followers, to take into the Gentile world the idea that God had spoken to man in a manner more direct than prophecy.

> And as he journeyed, he came near Damascus: and suddenly there shine'd round about him a light from heaven: and he fell to the earth, and heard a voice, saying unto him, Saul, Saul, why persecutest thou me? And he said, Who art thou, Lord? And the Lord said, I am Jesus whom thou persecutest: it is hard for thee to kick against the pricks.[3]

At no point in his writings does Paul distinguish between this visionary experience and the visions of the risen Jesus which were reportedly vouchsafed to Jesus's close friends Mary Magdalen, Peter, John, and the rest of the Twelve, including Doubting Thomas. Paul does not even suggest that his faith depends on the existence of an empty tomb. He does not advance any 'evidence' for the Resurrection. Once, when I visited the Garden Tomb in Jerusalem, there was a party of American tourists. Their tour leader was informing them that 'the Resurrection of Jesus Christ is the best-attested fact in human history'. This would not have been Paul's claim for whom it was a matter of faith. Nor for the author of the Fourth Gospel, who believed that there was blessedness in not having seen, while having believed.

The evangelists, whoever they were, and wherever they were writing, had all entered this same world of faith, inhabited by Paul, and by other believers who somehow or another are convinced that Jesus lives. We have reached the point in our narrative where we must

---

[1] Simone Weil: *Intimations of Christianity Among the Ancient Greeks* (ET 1957).
[2] I Cor. 10:4.
[3] Acts 9:3–5.

abandon our efforts to pursue 'what really happened'. Subjectivity is the only criterion of Gospel truth.

Those who had not seen, but had believed, wrote Resurrection-stories for the congregations whom they served. We need not surmise that the first to write such stories down were fabricating falsehoods. As we can tell from reading Paul's Letter to Corinth, a quarter of a century after Jesus's death, the Resurrection was a fully realised fact of the imaginative life of these communities.

Behind the stories, and the encounters with the risen Jesus, such as might be enjoyed today by believers, there lurked some older experiences. I find it impossible, given the nature of the stories which survive, to believe that the female friends of Jesus, who had been kept at such a distance during his last hours, did not come to the tomb early in the morning of the Third Day. I find it equally hard to believe that they did not find the tomb empty of the body which they sought. I say this, not because I find any of the 'Resurrection narratives' so inescapably plausible, or psychologically realistic. I say it because the first witnesses were women, and no first-century Jew, wishing to invent a good case which depended to some extent on evidence, would have chosen to concoct female false witnesses. Women were not even allowed to give evidence in Jewish courts; their testimony counted for absolutely nothing. If the Disciples had chosen to invent the story of the empty tomb, they would have said that the first witnesses were Peter, or James the brother of the Lord, or the rich men Nicodemus and Joseph of Arimathea. Christian piety has liked to see that history itself changed during that mysterious first Easter Eve: 'the world had died in the night. What they were looking at was the first day of a new creation, with a new heaven and a new earth and in the semblance of a gardener God walked again in the garden, in the cool not of the evening but the dawn.'[1] There is more than a metaphorical truth in the fancy.

Mark's narrative, supposed by many scholars to be the earliest, relates that Mary Magdalen, Mary the Mother of James, and Salome came to the Tomb, hoping to anoint the body with sweet spices. They found the stone which had been used to seal the door of the tomb was rolled away. Inside the sepulchre they found the *neaniskos* in a shroud or white garment, presumably the same mysterious young man who had run away three days before on the night of

[1] G. K. Chesterton: *The Everlasting Man* (1936).

Jesus's arrest. The young man told the women that Jesus was no longer there. 'But go your way, tell his disciples and Peter that he goeth before you into Galilee.'[1] The reaction of the women was to run away in terror. 'Neither said they any thing to any man; for they were afraid.'[2]

There Mark's Gospel ends.[3] We could take this to signify a number of things. Unless we read the story with the eyes of faith, we should not suppose that this narrative, mysterious as it is, suggested that Jesus had miraculously risen from the grave. It would make much more sense to think that the young man and his friends had decided to move the body to Galilee for burial. Perhaps they succeeded in their ambition, and the body of Jesus rests in Nazareth near his mother's house, or in Capernaum by the shores of the Lake where he and his friends went fishing. Perhaps they failed. Perhaps, having been disturbed by the women, and frightened for their lives by the possibility of an encounter with the Roman military, the young man and his friends abandoned the body in some nearby spot. We shall never know.

In Matthew's account, the young man has become an angel whose 'countenance was like lightning and his raiment white as snow'.[4] As the women run away from the garden, in Matthew's version, they meet Jesus himself, who tells them that he has risen from the dead and is making his way to Galilee. Matthew might have been writing his story anything up to sixty years after the death of Jesus; but he clearly retained memories of a less credulous tradition. In his account, the wicked unbelievers claim that the Disciples had in fact removed the corpse from the tomb. In order to dispel any such scepticism, Matthew's Jesus makes a final appearance on a Galilean hillside, the very spot where he had originally commissioned the Twelve. He tells them to go into the world, and to 'teach all nations, baptizing them in the name of the Father and of the Son and of the Holy Ghost'.[5] Jesus, in this version, has become the founder of the Catholic Church; it is not, therefore, surprising that believers in Catholic Christianity look for ways to persuade themselves that

[1] Mark 16:7.
[2] Mark 16:8.
[3] All scholars agree that verses 9–20 of Mark 16 belong to a later tradition. They are not found in many MSS.
[4] Matthew 28:3.
[5] Matthew 28:19.

Matthew's is the first, the ur-Gospel, from which the other three derive. [1]

Luke's account of two men walking to the village of Emmaus has a certain narrative plausibility. As they walked along, the men discussed the events of the previous three days, and their intense disappointment in Jesus whom they had 'trusted . . . should have redeemed Israel'. [2] Even as they spoke, they were joined by a stranger who told them that far from being disappointed by the death of Jesus, they should see that it was the natural fulfilment of the Jewish Scriptures. 'O fools and slow of heart to believe all that the prophets have spoken.' [3] In words which for English-speaking readers have become heavily overladen with memories of one of the best-loved hymns in their language, the two men turn to the stranger, as they reach their destination and say, 'Abide with us: for it is toward evening and the day is far spent'. [4] The stranger remained with them until they broke bread when he 'vanished out of their sight'. It is a magnificent story because it reveals so much of the nature of faith. The unbeliever, reading this account, will hardly be convinced that the Resurrection is a fact of history. Naturalistic explanations could be provided for all of it. We could point out the extreme oddness of the Disciples not recognising Jesus until after he had departed from them; this could rationally be explained by the fact that it was not Jesus at all, but a man who resembled him, such as a brother. Would not James, who in Luke's sequel to this story, Acts, emerged without introduction as the leader of the Jerusalem 'Church', have been likely to say exactly what this 'stranger' says to the two mournful Disciples? But for the believer, such questions would be facile. 'Did not our hearts burn within us while he talked with us by the way?' [5]

The Fourth Gospel contains the most dramatic Resurrection stories. That is what we should have expected. There are principally three. In the first, Mary Magdalen comes to the garden alone. She finds the empty tomb and runs back to fetch Peter and 'the other disciple whom Jesus loved'. They see the empty tomb and go home again. Then Mary meets a pair of angels sitting in the sepulchre

[1] See e.g. B. C. Butler: *The Originality of Matthew* (1951).
[2] Luke 24:21.
[3] Luke 24:25.
[4] Luke 24:29.
[5] Luke 24:32.

where the body of Jesus has been lain. After this, she goes out into the garden and meets a stranger whom she supposes to be the gardener. She says to him, 'Sir, if you have borne him hence, tell me where thou hast laid him and I will take him away'. [1] As with Luke's Emmaus story, it is hard to see why someone who had known Jesus quite well should have been so slow to recognise him. If, however, the stranger were not the dear friend, but the dear friend's brother, who bore a strong resemblance, then this is just the sort of 'double take' which we should expect. 'Jesus saith unto her, Mary. She turned herself and saith unto him, Rabboni which is to say, Master.' [2]

Tersely eloquent as only the Fourth Gospel can be, this is perhaps the most moving of all the Resurrection stories. As so often – as in the stories of Nicodemus, and of the Samaritan woman at Jacob's Well – it achieves so much of its power by reducing the cast list. The other women and the male Disciples who are all present in the garden of the Resurrection have been cut out by this supreme master of storytelling so that he can stage a purely individual encounter between Jesus and his closest female follower.

If the Fourth Gospel derives, as some believe, from Samaria, where the Hellenized Jews of the Diaspora had taken the Good News about Jesus, then it is not surprising that it should contain so much more insistence than the other New Testament books upon the physical reality of Jesus's arising. This is a Gospel which intends to lead the believer to a true worship of the Father in spirit and in truth. But it does not want us to lose sight of the earthly and the actual in our quest for the spiritual. The Word has been made flesh. Flesh he remains even after death. In the second generation after Jesus's death, particularly among those who had never had, or had abandoned, any ritualistic observance of Judaism, the community of belief which produced the Fourth Gospel must have felt peculiarly tempted to say that it did not matter whether Jesus had been raised in the flesh. Perhaps there were believers among them, who had never consciously defined what they meant by Christ's Resurrection and who had never spoken of, perhaps never heard of, the empty tomb. The Fourth Gospel, which believed that it was more important to believe not having seen, and to worship in spirit, inserts many correctives

[1] John 20:15.
[2] John 20:16.

against such an approach. There is, for example, the story of Lazarus, which Morton Smith plausibly argued began as the memory of a ritual and ended as a piece of history. There are then the stories of Mary Magdalen in the Garden. The famous *noli me tangere*[1] like so much in the Fourth Gospel bristles with double-meaning and self-contradiction. Is it a body speaking to her, or a spirit? Could she have touched it if she had chosen to do so? Later that week, Jesus in his resurrected form passed through a closed door or a wall to the room where the Disciples are gathered 'for fear of the Jews'. Thomas, one of the Twelve, was not present on that occasion which gave the evangelist the opportunity to construct his boldest theological fiction. The rite of Baptism, by which the believer, shrouded in white, was called forth into newness of life, was dramatised by this writer as the story of the raising of Lazarus. Had Lazarus risen from the dead as a matter of historical fact, it is unthinkable that the other Gospels would not have mentioned it. In rather the same manner, lest any should doubt that Jesus had arisen, the imagination of the evangelist creates the moving story of Doubting Thomas. 'Then saith he to Thomas, reach forth thy hand, and thrust it into my side: and be not faithless but believing. And Thomas answered and said unto him, My Lord and my God.'[2]

As with the story of Lazarus, it is almost unthinkable, if so memorable an event had happened in history, that the other evangelists should not have included the story in their accounts of Jesus in his Resurrection. In his third Resurrection-story, the evangelist takes us to Galilee. Jesus is seen on the shore of Lake Galilee after a night in which the Disciples have caught nothing. He urges them to cast their net over the right side of the boat, and when they do so, their nets are filled with the miraculous draught of fishes – 153 in number which must have mystic significance. As in the story of Mary Magdalen's encounter with Jesus near the garden tomb; and as in Luke's story of the journey to Emmaus, the Disciples do not recognise Jesus. Even more than with the other two narratives just mentioned, however, a naturalistic explanation for this would seem inapposite. By the time of his third appearance from the dead in the Fourth Gospel, Jesus is intent on passing over the Primacy of his Church to Peter, and the chapter concludes with his urging Peter to 'feed my lambs'.[3]

[1] John 20:17.
[2] John 20:21.
[3] John 21:15.

The draught of fishes which the Disciples have just landed is an emblem of the converts who will worship neither in Jerusalem nor on Mount Gerizim but in spirit and in truth. This is the Johannine equivalent of the story which Mark places at the very beginning of the Gospel, of Jesus walking beside the Sea of Galilee and saying to Simon and Andrew: 'Come ye after me and I will make you fishers of men.'[1]

What Jesus made of them is largely a matter of pious legend. What they made of Jesus has been the most astonishing theme in human history. Within three hundred years, the Roman Emperor himself would be convening the Council of Nicaea at which the bishops who claimed to trace their apostolic authority from the fishermen of Galilee solemnly proclaimed that Jesus was not merely divine, but 'God of God, Light of Light, Very God of Very God, Begotten, Not Made, Being of One Substance with the Father By Whom all things were made'.

It lies outside the scope of this book to tell the story of Christendom, or to investigate the development of Christian theology. It is a story which has been told to us, almost entirely, by the Christians, and not merely by the Christians, but by those who deemed themselves to be 'Orthodox'. It is therefore very usual for modern Christians to suppose that after Jesus died and ascended into the clouds, he sent the Holy Spirit to guide the Church into all truth. This was an event which was supposed to have taken place on the Day of Pentecost, fifty days after the Resurrection. Thereafter, it would seem, all was peace and joy among the apostolic community, who held together, albeit in a primitive form, the core of the Catholic faith.

In fact, as even the New Testament betrays, this was very far from being the case. From the beginning, there were probably several 'Christian' groups, and they did not all, by any means, share a common faith.

In the seventh chapter of the Acts of the Apostles, for instance, we read of Stephen, a Hellenizing Jew who did not believe in the necessity of Temple-worship. Stephen made a speech in Jerusalem which bitterly denounced the religious hierarchy in Jerusalem, and said that, throughout Jewish history, the leadership had misunderstood and killed the prophets, just as they had killed Jesus. That was

[1] Mark 1:17.

because they resisted the Holy Spirit and they did not understand that the Almighty does not live in a house made with hands. [1] Stephen's speech is thought by scholars to represent a very primitive form of belief in Jesus. It sees Jesus as a great prophet who might come to vindicate his people on the clouds, like Daniel's Son of Man, but it does not of course suggest that Jesus was divine, or even that he had risen from the dead. It is Stephen with his Hellenized Jewish faith, who attracts the persecution of the Orthodox, whose keenest representative is Saul, later known as Paul. At Saul's instigation, according to a somewhat questionable account in Acts, Stephen was stoned to death for blasphemy.

It is hard to know what attitude the Twelve took towards the Hellenizers. The Twelve, who had regrouped under the leadership of Jesus's brother James, remained in Jerusalem, and clearly did not share Stephen's distaste for Temple-worship. There are many references to their habits of Temple-worship in Acts. The Hellenizers, of whom Philip was one, went into Samaria, the region between Galilee and Jerusalem. All the Gospels attest to the tolerant attitude which Jesus took towards the Samaritans, and it is perhaps obvious that the Hellenizers, finding themselves persecuted in Jerusalem by Saul, should have gone north in search of converts. The Samaritans had never believed in Temple-worship, as is made clear by Jesus's conversation with the woman at Jacob's Well. They looked for the coming of an earthly Messiah – Ta'eb [2] – and they were easily persuadable that Jesus had been this figure. The Samaritans held a less rigid hold on monotheism than the Jews of Jerusalem and Judaea. After the destruction of the Northern Kingdom of Israel in 605 BCE five Babylonian tribes had been transplanted to Samaria, bringing their tribal gods with them. These people in the fulness of time, while not wholly abandoning their Babylonian gods, came to worship Yahweh as well. It was probably from this fertile soil that the Fourth Gospel, at least in its first manifestation, came to bud. Its story of Jesus talking to the Samaritan woman makes it clear that Jesus's Judaism was regarded as far from Orthodox by the Johannine community of faith. 'The hour cometh when neither in this mountain, nor in Jerusalem shall ye worship the father.' [3] Admittedly, he immediately adds that salvation is from the Jews, but it is no longer,

[1] Acts 7:48, 51.
[2] A. Merx: *Der Messias oder Ta'eb der Samaritaner* (1910).
[3] John 4:21.

in this book, their unique possession. Like all stories told by the Fourth evangelist, we do not know how much of metaphor there is. Should we regard the woman as a symbol of Samaria, her five unworthy husbands the five gods brought by her ancestors from Babylon, the true husband of her soul being the man who sits beside her, offering her the water of eternal life? The potent blend of Samaritan heterodoxy and Hellenistic ideas about the *logos* led to the idea of Jesus as the Eternal, Pre-Existent Word, walking about among his own, and his own receiving him not. He is specifically misunderstood by the Judaeans, the men of Jerusalem, translated always as 'Jews' but meaning, surely in this context, the people of Judaea who had always misunderstood the people of Israel, Samaria and Galilee. We can be fairly sure that there were Samaritan Christians for several centuries after the death of Jesus, but they were never great in number. [1]

The 'Christianity' of James, Jesus's brother, and of the Jerusalem 'Church' has likewise failed to survive. Clearly, to begin with, it was regarded as the mainstream. James and his followers were adamantly opposed to Paul's abandonment of the Jewish Torah. By the time of Irenaeus in the second century, however, these followers of James, known as the Ebionites, were themselves deemed 'heretical'. Irenaeus denounced them as little different from the Jews. From an early age, these Jewish Christians, if one can term them that, believed in the need to remain Jewish, and any new convert to 'the Way', as they called the religion of Jesus, would have to agree to submit to Jewish rituals, including circumcision, Jewish dietary laws, and Jewish beliefs. Religion was, for the Ebionites, Judaism, because they were Jews, as Jesus had been a Jew. They did not believe in the divinity of Christ – they were disputing it as late as the second century when Irenaeus denounced them as heretics. They did not believe that he was born of a Virgin – how could a sect which had as its leader one of Jesus's brothers believe anything so fantastic? [2]

It would seem as though, after his death, the family of Jesus were accorded particular status in the new sect. Eusebius, who was a fourth-century Orthodox Christian, describes James as 'entrusted with the throne of the episcopate at Jerusalem', though it can hardly have been much of a throne, or much of an episcopate at the time.

[1] Oscar Cullmann: 'Samaria and the Origins of the Christian Mission' in *The Early Church* (1956).
[2] Adolph Harnack: *History of Dogma* (1984), I. 299.

Acts does not make it clear how James met his end, though ecclesiastical tradition, again preserved in Eusebius, suggests that he met a
fate reminiscent of one of his brother's temptations in the wilderness.
He was cast down from a pinnacle and beaten to death with a club. [1]
According to his admirer Hegesippus, James was an ascetic,
abstaining both from strong drink and from shaving. The epistle
which is attributed to him might be written by someone else but it
reflects the Ebionite piety. [2] It is unmystical, ethical and accessible.
'Pure religion and undefiled before our God and Father is this, to
visit the fatherless and widows in their affliction and to keep himself
unspotted from the world.' [3]

So bitterly has this epistle been hated by Orthodox Christians that
they have even questioned whether it is Christian at all. Luther used
to tear it from the Bible whenever he found it, denouncing it as an
epistle of straw, for it advocates goodness and self-restraint and says
nothing about Justification by Faith Only. Jesus would doubtless
have found it puritanical, but closer in spirit to his own ideas than
those of Paul, Irenaeus or Luther, who in his vilely anti-Jewish tirades
anticipated the worst excesses of the Third Reich.

Forty years or so after the death of Jesus, Jerusalem was destroyed
by the Romans. Together with the Temple, and all the splendid
buildings, and most of the inhabitants, there went the little 'Church'
of Jewish Christians. They survived in pockets – large enough
pockets to be denounced by the Gentile Christians in the next century, but their attempts to insist that Jesus was merely trying to teach
the Jews how to be better Jews met with little enthusiasm among
Gentiles who had no ancestral reason for accepting Judaism and no
wish to submit to circumcision. 'The Jewish religion is a national
religion, and Christianity burst the bonds of nationality.' [4] It did so
very largely because of Paul. Once the idea of Jesus had been given
to the Gentiles, they adopted him as a saviour in whose human
biography they took small or no interest. For the Platonist author of
the Epistle to the Hebrews, all the Old Testament and all the Jewish
rituals were mere shadows and fore-ordinations of heaven. Jesus was
the great High Priest who had poured out not the blood of bulls and

[1] Eusebius 11:23.
[2] A case for the epistle being the actual work of James the brother of Jesus is made by J. A. T.
Robinson in *Redating the New Testament*.
[3] James 1:27.
[4] Harnack: op.cit., I. 289.

heifers in sacrifice but his own. Just as the sacrifice of the High Priest in the old religion made peace between men and God, so the blood of Jesus provided an everlasting covenant. The High Priest had passed through the veil on the Day of Atonement into the Holy of Holies. Jesus passed through the heavens, to prepare a place for his followers.

For another writer, probably from Asia Minor, and much imbued with the Jewish apocalyptic texts, Jesus was the Lamb of God, seated on a throne and adored by a choir of the redeemed. For this author, there seems to be as much pleasure in consigning the wicked to hell as in contemplating the joy of the blessed who worship the Lamb. The author detests the Jews, whom he denounced as the 'synagogue of Satan'. [1] Even more wicked were the Romans, and in particular Nero. The book, known variously as the Apocalypse and the Revelation of 'St John the Divine' probably dates from about the year 90. The Greek of the book is uncouth. The imagery is deranged. The ethical system, in so far as it has one, is irrational. It seems as far from the spirit of Jesus as it is possible to be, and yet it provides the conclusion of the Christian Bible.

Most of the history of Christendom may be seen as a series of extraordinary accidents, but it is not purely accidental that Jesus could so easily be adopted and transformed into the Gentile God that he became. It is precisely because he refused to define himself that he was so vulnerable to the assaults of theologians and fantasists. 'Who do men say that I am?' He asked the question, but he did not tell them what sort of answer they should have given.

Something with which Western minds have found it almost impossible to come to terms is the unsystematic nature of Jesus's thought. Since Jesus existed within an accepted religious framework, and was not setting out to found a new religion, still less to found a philosophical school, there is no need to search among his recorded sayings for a coherent metaphysic. He spoke in parables partly with the deliberate aim of baffling and disturbing his hearers, that hearing they might not understand. He did not wish to deliver them with a finished pattern which they could follow. The pattern was something which, if it existed, they must make for themselves. Most Christian schemes of thought have arisen from a passion to take some group of recorded sayings in the Gospels and to force

---

[1] Revelation 3:9.

them to their logical conclusion. The whole of Calvinism, for example, may be deduced from the parable of the woman looking for the lost coin. If, as Calvin did, you imagine that this story is a piece of theology, then certain terrible deductions can be made from it. The Almighty is the woman, and the human soul is the coin. It follows that all human impulses towards the divine are worthless, since the initiative, in the process of salvation, must always come, not from man, but from above. We cannot work for our own salvation; we must wait for it. It therefore follows that only those who have been called or elected to glory may be saved – with the cruel concomitant that those who are not so called must be elected to everlasting damnation.

Tolstoy, whose interpretation of the life and teachings of Jesus is so profoundly attractive, made a comparable, though far less terrible, mistake when he tried to rewrite the Gospel as if it were no more than an ethical system, a handbook for pacifist anarchists. He believed, as he did so, that it was the holy idiot in him, the peasant simpleton whom he never was but longed to become, that was able to reduce the Gospel to a mere injunction to refuse to accept oath-taking, civil government, war and violence of any kind. It was not. It was the Voltairean side of his nature, urging him on to take the teachings of Jesus to their logical conclusion. Rationalist that he was, Tolstoy could not imagine that there were some things to which there *is* no logical conclusion.

While it can be seen that there have been few figures in modern times who have come closer to the teachings of Jesus than did Tolstoy in his writings, there is yet an extraordinary disparity between his devastatingly cohesive ethical system, and the sheer muddle which we find in the Gospels. Who can not believe Tolstoy when he tells us that acts of violence, and in particular acts of war, are incompatible with the teachings of Jesus? Did Jesus not say that we should resist not evil, and turn the other cheek to aggressors? Yes, in all likelihood he did; and Tolstoy was right to find something blasphemous in the idea of Orthodox priests blessing the holy Russian armies before they went into battle, or forcing heretics, such as the Doukhobors, to be baptized at bayonet-point. And yet Jesus and his companions in the Garden of Gethsemane carried swords. Who can not believe Tolstoy when he says that the logical conclusion of taking no purse nor script for our journey, and laying not up treasure upon earth, is a life in which the ownership of personal property is an impossibility?

The early followers of Jesus themselves practised such a simple form of communism. And yet Jesus lived in a house, quite a large house if the archaeologists at Capernaum are to be believed, and his followers were probably prosperous fishermen, and, since he urged them to pay their taxes to Caesar, he must have assumed that they would have earned money in the first place in order to pay the tax. Who can not believe Tolstoy when he says that oath-taking is forbidden in the Gospel; that the kingdom is within us, and not of this world; that the true followers of Jesus can therefore never wish to take part in civil systems, and never seek political solutions to the problems which beset society? And yet Jesus, who told his followers to render to Caesar the things which are Caesar's, is never recorded as recommending a Tolstoyan policy of civil disobedience against Rome of the sort which inspired Mahatma Gandhi to defy, and ultimately to overthrow, the British Raj in India.

The truth is, that Jesus remains too disturbing a figure ever to be left to himself. Christianity in all its multifarious manifestations, Orthodox and heterodox, has been a repeated attempt to make sense of him, to cut him down to size. The extent to which no saying or story of Jesus can, in fact, be taken to its logical conclusion without being contradicted by some other saying or fact is perhaps less a symptom of how imperfectly the Gospels record him than how oblique and how terrifying a figure he actually was in history. Terrifying, because he really does undermine everything. He appeals to disruptive imaginations such as Tolstoy or Blake, but even they, in seeking to make his disruptiveness their own, systematise or enclose him. It cannot be done. 'Neither tell I you by what authority I do these things.' He will not tell us. We can accept some Church version of Jesus, or if it makes more appeal to us, we can accept a 'heretic' version; or we can make one up by ourselves. A patient and conscientious reading of the Gospels will always destroy any explanation which we devise. If it makes sense, it is wrong. That is the only reliable rule-of-thumb which we can use when testing the innumerable interpretations of Jesus's being and his place in human history.

The death of Jesus was a negligible fact in history. What was one crucifixion among so many? Alexander Jannaeus crucified 800 Pharisees in a single day. What matters is the imaginative use which the New Testament writers have made of this death, so that for the Epistle to the Hebrews, it can be the ultimate priestly sacrifice; for Paul, it can be the paying of the price for sin; for the Fourth Gospel it can be the saving of the world, the lifting up of the Son of Man just as the serpent was lifted up by Moses in the wilderness.

It is an astonishing testament to Jesus. No other death in history has attracted quite such a powerful range of Midrash, meditation, and theological exposition. And from reading the New Testament reflections on the death of Jesus, we realise that his death was much more important to the early Christians than his life; that is why so many scholars and believers would view the pursuit of the historical Jesus as irrelevant. Only in the most tangential fashion do the theological treatises allude to the virtue of Jesus. The Epistle to the Hebrews implies that he was a brave man, 'who endured the Cross, despising the shame',[1] but it tells us nothing which should make us admire Jesus as a human being. Very few, if any, of the New Testament writers, are trying to make us admire Jesus. They nearly all wish us to accept him as our Saviour or Messiah; but by stating his theological attributes, they tell us almost nothing about him as an historical being.

Yet, almost in spite of the Christ of the theologians, Jesus has survived: a man doodling in the dust with his finger, while all around him, self-righteous men are shouting for the death of a sinner; a man who could liken the love of God to a fussy Jewish mother searching a house high and low for a lost coin; a man with sudden outbursts of anger, and strange flashes of mysticism; an exorcist, and a spiritual healer, but also one who sits at meat with sinners, and is accused of being a wine-bibber and a glutton. This is a very distinctive figure indeed, even though there are so many things about him which we should like to know and do not know. His ideas have been incoherently pieced together by the evangelists. In so far as they are discernible in the Gospels, we can see that they have been almost the least influential ideas which were ever propounded. The course of human history has not been conspicuous for meek rulers of the earth, nor for the oppressed blessing their persecutors, nor for a widespread reluctance to lay up treasure. One could immediately name a dozen figures who had been of far greater influence on the human race than Jesus.[2] Few of the Christian Churches have ever viewed the teaching of Jesus with anything but contempt. And while Churches might think that they are returning to the teaching of Jesus it will invariably

[1] Hebrews 12:2.
[2] For example: Plato, Aristotle, Euclid, St Paul, St Augustine, Mahomet, Copernicus, Calvin, Marx, Darwin, Lenin and Freud.

be found that they are pursuing a distorted version of one or two of his ideas while contradicting the others. Today, for example, there is a widespread recovery of the idea of Christian pacifism, in Churches which would formerly have taught the doctrine of the just war. Rather late in the day Christians have developed the sense that there is something inherently wrong with war, and while this might be explained by collective panic about a nuclear catastrophe, the Christian witness against the arms race derives, at least in part, from such sayings as 'Resist not evil' in the Sermon on the Mount. But Christians who support pacifism on the grounds that it seems to have been the teaching of Jesus (in that chapter of Matthew at least) are often happy to disregard Jesus's teaching in other areas. He taught that virtue consisted in leaving wife and children and even dying parents for the sake of the Gospel. The modern Christian wisdom is that the family is all important, so the Churches teach the virtue of the family, even though Jesus, and the majority of Christians for the first three centuries of the faith's existence, were rather hostile to the family. In earlier generations, you would have been hard put to it to find any Christian body except the Religious Society of Friends who took Jesus's teachings about aggression seriously, but until the Middle Ages, Christians might have been much more literal in their interpretation of his injunction to sell all and give to the poor. In later years, Victorian moralists could cheerfully absorb the Manichean teachings about sex propounded by St Augustine and loosely based on Jesus's few known references to the sins of the flesh. Such puritans might have thought very little of the 'Franciscan' side of Jesus, his scoffing at those who save up wealth or array themselves in rich clothes. It could be said that this Jesus, the holy anarchist, is as much an imaginative projection as any other, bearing no more resemblance to the Jesus of History than does the Sacred Host in the Liturgy. One of the reasons for the spread and survival of Christianity has been its remarkable adaptability. The Epistle to the Hebrews speaks of 'Jesus Christ, the same, yesterday, today and forever'.[1] Jesus is actually different in every country and in every age. In Japan, he is seen as an oriental with smooth black hair; in American films such as *King of Kings*, he looks like the handsomest type of blonde-blue-eyed sportsman in some Ivy League university. In Byzantine art, he became the stern, bearded figure of the Pantocrator, raising

[1] Hebrews 13:8.

his hand to bless and to judge the world. In post-Renaissance European art, the humanity of Jesus has been so vividly and so continuously portrayed that in many Christians' minds there is, I suspect, an imagined difference between the historical Jesus and the 'Christ of faith'.

The two come together, for the Christian, in a mysterious way when contemplating the figure of the Crucified Christ, an emblem in which the suffering of humanity and the love of God are, for the believer, bound together in a manner which liturgy, and music, and silence can explain better than words. To every person's mind, however, there must recur the question of what Jesus of Nazareth would think if he could survey the whole of human history and contemplate the things which had been done in his name. Christianity gave to the human race a sense of the worth of the individual, slave or free, male or female, Gentile or Jew. Without it, there would have been no St Francis, kissing the beggar, and no Mother Teresa of Calcutta, living among the poorest of Calcutta's poor. In Christ's name, Wilberforce freed the slaves, and Elizabeth Fry campaigned for the prisoners, and Christian Aid attempts to feed the hungry. In Christ's name, 'little unremembered acts of kindness and of love' have been performed throughout the centuries. If Jesus saw the activities of the Salvation Army among urban slums or the work of Father Damien among the lepers, he would be thankful to the mystic heretic Paul who took Judaism to the Gentiles in Christ's name.

Had he attended the great Councils of Christendom – Nicaea, Chalcedon, Trent, or the First and Second Vatican Councils – his gratitude might have turned to dismay. 'Why call ye me Lord, Lord, and do not the things which I say?'[1] 'Why callest thou me good?'[2] If it were even half possible that an historical personage existed who said the words attributed to him in the Gospels, there could be no greater insult to his memory than to recite the creeds, invented in a Hellenized world which was, imaginatively speaking, light years away both from Jesus and from ourselves. Nor could one insult his memory by claiming that he had founded a Church which for many years of its history was devoted so intently to persecuting anyone who dared to question these creeds. Wars, crusades and inquisitions have been perpetrated in the name of Jesus. When the Gospels were

[1] Luke 6:46.
[2] Matthew 19:17.

written down, the Christians were scarcely distinguishable, in the eyes of the Romans, from the Jews, and the worshippers of Jesus did all in their power to distinguish themselves from his co-religionists. In St Matthew's Gospel, the Jews take upon themselves the blood-guilt for the death of Jesus, and in the Fourth Gospel, the Jews are repeatedly seen as the unenlightened enemies of Christ. It is easy to see how the evangelists felt the need to distort history in this way, since at the time, they were the embattled minority, fighting to save their skins from persecution. When the Church triumphed over the synagogue, however, the deadly legacy of anti-Semitism remained embodied in the Christian view of the world. Not until over twenty years after the Second World War did the Roman Catholic Church officially absolve the Jewish people from guilt in the death of Jesus. By then, there were millions of Jesus's fellow believers in Judaism who had died either directly or indirectly because of the idea that they had killed the Son of God. Were Jesus to contemplate the fate of his own people at the hands of the Christians, throughout the history of Catholic Europe, culminating in Hitler's Final Solution, it is unlikely that he would have viewed the missionary activities of St Paul with such equanimity. We are told that before Jesus died, he wept over the city of Jerusalem, and seemed to foresee its tragic fate. Matthew tells us that, his Messianic hopes in ruins, Jesus died with the words of the Psalmist on his lips: My God, my God, why hast thou forsaken me?[1] Perhaps if he had foreseen the whole of Christian history, his despair would have been even greater, and he would have exclaimed with Job, 'Why died I not from the womb? Why did I not give up the ghost when I came out of the belly? Why did the knees receive me? Or why the breasts that I should suck? For now should I have lien down and been quiet; I should have slept; then had I been at rest.'[2]

[1] Matthew 27:46.
[2] Job 3:11–13.

# BIBLIOGRAPHY

The place of publication, unless otherwise stated, is London.

ET = English Translation.

## I. PRIMARY SOURCES

*He Kaine Diatheke* (Greek New Testament) (The British and Foreign Bible Society, Second Edition 1964).

*The Apocryphal New Testament* (ed. M. R. James, Oxford 1924).

*The Apocrypha and Pseudepigrapha of the Old Testament* (in English, 2 vols) (ed. R. H. Charles, Oxford 1913).

*The Dead Sea Scrolls* (in English) (Geza Vermes, Harmondsworth 1962).

*The Zadokite Documents* (ed. Chaim Rabin, Oxford 1958).

*The Mishnah* (ET Jacob Neusner, Yale 1988).

– (ET H. Danby, Oxford 1933).

Josephus (Loeb Classical Library 1926–1965).

Josephus: *The Jewish War* (trans. G. A. Williamson, Harmondsworth 1959).

Philo: (Loeb Classical Library 1929–43).

Eusebius: *The Ecclesiastical History and Martyrs of Palestine* (trans. by Hugh Jackson Lawlor and John Leonard Oulton, 1927).

*The Holy Bible* (Revised Version) Oxford 1926.

*The New Jerusalem Bible* 1985.

## II. BIBLICAL COMMENTARIES AND SYNOPSES

Aland, Kurt. Synopsis Quattuor Evangeliorum (1964).

Allen, Willoughby C. *A Critical and Exegetical Commentary on the Gospel According to St Matthew* (Third Edition, Edinburgh 1974).

Barrett, C. K. *The Gospel According to St John* (1955).

Beasley-Murray, G. G. *A Commentary on Mark Thirteen* (1957).

Black, Matthew and Rowley, H. H. *Peake's Commentary on the Bible* (completely revised and reset 1966).

Brown, R. E. *The Gospel According to St John* (New York 1966).

Bultmann, R. *The Gospel of John: A Commentary* (ET Oxford 1971).

Cranfield, C. E. B. *The Gospel According to St Mark* (Cambridge 1959).

Derrett, J. D. M. *The Making of Mark* (Shipston on Stour 1985).

Farmer, W. G. *Synoptikon* (1969).

– 257 –

Fenton, J. C. *St Matthew* (Harmondsworth 1963).
Gore, Charles *et al.* *A New Commentary on Holy Scripture* (1928).
Holtzmann, H. J. *Die Synoptiker* (Tübingen 1901).
Hoskyns, E. C., ed. F. N. Davey. *The Fourth Gospel* (1940).
Johnson, S. E. *A Commentary on the Gospel According to St Mark* New York 1960.
Lightfoot, R. H. *St John's Gospel: A Commentary* (Oxford 1956).
Marsh, John. *Saint John* (Harmondsworth 1968).
Montefiore, C. G. *The Synoptic Gospels* (edited with an introduction and commentary 1927).
Smith, B. T. D. *The Gospel According to Saint Matthew* (Cambridge 1927).
Sparks, H. F. D. *The Synoptic Gospels and the Johannine Parallels* (1964).
Taylor, V. *The Gospel According to St Mark* (1952).
Westcott, B. F. *The Gospel According to John* (1908).

## III. GENERAL

Abrahams, I. *Studies in Pharisaism and the Gospel* (Cambridge 1917).
Allegro, John. *The Dead Sea Scrolls: A Reappraisal* (Harmondsworth 1966).
 – *The Sacred Mushroom and the Cross* (1970).
Alon, Gedalyahu. *Jews, Judaism and the Classical World.* (Jerusalem 1977).
Auerbach, E. *Mimesis: The Representation of Reality in Western Literature* (ET 1953).
Baltensweiler, H. *Die Verklärung Jesu: historisches Ereignis und synoptische Berichte* (Zurich 1959).
Barrett, C. K. *Luke the Historian in Recent Study* (1965).
Bauer, Walter. *Orthodoxy and Heresy in Earliest Christianity* (ET 1972).
Beare, Francis Wright. *The Earliest Records of Jesus* (Oxford 1962).
Beilner, W. *Christus und die Pharisäer: exegetische Untersuchung über Grund and Verlauf der Auseinandersetzungen* (Vienna 1959).
Black, M. *An Aramaic Approach to the Gospels and Acts* (Oxford 1967).
Blake, William (ed. Geoffrey Keynes). *Poetry and Prose* (1939).
Blinzler, Josef. *The Trial of Jesus* (ET 1959).
Bornkamm, G. *Jesus of Nazareth* (ET 1960).
 – *Paul* (ET 1969).
Bowker, J. *Jesus and the Pharisees* (Cambridge 1973).
Brandon, S. G. F. *The Fall of Jerusalem and the Christian Church* (1951).
 – *Jesus and the Zealots* (Manchester 1967).
 – *The Trial of Jesus of Nazareth* (1968).
Brownlee, W. H. *The Meaning of the Qumran Scrolls for the Bible* (New York 1964).
Bultmann, R. *Die Geschichte der synoptischen Tradition* (Göttingen 1967).
 – *The History of the Synoptic Tradition* (ET Oxford 1963).
 – *Jesus and the World* (ET 1958).
 – *Theology of the New Testament* (ET 1954).
 – *Essays, Philosophical and Theological* (ET 1955).
Burkitt, F. C. *The Gospel History and its Transmission* (1911).
 – *The Earliest Sources for the Life of Jesus* (1910).
 – *The Syriac Forms of New Testament Proper Names* (1906).
Burney, C. F. *The Aramaic Origin of the Fourth Gospel* (Oxford 1922).

Butler, B. C. *The Originality of St Matthew* (Cambridge 1951).

Casey, Maurice. *From Jewish Prophet to Gentile God* (Cambridge, England, and Louisville, Kentucky, 1991).

Cathchpole, David R. *The Trial of Jesus* (Leiden 1971).

Chesterton, G. K. *The Everlasting Man* (1936).

Conze, Edward (trans.). *Buddhist Scriptures* (Harmondsworth 1959).

Conzelmann, H. *Jesus* (ET 1973).

– *An Outline of the Theology of the New Testament.* (ET 1969).

Creed, J. M. *The Gospel According to Saint Luke* (1960).

Cross, F. L. (with E. A. Livingstone). *The Oxford Dictionary of the Christian Church* (Second Edition 1974).

Cullmann, Oscar. *The Early Church* (1956).

Davies, W. D. *Paul and Rabbinic Judaism* (1948).

Derrett, J. D. M. *Jesus's Audience* (1981).

Dibelius, M. *From Tradition to Gospel* (ET 1934).

Dodd, C. H. *The Interpretation of the Fourth Gospel* (Cambridge 1953).

– *Historical Tradition in the Fourth Gospel* (Cambridge 1963).

– *The Founder of Christianity* (1971).

– *The Parables of the Kingdom* (1935).

Doresse, Jean. *The Secret Books of the Egyptian Gnostics* (ET 1960).

Drury, John. *The Parables in the Gospels* (1985).

Dupont-Sommer, A. *The Essene Writings from Qumran* (ET Oxford 1961).

Emerton, J. A. 'The Hundred and Fifty-Three Fishes in John XXI:11' in *Journal of Theological Studies, New Series* ix (April 1958), 86–89.

Farmer, William R. *The Synoptic Problem* (1964).

Farrer, Austin. *St Matthew and St Mark* (1966).

Filson, Floyd V. *A New Testament History* (1965).

Finkel, A. *The Pharisees and the Teacher of Nazareth* (Leiden 1964).

Flender, Helmut. *St Luke Theologian of Redemptive History* (1967).

Freyne, Sean. *Galilee from Alexander the Great to Hadrian: 323 B.C.E. to 135 C.E.* (Notre Dame 1980).

Fredricksen, Paula. *From Jesus to Christ* (Yale 1988).

Frye, Northrop. *The Great Code: The Bible and Literature* (1982).

Gerhardsson, Birger. *The Origins of the Gospel Tradition* (Philadelphia 1979).

Goguel, Maurice. *The Life of Jesus* (ET 1959).

Goldstein, M. *Jesus in the Jewish Tradition* (New York 1950).

Goppelt, Leonhard. *Jesus, Paul and Judaism. An Introduction to New Testament Theology* (New York 1964).

Goulder, Michael. *Midrash and Lection in Matthew* (1974).

Grant, F. C. *The Gospels: Their Origin and Growth* (1957).

Grant, Robert M. *A Historical Introduction to the New Testament.* (1963).

Guilding, Aileen. *The Fourth Gospel and Jewish Worship* (Oxford 1960).

Harnack, Adolph. *History of Dogma* (ET 1894).

Harvey, A. E. *Jesus and the Constraints of History* (1982).

Hawkins, Sir John C. *Horae Synopticae* (1909).

Helfgott, B. W. *The Doctrine of Election in Tannaitic Literature* (New York 1954).

Hengel, Martin. *Was Jesus a Revolutionist?* (ET Philadelphia 1971).

Hick, John (ed.). *The Myth of God Incarnate* (1977).

Hill, David. *New Testament Prophecy* (1979).

Hogg, James. *The Domestic Manners of Sir Walter Scott* (Edinburgh 1909).

Hooker, M. D. *The Son of Man in Mark* (1967).

Hurst, L. D. *The Epistle to the Hebrews* (Cambridge 1990).

Inge, William Ralph 'Saint Paul'. *Outspoken Essays*, 205–229 (1927).

Isaac, J. *Jésus et Israël* (Paris 1948).

Jaubert, Annie. *La Date de la Cène* (Paris 1957).

Jeremias, J. *Jerusalem in the Time of Jesus* (ET 1969).

 – *The Parables of Jesus* (1963).

 – *The Eucharistic Words of Jesus* (ET Oxford 1955).

Johnson, Paul. *A History of the Jews* (1987).

Jones, Geraint Vaughan. *The Art and Truth of the Parables* (1964).

Käsemann, E. 'Blind Alleys in the "Jesus of History" Controversy' in *New Testament Questions of Today* (ET 1969).

Kenyon, K. *Jerusalem: Excavating 3,000 Years of History* (1967).

Kidd, B. J. *A History of the Church to A.D. 461* (Oxford 1922).

Kingsmill, Hugh. *The Poisoned Crown* (1944).

Kittel, G. *Jesus und die Rabbinen* (Berlin 1914).

 – *Theologisches Wörterbuch* (Berlin 1924).

Klausner, J. *From Jesus to Paul* (ET 1944).

 – *Jesus of Nazareth* (ET 1925).

Knox, Wilfrid. *Sources of the Synoptic Gospels* (Cambridge 1959).

 – *St Paul and the Church of the Gentiles* (1939).

 – *Some Hellenistic Elements in Primitive Christianity* (1944).

Kümmel, W. G. *Promise and Fulfilment* (ET 1957).

 – *Theology of the New Testament* (ET 1974).

Lewis, Lionel Snithett. *St Joseph of Arimathea at Glastonbury* (Cambridge 1976).

Lawrence, T. E. *The Seven Pillars of Wisdom* (1935).

Loffreda, Stanislao. *Recovering Capharnaum* (Jerusalem 1985).

Machen, J. Gresham. *The Origin of Paul's Religion* (Michigan 1947).

Mackey, J. P. *Jesus, the Man and the Myth* (1979).

Manson, T. W. *The Teaching of Jesus: Studies in Form and Content* (Cambridge 1935).

McKelvey, R. J. *The New Temple: The Church in the New Testament* (Oxford 1969).

Merx, A. *Der Messias oder Ta'eb der Samaritaner* (Berlin 1910).

Meyer, B. F. *The Aims of Jesus* (1979).

Montefiore, Hugh. 'Does L. hold water?' in *Journal of Theological Studies, New Series* iv (1953), 27–31.

Moule, C. F. D. *The Origin of Christology* (Cambridge 1977).

Morton, H. V. *In the Steps of the Master* (1934).

Neusner, Jacob. *From Politics to Piety* (Englewood Cliffs, New Jersey 1973).

Nineham, Dennis. *The Use and Abuse of the Bible* (1976).

 – *Historicity and Chronology in the New Testament* (1965).

Nolan, Albert. *Jesus before Christianity* (Capetown 1976).

Nygren, Anders. *Agape and Eros* (ET 1954).

Pasternak, Boris. *Doctor Zhivago* (ET 1958).

Pelikan, Jaroslav. *Jesus Through the Centuries* (Yale 1985).

Perrin, Norman. *Jesus and the Language of the Kingdom* (1976).
- *The Kingdom of God in the Teaching of Jesus* (1963).
- *Rediscovering the Teaching of Jesus* (1967).
Pines, Shlomo. 'An Arabic Version of the Testimonium Flavianum and its Implications' (Israel Academy of Science and Humanities, Jerusalem 1971).
Rajak, Tessa. *Josephus: The Historian and His Society* (1983).
Renan, Ernest. *La Vie de Jésus* (Paris 1863).
- *Oeuvres Complètes* (Paris 1949).
Reumann, John. *Jesus in the Church's Gospels: Modern Scholarship and the Earliest Sources.* (Philadelphia 1968).
Riches, John. *Jesus and the Transformation of Judaism* (1980).
Robinson, James. *A New Quest for the Historical Jesus* (Nashville 1959).
Robinson, John A. T. *Redating the New Testament* (1976).
- *The Priority of John* (1985).
- *The Human Face of God* (1972).
Rowland, Christopher. *Christian Origins* (1985).
Ruckstuhl, E. *The Chronology of the Last Days of Jesus* (ET New York 1965).
Sanders, E. P. *Jesus and Judaism* (1985).
- *Paul and Palestinian Judaism* (1977).
Schlosser, Jacques. *Le règne de Dieu dans les dits de Jésus* (2 vols.) (Paris 1980).
Schoeps, H. J. *Paul: The Theology of the Apostle in the Light of Jewish Religious History* (1961).
Schonfield, Hugh J. *The Passover Plot* (1966).
Schürer, Emil, Vermes, Geza, Millar, F. *The History of the Jewish People in the Age of Jesus Christ* (ET Vol. I 1973; Vol. II 1979).
Schweitzer, A. *The Mysticism of Paul the Apostle* (ET 1931).
- *The Quest for the Historical Jesus* (ET 1910).
Seeley, Sir J. R. *Ecce Homo* (1907).
Sidebottom, E. M. *The Christ of the Fourth Gospel* (1961).
Sloyan, G. *Jesus on Trial* (Philadelphia 1973).
Smith, Morton. *Jesus the Magician* (1978).
- *The Secret Gospel* (1974).
Stauffer, E. *Jesus and His Story* (ET 1960).
Strauss, D. F. *The Life of Jesus Critically Examined* (ET 1846.)
Streeter, B. H. *The Four Gospels: A Study in Origins* (1927).
Sweet, J. P. M. 'The Zealots and Jesus' in *Jesus and the Politics of His Day* (ed. Ernst Bammel and C. F. D. Moule) (Cambridge 1984).
Swetnam, James. *Jesus and Isaac* (1981).
Taylor, Vincent. *The Gospel According to St Mark* (1959).
- *The Origins of the Gospels* (1965).
Thackeray, H. St John. *St Paul and Contemporary Jewish Theology* (1900).
Tödt, H. E. *The Son of Man in the Synoptic Tradition* (ET 1965).
Tolstoy, L. N. *The Kingdom of God and Peace Essays* (ET Oxford 1936).
Trocmé, E. 'L'expulsion des marchands du temple' in *New Testament Studies* 15(1968), 1–22.
- *Jesus and His Contemporaries* (ET 1973).
- *The Formation of the Gospel According to St Mark* (ET 1975).

Vermes, Geza. *Jesus the Jew* (1973).
– *Jesus and the World of Judaism* (1983).
– *The Dead Sea Scrolls: Qumran in Perspective (1977).*
Wachsmann, Shelley (ed.). 'The Excavations of an Ancient Boat in the Sea of Galilee' in *Atiqot* Vol. XIX (Jerusalem 1990).
Weil, Simone. *Intimations of Christianity Among the Ancient Greeks* (ET 1957).
– *Waiting on God* (ET 1951).
Weiss, Johannes. *Die Predigt Jesu vom Reiche Gottes* (Göttingen 1892).
Wells, G. A. *The Jesus of the Early Christians* (1971).
Westerholm, Stephen. *Jesus and Scribal Authority* (Lund 1978).
Whiteley, D. E. H. *The Theology of St Paul* (Oxford 1964).
Wilder, A. *Eschatology in the Teaching of Jesus* (New York 1950).
Wilson, Ian. *Jesus the Evidence* (1984).
Wilson, R. McL. *Gnosis and the New Testament* (1968).
Winter, P. *On the Trial of Jesus* (Berlin 1961).
Witherington, Ben. *Women and the Genesis of Christianity* (Cambridge 1990).
Yadin, Yigael. *Masada: Herod's Last Fortress and the Zealots' Last Stand* (1966).
Yoder, J. H. *The Politics of Jesus* (1972).
Zahrnt, H. *The Historical Jesus* (ET 1963).

# INDEX